The Roots of Phonics

The Roots of Phonics

A Historical Introduction
Revised Edition

by

Miriam Balmuth, Ph.D.

·P A U L·H·
BROOKES
PUBLISHING Cº ®

Baltimore • London • Sydney

Paul H. Brookes Publishing Co.
Post Office Box 10624
Baltimore, Maryland 21285-0624
USA

www.brookespublishing.com

Copyright © 2009 by Paul H. Brookes Publishing Co., Inc.
All rights reserved.

"Paul H. Brookes Publishing Co." is a registered trademark
of Paul H. Brookes Publishing Co., Inc.

Typeset by Integrated Publishing Solutions, Grand Rapids, Michigan.
Manufactured in the United States of America by
Victor Graphics, Inc., Baltimore, Maryland.

This book was originally published in 1982 by McGraw-Hill (ISBN-10: 0-07-003490-7).
A second edition was published in 1992 by York Press (ISBN-10: 0-912752-32-7).

Library of Congress Cataloging-in-Publication Data
Balmuth, Miriam.
  The roots of phonics : a historical introduction / by Miriam Balmuth.—Rev. ed.
    p.   cm.
  Includes bibliographical references and index.
  ISBN-13: 978-1-59857-036-6 (pbk.)
  ISBN-10: 1-59857-036-6 (pbk.)
  1. English language—Phonology, Historical.   2. English language—Orthography and
  spelling.   3. English language—Pronunciation.   4. Reading—Phonetic method.
  I. Title.
  PE1133.B26 2009
  421′.5—dc22   2009000654

British Library Cataloguing in Publication data are available from the British Library.

2013   2012   2011   2010   2009
10   9   8   7   6   5   4   3   2   1

*To seven-year-old Michael Quinones
who, when asked, "And what is a teacher?",
calmly answered, "A teacher is for beautiful."*

Contents

About the Author

Miriam Balmuth, Ph.D., was Professor of Education and Coordinator of Corrective and Remedial Reading in the Division of Programs in Education at Hunter College of the City University of New York. She took her Ph.D. in educational psychology at New York University and an M.S. in elementary education with a specialization in developmental and remedial reading at The City College of New York. Dr. Balmuth has been a classroom teacher and reading clinician. Currently, she is Professor Emeritus of Hunter College.

Foreword

The word *phonics*, Balmuth begins, has two meanings. In its historically earlier sense, phonics refers to the way the letters and spelling patterns of a written language represent its speech sounds. In its second and more recent sense, phonics refers to instruction on those correspondences that is intended to help students learn to read and spell. In *The Roots of Phonics: A Historical Introduction, Revised Edition*, she takes us through the history of both senses of the word, with special care to helping us understand how the evolution of the former has shaped both the challenges and the politics of the latter.

Balmuth opens the book with a history and comparison of different writing systems. She tells us how the alphabetic system of writing evolved—first consonants, then vowels, and later spaces, punctuation, and far later, "correct" spelling—in a story that recalls the stages of children's development. By the seventh century A.D., when the Roman alphabet was brought to England by Irish missionaries, it was basically set, excepting a few graphemes. The Roman alphabet was used to spell English words by mapping letters to sounds. Even though the fit wasn't perfect, historians hold that Old English spellings were considerably more consistent and regular than today. What happened?

Balmuth takes us through time—through invasions, civil wars, alliances, social and religious upheavals, fashions, fads, and innovations. In consequence of these events, spoken English changed considerably in both pronunciation and grammar over the centuries. In contrast, because writing was primarily the responsibility of scribes, written English changed far less. It was, after all, the job of a scribe to write as has been writ. To be sure, new words entered the written lexicon over those many years. However, many of these new words also lacked consistent phonology or pattern as they were based on the era and the dialect or mother tongue of the individual scribes who rendered them.

Only in the sixteenth century, with the wars finally over, did the Renaissance blossom in England. The printing press had arrived and—with the embrace of the written vernacular, Protestantism, and the flowering of English literature—the desire to read and write moved into the mainstream. The increase in literature and literacy brought with it an increase in reading and writing instruction. There followed teacher's manuals, graded texts, glossaries, and eventually dictionaries. In addition, there arose a number of serious movements to clean up the disarray of English spelling. With notable exceptions, however, traditional spellings prevailed.

Even as Balmuth's treatment of historical events and characters is riveting, the plot of this saga is consistently fixed on their effects on the English language, spoken and spelled. A sampling of the mysteries that she explains in course include:

- How the schwa displaced the sound of the written vowels in so many words

- How long and short vowels used to be sounded—hence, their names

- Why some long vowels are signaled by final *e* and others by digraphs

- Why words such as *light, night,* and *sight* are spelled with *-ight*

- Why some English words end with doubled consonants

- How it came to be that *er, ir,* and *ur* are spelled differently but pronounced the same

- How the silent consonants arose

- Why phonics programs persist in teaching the distinction between voiced and unvoiced *th*

- How some prepositions evolved into prefixes

- How the apostrophe came to mark possessives

- When and why British and American pronunciation diverged and why some words are spelled differently in England and America

- Most of all, how the complexity of English phonics helped to shape the great debates about whether to teach phonics and, if so, what and how to teach children about it in the course of their reading and writing instruction

All of us who teach or study reading have wondered about such issues. Presenting them with cause, effect, and pattern, Balmuth does more than meet our quirkwise curiosity. She changes the way we understand and think about the English spelling system. She leads us to appreciate written language as the human invention it is.

I first read this book when writing *Beginning to Read: Thinking and Learning About Print* (MIT Press, 1990). So many times I have wanted to share it. So many times I have wanted to assign it. Alas, it was out of print.

I was therefore delighted when I heard that *The Roots of Phonics* was finally to be reprinted, and I was deeply honored to be asked to write the foreword. Yet, I was also a little nervous. Might the book be dated? True, history does not change. On the other hand, our knowledge and interpretations of it do.

Just to be sure, I have read the book yet again, this time with my most critical eye. I found myself yet again overawed. The sheer breadth of the scholarship that Balmuth would need to have undertaken to write this book is staggering. Across that vast literature, I can only imagine how difficult it must have been to find the pieces relevant to her thesis, much less to explain and thread them together. This book is the product of a truly prodigious and masterful effort. It is brilliantly informative, and it is ever considerate of the history, the historians, and the reader. It is an enduring treasure.

Marilyn Jager Adams, Ph.D.
Brown University

Foreword to the Previous Edition

This is an important book for teachers, reading professionals, and reading and language scholars and researchers. It takes one aspect of reading and language—English phonics—and presents it historically with depth, care, and compassion.

The book contributes to two current trends in reading research and practice—concern with language in the acquisition of reading and interest in the history of reading instruction. Through a historical presentation of the relation of English phonics to spelling, writing, and reading it brings to teachers and reading researchers insights into the importance of phonics in education over several centuries. It also treats the history of phonics as a method of teaching reading. Choice quotes from Noah Webster, Horace Mann, and many others help us realize why the seemingly minor issue of phonics in reading and spelling instruction tends from time to time to take on aspects of fierce partisanship.

The Roots of Phonics is a book in the humanistic tradition. It will enrich reading teachers and researchers with its broad perspective. The historical information will also be useful for students—whether in graduate programs on reading and language, high school students grappling with the harder aspects of advanced spelling, or primary grade children learning to read.

The Roots of Phonics will also bring to the readers—teachers or researchers—a sobering humility when it is realized how much those who preceded us sought solutions to problems similar to ours and how close they often came to solving them in similar ways.

Jeanne S. Chall, Ph.D.
Harvard University

Acknowledgments

This book about roots has its own roots. Many of them are the scholarly works identified in the text and bibliography. Others were set down by teachers who helped form my concepts about learning to read and language history. Those teachers, as well as friends and colleagues who helped with the book in its more recent stages, I am happy to acknowledge here.

The first acknowledgment goes to my students at Hunter College. For more than a decade they shared my enthusiasm for reading and the history of reading. Their contributions to class discussions deepened my understanding, led me to explore further, and inspired me to collate for others what they had valued.

The origins of the book go back much earlier, however. Long ago, my sister Anne taught me to read before I entered first grade by showing me how to sound out the letters. I was greatly intrigued, therefore, when Miss McCauley, the first-grade teacher, began by having us read whole words in sentences. That was the start of an awareness and a puzzlement that have never left me.

My high school teacher, Dr. Edward Horowitz, author of *How the Hebrew Language Grew*, first opened the world of language history. His great relish for the subject as well as for the principles of language change that he clarified are treasured gifts. I was also fortunate to be a student of Daniel Persky, an eminent Hebrew grammarian. The quintessential enthusiastic teacher, he brought delight to punctuation and permanent grace to syllabic stress.

When I became a teacher myself, a new source of knowledge became available. I found that students of all ages, by opening themselves to learning from me, taught me in return. I had had a variety of experiences as a classroom teacher when Helen Stockvis, then coordinator of reading on the West Side of Manhattan, gave me the chance to work with children with reading problems. She helped me set up a remedial reading program and marvelously combined compassion with professional competence. The children in the program revealed some of the mysteries of reading acquisition and taught me ways of meeting their needs that I was later able to use with other struggling readers.

My dear teacher, Florence Roswell, gave me the chance to translate my experiences with children into teaching teachers, showing a faith I cherish as much as her great gift in "freeing" me in the world of reading. I was one of the fortunate students in her classes at The City College whom she taught to let go of stale misconceptions and to look objectively at the reader and the reading process.

The world of research in reading was opened for me by Jeanne Chall, first when she chaired the committee for my master's thesis and later when she invited me to join her assistants on the Carnegie study that resulted in *Learning to Read: The*

Great Debate. Her understanding of the field of reading is immeasurable, as is the gratitude I feel for the wisdom and inspiration she has provided in the years since then. I consulted with her at various stages of the book and she never failed to meet my needs in just the right way and just the right measure.

Josephine Piekarz Ives first made me aware of how modern linguistics relates to reading. At New York University, she was a model of how to guide doctoral students and responded immediately when I asked for help in the first stages of the book. She has my gratitude and affection.

My understanding of the ties between British and American language history was greatly extended because Vera Southgate Booth invited me to work with her in Bermuda one summer and then to lecture and visit in England. I learned much from those shared experiences and treasure her wisdom and encouragement during the years of our friendship.

In Tom Quinn, my publisher of the first edition at McGraw-Hill, I have seen how a great teacher functions outside a school or university. Impeccable respect for others and deep understanding of his profession lead him to guide and support rather than to impose or cramp. I shall never forget his kindness.

For direct help with the text and the manuscript, my thanks and gratitude go to Naomi C. Miller, who reviewed the sections on British history, to Harvey A. Minkoff, who examined the sections on Old and Middle English, to E. Jennifer Monaghan, who reviewed the section on Noah Webster, and to Katherine S. Harris, for her help with the section on the production of a syllable. I am grateful also to Richard L. Venezky for his most helpful comments on the manuscript as a whole. My friend Fran Cohen's work in typing the manuscript was invaluable, as were her reactions to the early drafts.

For the second edition, Elinor J. Hartwig, the publisher of York Press, provided an unparalleled professionalism with her appreciation and support of the book as she reached out to wider audiences. Her warmth and astuteness added my affection to that of all who know and love her.

Finally, at Brookes Publishing Co., my heart was gladdened first by Sarah Shepke, Acquisitions Editor, who first supported and effected the idea of a new edition, and then by all of the staff, including Janet Wehner, Senior Production Editor, and Jen Lillis, Copy Manager, who worked assiduously and most sensitively on all aspects of the final volume. It was at Brookes, too, that the idea of including some exercises originated. It was a new idea, and I wondered if it would fit in with the flow of the book. I agreed to the exercises, however, after consulting with my friend Sandra Priest Rose and recalling a conversation with Jeanne Chall, both of whom thought that new teachers would appreciate greater grounding in basic technical terms. Therefore, Tara Gebhardt's exercises in the first chapters of this edition were designed to broaden the book's usefulness.

The book could never have been produced without the help of all who have been mentioned, as well as of others who have been of help in myriad ways throughout the years. Although their contributions and suggestions are integrated within the book, all choices that were made were my own, however, and so responsibility for the book's contents is entirely my own as well.

Introduction

The book has an ambitious aim: to present a clear and accurate history of the complex phenomenon that is English phonics.

It started out as a source book for the teaching of phonics, consisting of teaching techniques and a listing of words according to their English spelling patterns. One part of the book's original design was a brief survey of the development of present-day English phonics. Despite years of exposure to information about our language, a great deal of intriguing information came to light as I began to explore the origins of the phonics we teach. Each unearthed fact seemed to raise additional questions so I found myself digging more and more deeply to track down answers. Of even greater fascination than the isolated details that turned up were the striking connections between various aspects of phonics and the cultural, economic, and political environments of the past. I was continually moved to include such information for the benefit of prospective readers who, like myself and my students, might find it of great interest. The survey section began to expand.

Furthermore, in searching out specific information, I found it necessary to consult a wide range of sources. Works in historical linguistics were of prime importance, but writings on general history, descriptive linguistics, phonetics, psycholinguistics, history of education, various etymological and foreign language dictionaries, and many works on specific topics were required as well. I came to realize that having this information in one convenient volume would provide a useful central reference—perhaps after an initial introductory reading. This consideration, too, prompted the inclusion of additional material.

Gradually, the focus of the book began to shift from its proposed outline. The historical section grew and grew—becoming large enough to comprise a book in itself. The original source book was set aside for another day.

The major reason for compiling this book, then, is to offer to teachers and other practitioners in education ready access to both the gratification and the information I found in seeking out the origins of what is unquestionably the threshold to the storehouse of our civilization's riches. Such a characterization may sound grandiose for phonics, a subject whose name evokes drab echoes for all but its most bemused infatuates, yet the simple fact is that, for those who are learning to read and spell, phonics is the inescapable essence of every word.

Moreover, while phonics finds a fair degree of acceptance in the present climate of eclecticism in reading methodology, this has not always been the case. In the back-and-forth swing of teaching fashions (like the swings of fashion in clothing, always with modern touches added to the recycled styles of earlier periods) phonics has known times of neglect, times of exalted praise, and times of scathing vituperation. It has also been peculiarly vulnerable to the general societal moods of each era. At any rate, phonics never goes completely "out of style"—even when out of favor except with a small number of nonconformists—and more chapters will no doubt be added to its venerable history.

THE PROSPECTIVE AUDIENCE

Recent years have seen an accelerating trend, culminating in what Morrison and Austin call "giant steps,"[1] toward requiring schoolteachers—especially at the elementary school level—to undergo substantial preservice training in the teaching of reading. Even more striking has been the increase in postbaccalaureate study for all teachers, often including advanced coursework in the teaching of reading. Add to this the proliferation of graduate programs expressly for the training of teachers, supervisors, and researchers in reading as well as in such related fields as educational psychology, linguistics, speech pathology, and special education (including learning disabilities). The result is a far larger group of scholarly and academically sophisticated teachers and other educators concerned with reading than existed a generation ago, ones who are open to a more profound understanding of the subjects relevant to their work. It is mainly for such educators that this book is intended.

For many of those readers, the book might provide benefits beyond the pleasure of acquiring knowledge for its own sake. Those who are actively engaged in teaching phonics should find a good deal that can enrich their instruction—either through new insights they may use in approaching the subject or by information they can transmit directly to their pupils. Some notice has been taken in this regard throughout the book, usually by comments addressed to "teachers of reading," although they will no doubt pick up a great number of relevant points independently. Similarly, much in this book can be used in the teaching of such related subjects as spelling, handwriting, grammar, vocabulary, and speech; here, too, it is expected that individual readers will make their own pertinent correlations.

THE DEFINITION OF PHONICS

Contributing to the complexity of phonics is the fact that the term *phonics* has two meanings. In the historically earlier sense, the phonics of a written language are the letters and spelling patterns of that language's alphabet and the speech sounds they represent—put very simply, the sounds that the letters make. Different written languages have different phonics systems. Even languages that use the same letters

---

[1]Coleman Morrison and Mary C. Austin, *The Torch Lighters Revisited*, International Reading Association, Newark, DE, 1977, p. 35.

may assign different speech sounds to some of them. Thus, the *soft g* (before *e*, *i*, or *y*) of English phonics is pronounced as in *page*, but the *soft g* of French phonics is pronounced as in *rouge*. Similarly, in English phonics the *final e* is usually silent, as in *joke*, and generally indicates that the preceding vowel is long. In Spanish phonics, however, the *final e* is always sounded, as in the name *Jose*, and gives no special clue to the preceding vowel.

The second and historically more recent meaning of the term *phonics* refers to a technique of reading instruction. As Charles Fries puts it, phonics in this sense means "those practices in the teaching of reading that have aimed at matching the individual letters of the alphabet with specific sounds of English pronunciation."[2] (It should be noted, however, that although both Fries and I focus on the phonics of English, phonics as a methodology is often used in the teaching of written languages other than English.)

While phonics in the first sense goes back further in time than does phonics as an instructional method, the two are currently intermingled in the day-to-day teaching of reading. For that reason, this book is addressed to events and influences that have borne on both of them.

GATHERING AND SELECTING THE INFORMATION IN THE BOOK

In its first sense, phonics is a connecting of spoken and written forms, and so it follows that the history of English phonics rests on the history of spoken and written English. Unfortunately, those histories are hard to present cohesively because of the diverse factors that affect any sort of language development. Aside from the assortment of physiological processes that underlie the production and reception of all language, a great variety of cultural and historical forces come into play. For this book, information about those factors needed to be gathered from the fields of linguistics, speech, and ancient and modern history.

Moreover, for the more recent meaning of *phonics*, wholly different bodies of information exist, information about pedagogical practices not met in standard works of historical linguistics. One major body of information concerns the way English phonics has been perceived by its users and teachers, while another major body relates to the development of phonics methods within the history of beginning reading instruction. Other information, such as the roles played by principal advocates of different methods of teaching reading, also has a place here.

Gathering the necessary information for this book was an activity of unexpected pleasure. What had augured to be an amassing of details about a moderately interesting subject ended up as a true example of George Philip Krapp's depiction of the same process: "The historical student in one corner of his heart is not altogether unlike the stamp or curio collector. He finds it hard to resist the charm of a specimen. A specimen attracts for various reasons, the situation in which it was

---

[2]Charles C. Fries, *Linguistics and Reading*, Holt, Rinehart and Winston, New York, 1963, pp. 143–144. Also, see pp. 164, 175 n. 10, and 183 below for further discussion of the origin and use of the term *phonics*.

found, the shading of value which it acquires from context, or merely because it has never before been put on record."[3]

I soon became aware of the attraction that Krapp describes and of a danger that may be inferred: the danger of finding too many "specimens" too enticing. The main task was to select the best specimens and then organize them so as to avoid an overdetailed confusion. I tried to do so by separating the major topics and pursuing each one in historical perspective, seeking out the most reliable sources.

TECHNICAL TERMS

Another series of decisions concerned the technical terms arising in connection with a number of the topics. The questions of which terms to use, which definitions to provide, and where in the book to provide them were all thorny. Many technical terms, particularly linguistic ones, have lately entered the field of reading, and understanding them is necessary for following some of the current writings on reading.

The great number of coined words in linguistic literature alone makes it impossible to know them all. Crystal, for example, after giving an overview of three current linguistic theories, comments, "I doubt whether there is any linguist alive capable of giving a detailed account of all three . . . and the complex terminology involved is alone a major deterrent to any amateur linguistic investigator."[4]

Deciding where in the text to set down definitions of technical or complicated terms was also a problem. Two ways of doing so were adopted. For terms that are so technical or confined to such a narrow area of scholarship that few readers might be expected to know them, explanations are woven directly into the text. There are other, less obscure terms, however, whose meaning might be known to some readers though they are unfamiliar or unclear to others. The explanations for such terms are set off in parentheses or in a footnote when the definition is brief and fairly simple and in a separate section within the text when the concept is intricate and calls for a long explanation. The informed reader may easily skip the explanatory section and move directly to the thread of the text.

For those who wish to check on the meaning of a specific term, the index at the back tells where the definition for that term may be found.

---

[3]George Philip Krapp, *The English Language in America*, 2 vols., Frederick Ungar, New York, 1925, Vol. 1, p. vii.
[4]David Crystal, *Linguistics*, Penguin Books, Baltimore, 1971, p. 216.

Characteristics
of Writing Systems

In its present form, English phonics may be viewed as a curious growth rooted in four historical processes:

1. The development of writing systems

2. The development of our particular writing system

3. The development of spoken English

4. The development of English spelling patterns

Although each of these processes originated in a different place and at a different time, they ultimately came together to form the written language we find today. In the following chapters, these processes are examined individually, in order of their initial emergence, with some integration of them given whenever possible.

Because it was the first of the processes to be set in motion, we will start with the development of writing systems.

DEFINITIONS OF WRITING

In preparing to describe the evolution of writing systems, I soon found that a significant problem for language scholars is the definition of exactly what constitutes "writing." In the end, the most useful definition seems to be that of I.J. Gelb. A second definition, that of H.A. Gleason, is more limited but valuable because it incorporates the perceptions and terminology of modern descriptive/structural linguistics.

Gelb's Definition

Gelb defines *writing* as "a system of human intercommunication by means of conventional visible marks."[1] Gelb's use of the words "intercommunication" and "conventional" implies that a writing system cannot be limited to one person but must be consciously adopted by a group, even a small one. (Individuals have helped develop a writing system that is adopted by others, however.[2]) By contrast, artists' pictures are not "conventional," because each has personal meanings that often can be understood only through intimate knowledge of its creator's life.

By his use of the word "visible," Gelb separates writing from communication systems that use nonvisual senses—from auditory systems such as spoken language or drumbeat systems, for example, or from kinesthetic systems like the hand language used by Helen Keller and her close associates. In addition, Gelb's "marks" exclude such visible languages as the signs used by the deaf as well as signal systems based on smoke, lights, flags, and the like.[3]

Epigraphic and Paleographic Media

Gelb's definition also unites two types of writing media. One type, called *epigraphic*, stems from earliest times and includes inscriptions cut into such substances as clay, stone, metal, and wood. The other type, called *paleographic*, is more recent and includes writings drawn or painted on the surface of such materials as paper, parchment, and papyrus. Because investigations of ancient civilizations tend to be compartmentalized and because one type of writing arose in an earlier age than the other, these two kinds of source material tend to be studied separately. Nevertheless, although they may be very different in appearance, the markings in both kinds of media have all the necessary features of written language so Gelb's definition provides for this.[4]

As Doblhofer[5] and Ogg[6] point out, the differences in media had a substantial effect on the form symbols took. The greater fragility of the paleographic materials, for example, as well as the greater ease of writing on them, encouraged the development of simpler forms and gave impetus to the evolutionary changes discussed in the next chapter.

The instruments used also had an effect: Just as nowadays we modify our individual handwritings when we change from pencil or ball-point pen to the easier flow of a felt-tipped pen, so did the earlier changes from sharp, cutting epigraphic instruments to gentler paleographic instruments lead to changes in the forms of written symbols.[7]

---

[1] I.J. Gelb, *A Study of Writing*, University of Chicago Press, 1963, p. 12.

[2] David Diringer, *The Alphabet*, Third Edition completely revised with the collaboration of Reinhold Regensburger, Hutchinson, London, 1968, p. 442.

[3] Quite a few of the nonwriting systems of communication mentioned in this paragraph are, like braille, what Gelb considers "secondary systems" because, although designed for auditory or tactual reception, they are developed from "primary systems," or those designed for visual reception (Gelb, 1963, pp. 7–9).

[4] Gelb, 1963, p. 22. (See also Diringer, 1968, p. 2.)

[5] Ernst Doblhofer, *Voices in Stone*, Viking, New York, 1961, p. 29.

[6] Oscar Ogg, *The 26 Letters*, Crowell, New York, 1971, p. 61ff.

[7] See pp. 43–45 below for discussion of cursive writing.

Gleason's Definition: The Concept of a Grapheme

In a definition much more technical than Gelb's, Gleason states: "A writing system consists of a set of *graphemes* plus certain characteristic features of their use. Each grapheme may have one or more *allographs*."[8]

In this definition, Gleason is primarily trying to explain the term *grapheme*. For descriptive/structural linguists, a grapheme is a group of related *graphs* (defined as "markings in a writing system"), often similar in appearance, which, in a particular written language, are normally treated as if they were the same. The related graphs of a grapheme are called *allographs*.

Definition of Allographs

Allographs occur through differences in calligraphies, individual handwritings, typewriters, and typefaces. Thus, the lowercase form of the letter *t* may appear as a simple cross in one calligraphy and with a curve at the bottom in another. Each of these two variations is called an allograph of the grapheme that is written as ⟨t⟩ by linguists.

Similarly, there are many allographs of lowercase *t* in the assorted typefaces found on printing presses or typewriter keys. Comparison of the forms in any book on typography reveals great diversity in the thickness of the lines and the method of finishing off the extremities of each letter within the different types.[9] In individual handwritings, the variations of slant, additions or omissions of little curls or strokes, positionings of the *t*'s cross or the *i*'s dot—in short, most of the raw material of graphology—result in allographs. Some authors refer to such personal allographs as *free variations*.

EXERCISE

In the space provided below, write two allographs for the grapheme ⟨f⟩.

_____

The Graphemes of Written English

W. Nelson Francis, in the same linguistic tradition as Gleason, lists 41 graphemes for the written English language. These include the 26 consonant and vowel letters, 11 punctuation marks (, . ; : ? ! (" ' - and —)[10] and 4 graphemes, called *suprasegmen-*

---

[8]H.A. Gleason, *An Introduction to Descriptive Linguistics*, Holt, Rinehart and Winston, New York, 1961, p. 409.

[9]Tommy Thompson's *How to Render Roman Letter Forms* (American Studio Books, New York, 1946) and Ogg (1971) contain a number of sample types.

[10]See Chapter 7 for discussion of the origins of most of these punctuation marks.

tal graphemes, which occur only in combination with the other (that is, the segmental) graphemes. The suprasegmental graphemes are lowercase form, italic form, small cap form, and capital form. Francis then adds *space* as another "graphemic feature."[11] In addition, some authors refer to *compound graphemes*, where two single graphemes function as one in the spoken language (e.g., *th* and *aw* in English).[12]

EXERCISE

In the space provided below, write three compound graphemes.

_____

Use of the Term Grapheme

As Francis's list of English graphemes indicates and as Gleason's definition implies, markings other than alphabet letters may be graphemes. Moreover, in addition to the punctuation marks and other nonletter graphemes of primarily alphabetic systems like written English, the characters of the nonalphabetic writing systems described in the next chapters (pictographic, logographic, and syllabic writing) are also nonletter graphemes.

It should be noted that discussions of both the concept and the use of the term *grapheme* are found far less frequently in the writings of linguists than are the related concepts of phoneme and morpheme (defined below on pp. 27–28 and 198–199). The term *grapheme* originated later and is less often needed because linguistic discussions tend to center about spoken rather than written language, which may be why explanations of graphemes are often vague or contradictory. Thus, some authors refer to upper- and lowercase, italics, and capital forms as allographs, rather than as suprasegmental graphemes in the way that Francis does.[13] Others consider allographs to be spelling patterns that are pronounced in the same way, as *ee* and *ea*, or *f* and *ph*, rather than variations in the form of specific characters. Lefevre also relates graphemes directly to phonemes, stating, "Graphemes are the letters and combinations of letters that represent phonemes in standard spellings."[14]

In addition, the term *grapheme* is used, erroneously, by some as a synonym for what is commonly known as "letter of the alphabet." Still other authors are aware

---

[11]W. Nelson Francis, *The Structure of American English*, Ronald Press, New York, 1958, p. 447.

[12]Robert A. Hall, Jr., *Sound and Spelling in English*, Chilton Books, Philadelphia, 1961, pp. 3, 14–15.

[13]Dwight L. Bolinger, *Aspects of Language*, Harcourt Brace Jovanovich, New York, 1975, p. 476 n.15. Also, for a discussion of the issues surrounding the term grapheme, see H. Minkoff, "Graphemics and Diachrony: Some Evidence from Hebrew Cursive," *Afroasiatic Linguistics*, Vol. 1, Issue 7, March 1975, pp. 2–3.

[14]Carl A. Lefevre, *Linguistics, English, and the English Language Arts*, Allyn & Bacon, Boston, 1970, p. 67.

of the shortcomings of the term *grapheme* but prefer it to *letter* because of their concern about certain variations in meaning that the term *letter* acquires in everyday use.[15] Since no fully accepted, precise term exists, readers of this book may best be served by the use of commonly understood albeit imprecise terms. For that reason, unless the term *grapheme* is obviously called for, the terms *character, mark, sign,* or *symbol*—none of which is perfect—will be used to mean a unit of a writing system. The term *letter* will also be used for the characters of an alphabet.

THE "DIRECTIONALITY" OF WRITTEN LANGUAGE

Both Gelb and Gleason omit from their definitions a vital characteristic that differentiates written communications from ordinary drawings, a characteristic that has special implications for teachers of beginning reading: The symbols of all true writing systems are carefully aligned so that the reader's eyes must move in a prescribed direction to make sense of the message. By contrast, an artist presents a scene that fills a designated area. A person looking at the picture can focus on any part of it in any sequence—can even get an overview of the picture as a whole. In fact, artists often try to counteract this autonomy by composing their work so that the viewer's eyes will be led along a specific route.

Speech Basis of Writing Directionality

The directionality of written language probably stems from its parallel to spoken language, a relationship recognized at least as early as the fourth century B.C., when Aristotle pointed out that "spoken words are the symbols of mental experience and written words are the symbols of spoken words."[16]

By its nature, all speech is emitted on a stream of exhaled air.[17] Even though an idea may occur as a whole—in a global form, as it were, rather than in sequential bits—it must be squeezed into a verbal "ribbon" to be communicated through spoken language.[18] As a result, all writing systems are also set down in a ribbon, symbol by symbol. Despite the strict sequence in which spoken language is produced, however, under normal circumstances the speaker has little control over the direction it takes. It simply fans out into the air, to be picked up by anyone within hearing distance. Writing, on the other hand, being visible, must be placed in some definite direction, with built-in control of the reader's visual route.

---

[15]Richard L. Venezky, *The Structure of English Orthography*, Mouton, The Hague, 1970, p. 50, n. 6.

[16]Gelb, 1963, p. 13.

[17]A small number of utterances—called *suction-sounds or clicks* by Bloomfield—are used in certain African languages and in various kinds of gasps. These are emitted on inhaled air. (Leonard Bloomfield, *Language*, Holt, New York, 1933, pp. 93–94.)

[18]The listener must then absorb the "ribbon" in some form comprehensible to him or her, thus compounding the difficulty of trying to communicate an idea accurately. For some further discussion of this point, especially as it relates to reading, see Miriam Balmuth, "Reading Comprehension: Reading or Comprehension?" in *Literacy at All Levels*, Vera Southgate (Ed.), Ward Locke, London, 1972, p. 113.

Consequences of Writing Directionality

The strictly sequential, carefully directed format of written language has vast implications for attempts to master the reading process. After years of reading, our eyes learn to accommodate the printed word in an almost frighteningly rigid manner.

I first became aware of this by-product of written language through an exercise performed at a trial session of the Evelyn Woods Reading Dynamics Institute in the early 1960s. Participants in the session were asked to look at any page of print in a book and try to see the page as a whole, without focusing on any one part of it. Efforts to do this brought reactions ranging from "difficult" to "impossible"; our eyes insisted on focusing on one point or another, and we could not force them (or free them) to take in the entire page at one time. We were then asked to turn the book upside down and, again, to try to see the page as a whole. When we did so, our eyes were suddenly able to take in the entire, *now unreadable*, page with ease.

It is difficult even today for me to decide which was the more striking insight: that eyes apparently acquire an ability (or compulsion) to focus relentlessly on one point or that they seemed to differentiate automatically between meaningful and non-meaningful writing. The teachers of reading among us have been engaged (until now, perhaps, unconsciously) in producing this "reading of writing" skill in our students.[19]

Varieties of Writing Directions

The last aspect of writing directionality we will consider here is its eccentricity. This is the diversity of the directions in which written languages have been set down.[20] Some go from right to left, some, like ours, from left to right. Others go downward while still others go upward. During one period, for symmetry, Egyptian hieroglyphics would be placed in two columns, with the signs in the right column to be read from left to right and those in the left column, vice versa.

A number of languages have been set down in what is known as *boustrophedón* (like the back-and-forth route of an ox as it plows a field). In such systems, the writer alternates in left/right—right/left fashion, with the individual symbols reversing direction each time as well. This might be thought of as a time- and energy-saving technique, since it eliminates the motion of lifting the hand back to the beginning margin—necessary in one-direction writing. In *boustrophedón*, the hand simply moves directly below (or in some scripts, above or next to) the completed line and goes on writing in the opposite direction. One wonders about the effect of such a system on persons with directional confusion.[21]

One famous artifact, the Phaistos disc of 1700 B.C., is a unique example of writing set down in a spiral, starting on the rim of the disc and coiling counterclockwise

---

[19]Some authors believe that developing such focusing abilities is the key to helping individuals with reading difficulties. Thus, Ross states that "Selective attention is probably the most basic of the skills required for reading." (Alan O. Ross, *Psychological Aspects of Learning Disabilities & Reading Disorders*, McGraw-Hill, New York, 1976, p. 165.)

[20]Diringer (1968) is meticulous about specifying the direction of each writing system he describes.

[21]That is, difficulty in determining left and right in relation to themselves, in space, or both. Much study has been done on the relationship between such confusion and language difficulties—including reading and spelling.

to the center.[22] Finally, rather than always going in the same direction, some languages have nonchalantly varied direction, probably depending on the best way to fit a message into a particular space. Greek writing, from which our own is descended, was changeable in this way until about the sixth century B.C., when it settled into the left-to-right direction we inherited.

An intriguing question prompted by this variation in writing direction relates to the normal tendency of young children to vary the direction in which they string out a series of written characters and in which they write each individual one. Is this another illustration of the recapitulation phenomenon in which the development of the individual is patterned after the evolution of the species?[23] Perhaps adults would feel less dismay at "reversals" in children's early writings if they could view "flexible directionality" as a stage in a venerable process.

THE RELATION OF WRITTEN SYMBOLS TO UNITS OF SPEECH

One final question on the nature of written language relates to that large body of pictorial markings, each of which represents an idea rather than a specific unit of spoken language. An example would be an arrow in an airline terminal, pointing the way from the landing gate to the baggage claim area. In such a case, no specific word or phrase is represented, but passengers from all parts of the world can "read" the arrow. Only a person from some isolated culture in which the arrow convention is unknown would be "illiterate" in this instance. (See p. 14 below for additional examples of this kind of marking in modern times.)

The question raised is: Can a marking that conveys a general idea be called writing, or must all writing represent specific units of speech?

Bloomfield's Response

To this question, the great linguist Leonard Bloomfield apparently gives his answer when he states, "Writing is merely a device for recording speech."[24] This statement

---

[22]Diringer, 1968, p. 44 and Gelb, 1963, p. 155f. The idea has been put forth (Otto Schroeder, cited in Gelb, p. 157) that the Phaistos disc might be unique in yet another way: The individual signs were stamped rather than incised on the clay disc. This would make it the earliest known instance, with no discovered parallel, of writing with movable type. More recently, however, Pomerance reported on work he has been doing to test his hypothesis that the Phaistos disc is actually an astronomical, agricultural tablet. He stated that the entire disc might have been stamped as a unit instead of each symbol having been stamped individually. (Leon Pomerance, "Phaistos Disc—An Interpretation in Astronomical Symbols." Lecture delivered at the Explorers Club, New York City, February 9, 1976.)

[23]The idea that "ontogeny recapitulates phylogeny" was first articulated by Ernst Heinreich Haeckel in *The History of Creation* (1868), a work dealing with evolutionary theory. (John Bartlett, *Familiar Quotations*, 14th Edition, Emily Morison Beck (Ed.), Little, Brown, Boston, 1968, p. 752b.) With respect to writing directionality, the fact that each current written language has settled into a consistent direction might indicate that this consistency is the "mature" circumstance.

[24]Leonard Bloomfield, "Teaching Children to Read," essay in Leonard Bloomfield and Clarence L. Barnhart, *Let's Read: A Linguistic Approach*, Wayne State University Press, Detroit, 1961, p. 20. (Parts of this essay appeared as an article entitled "Linguistics and Reading," in *The Elementary English Review*, Vol. 19, No. 4 [April 1942], pp. 125–130, and Vol. 19, No. 5 [May 1942], pp. 183–186.)

narrows writing down to only those markings that are directly related to spoken language. It reflects the attitude of linguistic theoreticians from the mid-nineteenth to the mid-twentieth century. Bloomfield, however, in obvious contradiction, goes on to classify idea symbols (e.g., the pictorial markings described above) as one type of writing, which he calls *picture writing* (called *pictographic* by others). He tries to account for the inconsistency by stating that with picture writing, the reader gets the ideas that would have been gotten from hearing the speech sounds in conversation with the writer.[25]

Gelb's Designation of Semasiographic and Phonographic Writing

Gelb uses a different approach to the question of whether idea symbols can be considered true writing. He focuses on whether a symbol stands for an idea or for a linguistic unit, such as a syllable or a word, regardless of whether the symbol is pictorial. Thus, Gelb separates the development of written language into two stages: the *semasiographic* and the *phonographic*. In the semasiographic stage (from the Greek root *semasia*, i.e., the signification or meaning of a word), markings express ideas and meanings only loosely related to speech. In the phonographic stage (from the Greek root *phone*, i.e., voice or sound), markings represent exact forms of spoken language, with each symbol in such systems standing for a specific phrase, word, syllable, or individual speech sound.[26]

This distinction will be made even clearer in Chapter 2, in the discussion of the four types of written language.

---

[25]Bloomfield, 1961, p. 22.
[26]Gelb, 1963, p. 11.

2

Pictograms
and Logograms

A surprising fact about the writing system we use in English is how recently it was invented: The first alphabet came into being only about 1500 B.C. For thousands of years before, however, many groups of people communicated graphically through other systems. The usefulness of those other systems may be one reason that the alphabet did not arise sooner. So useful can other systems be, in fact, that some of them are the standard written form of certain contemporary languages (e.g., Chinese and Japanese). Furthermore, vestiges of those other systems can be found in current American communication.

In the three chapters that follow, we examine systems based on *pictograms*, *logograms*, *syllables*, and an *alphabet*. Each type of system is discussed, together with examples of vestiges of the older systems as they appear in our own. The information presented is based on what seems to be the overall consensus of scholars in the field—despite some divergence on almost every point. Divergence is especially frequent on points relating to the early systems, often because there simply is not enough data for conclusive opinions to be established. For finding more data, much depends on the happenstance of archaeological discovery.

PICTOGRAMS

In the pictogram system, alternatively called *pictography*, *pictorial writing*, or *picture writing*, each symbol or pictogram[1] stands for a designated idea rather than

---

[1]The words *pictogram* and *pictograph* are used by different authors for the same thing. Thus, Roger Brown (*Words and Things*, Macmillan, 1958), Doblhofer (1961), and Alfred C. Moorhouse (*The Triumph of the Alphabet*, Henry Schuman, New York, 1953) all use the term *pictogram*. Diringer (1968), Fries (1963), Gelb (1963), and Hans Jensen (*Sign, Symbol and Script*, Putnam, New York, 1969) all use the term *pictograph*. Bloomfield (1933) and Ogg (1971) use neither, but refer to *picture writing*. I have settled here on *pictogram* as a parallel to the uniformly adopted *logogram* (see p. 15 below). Therefore, we have: *logogram/logography/logographic* and *pictogram/pictography/pictographic*.

for a specific unit of spoken language. The example given on p. 11 above of an arrow signaling direction is one pictogram in current use. Another modern pictogram is the classic cartoon sign of a saw in a log with "z-z-z" hovering above. This pictogram gives the idea of someone sound asleep, probably snoring, but there is no one-to-one correspondence with any specific words or parts of words.

Still another example of a pictogram is the sign of a brightly lit electric light bulb above a cartoon character's head. Here, too, no specific words are set down; the meaning might be expressed by various combinations of words and in any language. A practiced reader of cartoons, however, knows immediately that the character had a sudden or a bright idea.

While pictograms do not correspond directly to specific units of spoken language, they acted, historically, as a bridge between the earlier simple drawings and the later writing that did correspond to spoken language units. On the one hand, they retained the pictorial element of the drawings (although usually stylized) and on the other hand, they were set down sequentially, one pictogram after the other, in the fashion of all true writing.

The lack of direct correspondence to specific spoken language units leads some scholars to suspect that pictographic systems are not true writing systems (see p. 11–12). In a sense, the problem seems to be mainly one of deciding at exactly which point an egg became a chicken. For practical purposes, it is useful simply to be aware of the characteristics of pictography, sequence it correctly in the history of writing systems, and not worry too much about whether it is pure enough to be considered true writing.

EXERCISE

In the space provided below, draw a common pictogram.

Languages Using Pictograms

Various kinds of pictorial markings have been found dating from 20,000 to 25,000 years ago (Upper Paleolithic or very early Stone Age). Those were probably used for sympathetic magic or ritual practices, however, rather than to record events or communicate ideas; they are not, therefore, considered writing. True pictographic writing, which did serve for communication and record-keeping, came on the scene many years later, probably not much before 3500 B.C., according to Diringer, who notes that "there is no evidence to prove that any complete system of writing was employed before the middle of the fourth millennium B.C."[2] Diringer finds that pic-

---

[2]Diringer, 1968, p. 4.

tography was used by the early inhabitants of Egypt, Mesopotamia, Crete, Phoenicia, Spain, France, and in many other locations, as well as by the more modern peoples in North America, Africa, and Australia.[3] Moreover, individual pictograms have continued to be used in other written systems throughout the ages; examples of those used in modern society were given above.

Pictographic Reading of Alphabetic Writing

In addition to the use in current communication of isolated pictograms, there are daily instances in which readers of our alphabetic system respond to alphabetically written words as if they were reading pictograms. Thus, for example, fluent readers often manage to abandon their carefully learned responses to words as specific units of speech and respond instead to the ideas in groups of words. Certain speed-reading courses, like the Evelyn Wood program mentioned earlier, use this approach to increase speed while retaining comprehension.

A somewhat different example of the same interaction with printed words can often be observed by reading teachers as they analyze the oral reading errors or "miscues" of certain readers. Such substitutions may make sense in light of some meaning within the reader's understanding but are totally different in appearance or sound from the words on the page. A child I once knew read the word *cookie* for the word *like* in his primer. He was clearly responding to his recollection that *like* represented some pleasurable concept. The word *cookie* was also used in that primer, and, in hastily reviewing his meager store of reading words, he retrieved *cookie* because it, too, represented pleasure.

LOGOGRAMS

In identifying one major category of writing system by the term *logogram*, I am adopting the structure set down by Gelb and strongly championed by Fries. A number of other scholars do not use the term in this way, if at all. Even Bloomfield, who is credited with helping to make the term *logogram* popular,[4] at times uses the term *word writing* in its place, particularly when addressing nonlinguists. Also, in quite a few sources the term *ideogram* is used to mean a similar but not identical type of symbol.

Definition of Logogram

A *logogram* is a written symbol that stands for a specific word or phrase. Examples of logograms in our current writing are numerous. Such characters as *$* (dollars),

---

[3]Diringer, 1968, pp. 10–11.

[4]Samuel E. Martin, "Nonalphabetic Writing Systems: Some Observations," in *Language by Ear and by Eye*, James F. Kavanagh and Ignatius G. Mattingly (Eds.), MIT Press, Cambridge, MA, 1972, p. 81. According to Martin, the term *logogram* seems to have been taken from Peter Duponceau's dissertation (1838) by Bloomfield and A.G. Kennedy.

9 (nine)—as well as all the other Arabic numerals—and *?* (question mark) are a few. Each of these symbols records a specific spoken word or phrase, not simply a general idea.

EXERCISE

In the space provided below, write three logograms.

_____

Notice that the word or phrase represented by a logogram can also be recorded alphabetically (i.e., either *9* or *nine*). The logogram is merely one possible method of representing speech. Furthermore, each logogram can be used to represent different words and often does, in actuality, stand for different words in different languages. The logogram *9*, for example, can be vocalized as "nine" or "nueve" or "neuf." (In alphabetic writing, on the other hand, each word adheres with great strictness to the sounds represented by its spelling patterns so that written English *nine* is always pronounced in the same way, with only inconsequential dialect variations.)[5]

Mathematical logograms like *%*, *0*, and the numerals are particularly useful since they enable persons who do not speak the same language to communicate about fairly intricate matters. This aspect of logographic language is reminiscent of pictographic language. Because pictograms are less precise, however, they tend to be less useful for the subtle kind of interlanguage communication that logograms can provide.

Rebuses

Another way to conceptualize a logogram is to think of it as a rebus, as in " bought some c&y *4* my friend." Rebuses are nonalphabetic symbols, often pictorial, that stand for words or parts of words. They are frequently used to represent homonyms. For example, in different contexts the symbol *4* can represent either the word *four* or the word *for*, and the sign *¢* can represent either the word *cents* or the word *sense*. In the same way, logograms can and have been used in all logographic languages to represent homonyms.

_____

[5]There are some words in alphabetic notation that are not read alphabetically. Examples in English are the symbols *pp.*, which is read as "pages," and *viz.*, which is usually read as "namely." In such cases, what seems to have happened is that a logogram from one language grew out of the alphabetic symbols of another language. See Moorhouse, 1953, p. 26.

Rebuses appeared in England as early as the sixteenth century, when they were scorned as being cheap substitutes for real words, used to disguise illiteracy.[6] In time, they came to be a game-like technique found in puzzles and children's books.[7]

EXERCISE

In the space provided below, write a sentence containing two rebuses.

_____

_____

Rise of Logographic Writing

It is believed that logographic writing began with individual logograms that were used as identity seals in the way that cattle ownership brands are used to identify cattle (the early logograms were used to identify a variety of possessions). Our word *logo* (an abbreviation of logogram), in fact, means a trade seal or an insignia.

It has been hypothesized that these early forms—in which a specific mark was identified with a specific vocal unit—then evolved into fuller systems by the gradual replacement of markings that stood for concrete words by markings that stood for more abstract, sound-alike words in the way that modern rebuses do.

Phonetization

With the continued use of logograms, the practice arose of putting together two or more logograms to make a new word. Often this was done to write foreign names or new words for which no logogram existed and that, perhaps, were composed of sounds not already in the spoken language. In this way, English speakers might

---

[6]See "rebus" in *The Oxford English Dictionary*, 13 vols., and *Supplement*, James H. Murray et al. (Eds.), Oxford, 1933. (Originally published in 1884–1928 as *A New English Dictionary on Historical Principles*.)

[7]A modern program of teaching reading by using rebuses has been published: *The Peabody REBUS Reading Program*, American Guidance Service, Circle Pines, MN, 1969. It is based on an experimental beginning reading program developed for children with mental retardation by R.W. Woodcock at the George Peabody College for Teachers. In it, the concrete words *box* and *table* are represented by pictures of a box and a table, while the abstract words *is* and *are* appear as one horizontal line (–) and two horizontal lines (=) respectively, demonstrating both pictorial and nonpictorial logograms. For further discussion, see Robert C. Aukerman, *Approaches to Beginning Reading*, John Wiley, New York, 1971, pp. 370–374.

write the French word *croissant* as + & (cross-and)—an inexact replication, but close enough so that, with some initial guidance, a reader of the language could make sense of the combination and gradually assimilate the word into his sight recognition vocabulary. This process of phonetization lies at the base of all subsequent writing systems.[8]

Gelb's example of the word *discord* is excellent for illustrating this phonetization process, as well as for underscoring the difference between the ways that pictograms and logograms function. To expand on his description: a pictogram for the word *discord* might show two persons facing each other with hands raised in a stylized manner. The pictogram would stand for "discord, quarrel, litigation."[9] A phoneticized logogram for the same word, however, might show a combined sign of a round disc and a cord, to be read as "discord." (Both symbols for the word *discord* have pictorial features, however, demonstrating why pictograms and logograms might easily be confused if judged solely on external appearance.)

Early Logographic Languages

Once this process of phonetization was functioning within them, some languages continued to incorporate more and more logograms. Other written languages retained the pictographic system and used logograms for limited purposes.

Among the written languages in which logograms came to be of major importance, the earliest and most influential originated in Asia Minor about 3100 b.c., with the Sumerians of southern Mesopotamia. There is strong evidence that all other logographic writing was derived from this one system. The Egyptian, the Hittite, and even the Chinese logographic writing probably came about through the influence of the Sumerians. Of these four written languages, Chinese, still alive today, contains by far the largest number of logograms. While the other three had a preponderance of logograms, they also had a fairly large number of the syllabic.

Logograms in Use Today

Among current written languages in which logograms are the prevailing symbolic unit, Chinese is the most famous. It has been in existence since at least 1500 b.c. and, despite many changes in its outer form, its inner characteristics have remained the same. The modern Japanese writing called *kanji* is also logographic. It is used mainly to represent nouns, verbs, adjectives, and adverbs in a written language that also contains syllabic signs. (See p. 25 below.) The symbols of *kanji* are actually old Chinese logograms that were taken over centuries ago, by way of Korea.

Just as individual pictograms have been adopted in modern written communication (see p. 14 above), individual logograms have been found useful for contemporary writing. The mathematical symbols mentioned earlier, for example, and road signs alerting drivers to conditions ahead are reminders of the value of logographic markings.

---

[8]Doblhofer, 1961, p. 29, among others.
[9]Gelb, 1963, p. 67.

Logograms and the Whole Word Reading Approach

The logographic concept also affects how we learn to read. This is manifested in our efforts to learn to read individual words as if they were logograms—solid word units, that is—rather than as the blends of isolated speech sounds they actually are. Opponents as well as advocates of the whole word approach have likened it to teaching by a "Chinese-writing" method. More is said on this point in Chapters 17 and 18.

Double-Duty Logograms

While true logograms are pronounced and function as words in every way, certain logograms hover between being logograms and being pictograms. Thus, punctuation marks like ? (question mark) and - (hyphen) may be pronounced as words, but they usually function silently, conveying ideas but not themselves being pronounced as part of a message.

EXERCISE

In the space provided below, write three double-duty logograms.

_____

Punctuation and other partially logographic markings stem from another writing symbol tradition that arose during the same era in which logograms arose—starting in about 3100 B.C. At that time, punctuation marks and certain silent markings called *determinatives* were used as they are today—to deliver silent messages within the written material. Determinatives, specifically, were placed before or after *homographs* (words with the same form but different meanings) to tell the reader which meaning was intended. For example, if determinatives existed in Modern English writing, we might distinguish between the two commonest meanings of the word *box* by using different determinative signs standing for "container" and "sport." In Egyptian writing, determinatives became so popular that they were often added to unambiguous words as well.[10]

---

[10]Hans Jensen, 1969, pp. 64–65, 96. (Also see pp. 49–53 below for the origins of modern English punctuation marks.)

3

Syllables

The third type of writing system, that based on syllables, was a further development of the trend toward using written forms to represent spoken language that was initiated by the logograms.

THE DEFINITION OF A SYLLABLE

The term *syllable* might seem too obvious to need further definition here. The nature of a syllable is fairly complex, however, and understanding it will shed light on why syllables have formed the basis of major written languages.

According to the *Oxford English Dictionary*, a *syllable* is "a vocal sound or set of sounds uttered with a single effort of articulation and forming a word or an element of a word."[1] This definition includes the ideas that spoken language is structured on syllables and that every syllable is the by-product of a physiological event. The fact that words can be analyzed into syllables is well known. In need of further clarification is the specific physiological process that takes place when a syllable is uttered.

How a Syllable Is Produced

To understand the physiological origin of a syllable, one must first think of human speech as being not much more than exhaled air or breath:[2] Exhalations provide the power for speech. All exhalations do not produce speech, however. During ordinary, peaceful respiration, the air is automatically drawn in (inhaled) and expelled (exhaled) by the expansion and contraction of the chest and lungs.[3] Little effort is

---

[1]*The Oxford English Dictionary*, Vol. *Su–Sz*, p. 358.
[2]See p. 9 n. 17 above for reference to inhaled speech sounds.
[3]For a thorough description of speech production, see Gloria J. Borden and Katherine S. Harris, *Speech Science Primer*, Williams & Wilkins, Baltimore, 1980, Ch. 4.

needed to send the breath stream on its way out through the nose or mouth, and ex-halations last only a bit longer than inhalations.[4]

When speech occurs, the process is modified. At those times, rapid inhalations are followed by slower, more controlled exhalations, on which utterances are borne.[5] To make the breath stream audible, certain muscles of the head and neck become active. One group of muscles brings the elastic vocal folds[6] into speech po-sition in the path of the exhaled air. From that position, the vocal folds alternately separate (as well as vibrate because of the pressure of the exhaled air) and then come closer together (ceasing to vibrate). That alternate opening and closing of the vocal tract divides the speech stream into subdivisions called *syllables.*

Structure of a Syllable

At the center of each syllable is a *vowel*—heard when the vocal tract is relatively open and the vocal folds vibrate. *Consonants* may be considered vocal tract clo-sures, clinging to either or both ends of the vowel nucleus.[7] The variety of conso-nants and vowels in human speech results from the action of other muscles, above the vocal folds, that move the jaw and tongue as the air stream moves outward.

Although each syllable must have a vowel, consonants are not necessary. Ex-amples of Modern English one-syllable words that illustrate some typical vowel and consonant patterns are shown in Table 3.1.

It might be further noted that it often is difficult to ascertain the beginning and end of a given syllable. The fuzziness of syllabic borders still troubles speech scien-tists, while for written languages like ours, "correct" syllabication was a bone of contention for spelling theoreticians long before Noah Webster became involved. (See p. 158 below.)

· · · · ·

The foregoing description of a syllable is a simplification of the subject, but is offered to emphasize the underlying physiological base in seeking to understand the appeal of syllables in the development of spoken and written language. This physi-ological aspect is recognized by teachers who show children how to determine the number of syllables in a word by clapping out the syllables. Children usually catch on to that technique surprisingly quickly, even though they may find the later study of written syllables difficult.

---

[4]Borden and Harris, 1980, pp. 63–69.

[5]Also, the amount of air inhaled varies with each utterance, depending on how long and how loud the speaker intends the utterance to be.

[6]Commonly known as *vocal cords*, they are a set of complex muscles located, roughly, in the part of the breathing passage behind the Adam's apple. (Giles W. Gray and Claude M. Wise, *The Bases of Speech*, Harper & Row, New York, 1959, p. 163.)

[7]See p. 67 n. 11, 12, 13 and 15 for further discussion of consonants.

Table 3.1.   Vowel and consonant patterns
of Modern English one-syllable words

WORD	VOWEL/CONSONANT PATTERN
ah	one V
big	one C, one V, one C
out	two V[1], one C
kept	one C, one V, two C[2]
trap	two C[2], one V, one C

[1]Or one *diphthong.* See p. 81 n. 6 below for further
definition of diphthongs.
[2]Or one *consonant cluster,* often called *blend* by reading teachers.
Key: C, consonant; V, vowel.

Development of Syllabic Writing Systems

In light of the natural way that syllables are produced, it was almost inevitable that they should have become the "hooks" upon which spoken words are hung. More-over, it should not be surprising that syllables should also have been used as sym-bolized units in many written languages. As a matter of fact, syllables were found to be so convenient for this purpose that Diringer observed, "The syllabic system in-deed, developed more easily and appeared as a creation more often than did an al-phabet."[8]

Syllabic writing developed gradually and probably in the following fashion: First, as was described with the word *discord* (p. 18 above), monosyllabic logo-grams—which represented whole words—would be combined in certain instances to form new polysyllabic words (disc + cord = discord). Next, such specific mono-syllabic word symbols were formalized to represent syllabic units—not just adopted to fill the need for one new word. Finally, these now-syllabic signs (called *syllabo-grams* by Gelb) would be juggled on a more extensive basis to represent a wider range of words. Thus, an ever-increasing body of words that were written syllabi-cally would grow up in an otherwise logographic or logographic-pictographic writ-ten language—in different degrees in different languages.

Over a period of time, as written forms were simplified to achieve greater speed and as different kinds of writing materials were devised, the syllabic signs lost much of their resemblance to the pictorial logographic forms, just as the lo-gograms had lost much of their resemblance to earlier pictographic forms.

Such an evolution was particularly characteristic and seemed to work particu-larly well for certain spoken languages whose words were mainly monosyllabic or lacked many consonant clusters.[9] The reason for this was that the syllables repre-sented in most of the ancient syllabaries (that is, tables of syllables) tended to be

---

[8]Diringer, 1968, p. 12.
[9]Doblhofer, 1961, p. 31.

"open."[10] That is, they tended to end with vowels rather than with consonant sounds (*fee*, *fie*, and *foe* are open syllables, while *fum* is a closed syllable). Apparently, at least some of the languages in which early syllabic signs originated were composed of many monosyllabic words.

In time, when a new group, speaking another language, adopted the already functioning syllabic signs—a common occurrence—it was helpful for the spoken words in the adopting language to be similarly simple in form, preferably with many open syllables. Diringer has an excellent example to illustrate the reasons for this: The word *family*, which has a vowel between each consonant, would be represented by the written syllables *fa-mi-ly*, while a word like *strength*, with its clustered consonants, could only be represented by the written syllables *se-te-re-ne-ge-the.*[11]

Early Syllabic Systems

One of the most important early writing systems in which syllabic signs were used extensively was the famous Mesopotamian (or Babylonian) cuneiform—from the Latin word *cuneus*, meaning "wedge." The people most closely associated with the origin of this oft-cited writing technique were the Sumerians, mentioned earlier in connection with logographic writing (p. 18). Although it is not certain whether they invented cuneiform, the Sumerians are its earliest known users.

It is believed that the Sumerians came from outside Mesopotamia in the fourth millennium B.C. and conquered the whole area from the Semitic peoples who had been living there. The invaders brought with them their pictographic writing system and continued to use it to record in Sumerian, even though the spoken languages in Mesopotamia were entirely different.

In their new location, the Sumerians found a plentiful supply of clay and, instead of cutting their markings in stone, as they had done originally, they learned to use clay and a sharp wedge for their recording. The softer clay, which could be easily and quickly impressed with the new implement, led to a change from the original, rounded pictorial signs to the wedge-shaped cuneiform. In time, the newer method spread from the Sumerians to their neighbors, and a number of other languages in that region also came to be set down in cuneiform. The term *cuneiform*, then, refers only to the shape of the markings and not to any spoken language the markings represent, nor to any writing system. In this cuneiform style, Sumerian syllabic writing signs proliferated, although they were always used along with logographic signs as well.

Noncuneiform writings in which syllabaries developed in ancient times include those of the Phoenicians, the Cypriotes, and the famous Linear B writings of Crete.[12] Egyptian hieroglyphics (or sacred carvings) also developed a number of syllabic signs, starting about 2100 B.C. At that time, they were used in texts of curses cast

---

[10]Diringer, 1968, p. 12. According to Gelb (1963, pp. 195–196), while all syllabaries include open syllable signs, ending in a vowel sound, some also include syllabic signs for closed syllables, ending in a consonant sound.

[11]Or, more phonetically accurate, "se-te-re-ge-ke-the" (Diringer, 1968, p. 12).

[12]Further details about these writings can be found in the cited works by Gelb, Diringer, Doblhofer, Jensen, and Moorhouse, among many others.

upon rulers of foreign lands. Apparently, the problem of recording so many foreign names was resolved by making combinations of existing logographic signs that sounded like the syllables in the various names. (There is a great deal of controversy about the extent to which the Egyptian system was syllabic, although there is evidence of at least some syllabic signs.)

Recent Syllabic Systems

The most outstanding instance of the use of syllabic signs in modern times are the two Japanese *kana*. One, called *katakana*, is used mainly for foreign names and words as well as for the names of cities and countries. The other, called *hiragana*, is the first writing system taught to children. It is supplemented by later instruction in the logographic *kanji* symbols mentioned above (p. 18). The *katakana* and *hiragana* symbols themselves are simplified forms of the older logographic *kanji* symbols. Although each of the three types of writing may be found individually or in any combination with the others, the standard writing system of modern Japanese is a combination of *kanji* and *hiragana*.[13] The entire system was formalized in the ninth century.

Other examples of modern syllabaries can be found in West Africa and among a number of North American Indian peoples. A famous example of the North American Indian syllabaries is that invented in 1821 by Sequoya, a member of the Cherokee tribe.[14] Other American Indian syllabaries—like that of the Cree—were devised by missionaries who hoped to use them in leading the native peoples to Christianity.

Even more recently, the Brazilian educator and philosopher Paulo Freire developed a syllabic method for teaching illiterate adults to read, albeit with groups of alphabetic characters. (See p. 179 n. 5 below for a description of Freire's approach.)

Use of Syllabic Writing In English

In a language such as English, with its considerable number of consonant clusters and great numbers of vowel variations, a syllabary would seem to be of limited value. For many years, however, a form of syllabary, called a *syllabarium*, was used for reading and spelling instruction. These syllabariums can be seen in children's instructional materials like the famous hornbooks used in England from the fourteenth century and through the Colonial period, both there and in this country. A syllabarium was also included in the equally famous *New England Primer* (see pp. 156–157 below). With both of these materials, children who mastered the names of the alphabet were next given exercises with syllables like *ab, eb, ib, ob, ub,* and *ba, be, bi, bo, bu,* and so forth.

---

[13]Takahiko Sakamoto and Kiyoshi Makita, "Japan," in *Comparative Reading*, John Downing (Ed.), Macmillan, New York, 1973, pp. 440–443.

[14]Frances Willard von Maltitz, *Living and Learning in Two Languages*, McGraw-Hill, New York, 1975, p. 152.

EXERCISE

In the space provided below, write five syllables with the letter *d*.

This method of syllable learning as part of reading instruction can be traced back to the Greeks of the fourth and fifth centuries B.C. At that time, too, after mastering the alphabet (through such devices as memorization in written sequence, chanting, and singing) pupils were taught to pronounce two- and three-letter syllables.[15]

The use of syllables in the reading instruction of the last century can be observed in the tradition of word family or phonogram instruction. This tradition has had a life of its own, no matter whether the major approach used by a teacher was alphabetic, phonics, or whole word. Part of its tenacious hold may be attributed to the great popularity of Noah Webster's *American Spelling Book* (also known as the *Blue-Backed Speller)* during the late eighteenth and much of the nineteenth century. Webster's approach began with lists of syllables, which were followed by lists of monosyllabic word families. That technique was rooted in a tradition of teaching syllables that is found in early English and American school texts, including the hornbook, the *New England Primer,* and the exceedingly popular *New Guide to the English Tongue,* by Thomas Dilworth. (See pp. 157–159 below for further discussion.)

Even more recently, syllabic teaching has been given new life and a new theoretical basis in such current "linguistic" reading programs as the *Let's Read* series, derived from the theories of Leonard Bloomfield,[16] and the *Merrill Linguistics Readers,*[17] devised by Charles Fries. Both series use syllables extensively, based on carefully structured linguistics rationales. A number of recent basal programs also include word families in a way that basal readers of 20 years ago would have shunned, reflecting the influence of linguistic programs as well as the more eclectic attitudes of today.

In addition, Gleitman and Rozin have developed a modern syllabary for reading instruction. They base their work on an examination of the historical uses of syllabaries and on recent evidence that "bolsters the suggestion that the syllable is a natural unit for representation in an orthography."[18] Further experimentation along these lines has also been reported by Harrigan.[19]

---

[15]Mitford M. Mathews, *Teaching to Read Historically Considered,* University of Chicago Press, 1966, p. 5.

[16]Leonard Bloomfield and Clarence Barnhart, *Let's Read* (series), Clarence L. Barnhart, Inc., Bronxville, NY, 1966.

[17]Charles C. Fries, Rosemary G. Wilson, and Mildred K. Rudolph (Eds.), *Merrill Linguistic Readers,* Charles E. Merrill, Columbus, OH, 1967.

[18]Lila R. Gleitman and Paul Rozin, "Teaching Reading by Use of a Syllabary," *Reading Research Quarterly,* Summer 1973, p. 464. See also Linda R. Gleitman and Paul Rozin, "The Structure and Acquisition of Reading I: Relations between Orthographies and the Structure of Language" and Paul Rozin and Linda R. Gleitman, "The Structure and Acquisition of Reading II: The Reading Process and the Acquisition of the Alphabetic Principle," in *Toward a Psychology of Reading,* Arthur S. Reber and Don L. Scarborough (Eds.), Erlbaum, Hillsdale, NJ, 1977.

[19]John A. Harrigan, "Initial Reading Instruction: Phonemes, Syllables or Ideographs?" *Journal of Learning Disabilities,* February 1976, pp. 74–80. (See also Patrick Groff, "Teaching Reading by Syllables," *Reading Teacher,* March 1981, pp. 659–663. Groff's review of research on the subject led him to conclude that "reading authorities who currently oppose syllable teaching may be in error" [p. 663].)

4

Alphabets

The fourth and last type of writing system is that based on an alphabet. In view of its overwhelmingly wide use in modern times, this type is the most important of all. Indeed, in many parts of the world, it long ago replaced other types of written language and continues to be firmly established.

The term *alphabet* itself is derived from the first two characters in the conventional sequence of the Greek alphabet: *alpha*, *beta*, *gamma*, and so forth. It stands for a body of characters in a writing system in which each character represents a specific phoneme. Although there is controversy among linguists regarding the concept of a phoneme, it is still widely accepted by descriptive linguists and extensively used in much of the literature in the field of reading.

THE CONCEPT OF A PHONEME

The term *phoneme* refers to a group or class of individual speech sounds (or *phones*) that, in a given language, are considered by speakers of that language to be variations of the same sound (although even so superficially simple a question as what constitutes an individual speech sound is highly complex and controversial).[1] Each of the related phones in such a group is called an *allophone* of the same phoneme.

Thus, the first sound in the word *ten*, the second sound in the word *stop*, the third sound in the word *matter*, and the last sound in the word *bit* are all allophones of the same English consonant phoneme, the one designated /t/. Conventionally, slashes are used to set off phonemes—which refer only to spoken language groups regardless of spelling—to distinguish them from letters of the alphabet, which relate to written spelling forms and may not necessarily correspond to phonemes on a one-to-one basis. This lack of correspondence between spelling forms and phonemes occurs frequently in English. The same letter of the alphabet does not al-

---

[1]For a clear, detailed discussion, see Kenneth L. Pike, *Phonetics*, University of Michigan Press, Ann Arbor, 1943, Ch. 3.

ways represent the same phoneme, and a phoneme may have a variety of spellings. Thus, the letter *t* has no sound in the word *whistle*, while in the word *this* it is part of the digraph *th*, which is pronounced as the phoneme /d̶/.

EXERCISE

In the space provided below, write three words containing the allophones of the English consonant phoneme /b/—one at the beginning of a word, one in the middle of a word, and one at the end of a word.

_____

_____

Similarly, there are vowel phonemes. The sounds represented by the letter *i* in *bite*, *hide*, and *tile* are all allophones of the same English phoneme even though they are considerably different from each other to the ear of a careful listener. Vowels, like consonants, are segmental phonemes.[2]

Different languages have different phonemic systems so that two given phones may be allophones of the same phoneme in one language and of different phonemes in another. For example, the sounds represented by the letters *b* and *v* belong to two phonemes in English, although in Spanish they are allophones of the same phoneme. That is why many persons whose native tongue is Spanish find it difficult to differentiate between these sounds in languages like English. In general, speakers of any language who are without linguistic training are rarely aware of allophonic variations.

In descriptive linguistics, phonology deals with phonemes and sequences of phonemes.

THE STRUCTURE OF AN ALPHABET

In a classically structured alphabetic system (ignoring for now such evolved inconsistencies as we have noted in written English), a different written character is assigned to each phoneme in the spoken language. For writing purposes, therefore, each word to be recorded must be separated into the speech sounds of which it is

---

[2]Suprasegmental phonemes are stress and pitch. See pp. 7–8 above for segmental and suprasegmental graphemes.

composed. The characters for those speech sounds are then set down in the same sequence in which they are produced in the spoken word. The reader of such a system must perceive each character in turn, blend their sounds in strict sequence, and so reconstruct the original word.

This procedure would be tedious for a written selection of any length if a fortunate process did not generally take place. That is, with repeated experience, the string of characters seems eventually to be perceived as a whole unit—almost as a logogram—making the process a good deal easier than it would be if every word had to be sounded out anew each time. Exactly how this occurs is not yet clear. There is evidence that, despite this apparently unified perception, the blending of individual units continues to take place, although at an extremely rapid rate. Geschwind reports several cases of adults who had lost their ability to read as a result of traumatic brain injury. These persons retained the ability to read numbers, however, so that while the word *seven* written alphabetically would not be recognized, the written symbol *7* would be read with ease.[3]

Such cases suggest that, since the subjects were able to function better with logographic symbols, perhaps the blending of visually symbolized sounds of alphabetic language reading can be divorced from whatever sensory and associative processes are necessary for reading other types of written language systems.

THE ADVANTAGES OF AN ALPHABET

A feature of the alphabetic writing system that sets it dramatically apart from the preceding systems is the small number of characters it requires. Since there are considerably fewer phonemes in any spoken language than there are ideas, words, or syllables, many fewer characters are needed in alphabetic writing than in the writing systems that symbolize those more complex linguistic units. Thus, there was a total of about 600 logographic and syllabic signs in the most recent Sumerian writing, about 700 in the Egyptian, and more than 450 in the Hittite,[4] while the letters of the various alphabets have characteristically totaled between 20 and 35. Furthermore, with the passage of time, the older systems tended to acquire many determinatives and additional markings to clarify the meanings of individual symbols, causing the systems to become increasingly cumbersome.

Another striking characteristic of the alphabetic system, one that relates to learning how to read it, is the fact that, after the relatively few symbols of a particular language have been mastered, any reader can thereafter, theoretically, unlock independently all the written words in that language. That independence was a crucial departure from the earlier systems, which required every new reader to depend on others to provide the key for each of the numerous symbols. This feature may also have been an important stimulus for the adoption of alphabetic systems by so much of the literate world.

---

[3]Norman Geschwind, "Anatomical Mechanisms of Acquired Disorders of Reading," Invited Address, 78th Annual Convention of the American Psychological Association, Miami Beach, FL, 1970.
[4]Gelb, 1963, p. 115.

THE FIRST ALPHABET: PROTO-SEMITIC

Although there are many alphabets to be found in the world today, all of them have been derived from the same source, from one single, ancient, prototypic system. That oneness of origin or monogenesis is true of the alphabets of such widely differing appearance and geographic location as the English, the Arabic, the Greek, the East Indian, the old Norse runes, and the Korean, among others. In most cases those were arrived at directly, and at some point in history they were similar to the ancient alphabet, although a number of alphabets were derived indirectly, using the same concepts, with newly invented characters.[5]

Actually, this ancient alphabet is imaginary: There are no records of it. Its existence has been deduced by scholars solely from evidence within later alphabetic systems. Such prototypes are traditionally posited by scholars in various fields. This is done when an original source is not in existence and there is no direct evidence of its prior existence; the probability of its having existed is deduced from evidence within available material from a later date. (See Proto-Indo-European on pp. 56–61 below.) This prototype was the first fully alphabetic system, although it should be noted that earlier Egyptian writing, which contained many different kinds of symbols, contained some symbols that represented individual sounds. These had never been systematized, however, as the alphabet was, nor had they been used independently of the many symbols of other types.

Diringer terms this first alphabet *Proto-Semitic*, stating that it was invented by one of the Semitic peoples living in the area bordering the eastern shore of the Mediterranean in what is now Syria, Lebanon, and Israel/Jordan. The precise nationality of this people is not known, although the time of the invention has been placed by Diringer within the Hyksos period (1730–1580 B.C.).[6] Agreement is far from universal on the origin of this script, however, a question Jensen describes as "one of the most debated problems in the history of writing."[7]

Nevertheless, a good deal is known about the political, economic, and social life of that part of the world at that time. Commercial activity was spreading, with a resultant rise of a class of energetic merchants and tradespeople who needed to communicate about their enterprises. Diringer saw this need in relation to the "independence" feature of alphabetic notation mentioned above, the feature that makes it potentially accessible to large numbers of persons. He writes, "The political situation in the Near East at that period favoured the creation of a 'revolutionary' writing, a script which we can perhaps term 'democratic' (or rather, a 'people's script'), as against the 'theocratic' scripts of Egypt, Mesopotamia, or China."[8] Each of these three earlier scripts had been in the sole possession of an elite few and continued to be so—down to recent times, in fact, in the case of the Chinese.

---

[5]The monogenesis of the alphabet, "now global in extent and multifarious both in form and in the order of its constituent letters," strengthened Westcott's belief in the monogenesis of spoken language as well. (Roger W. Westcott, "Protolinguistics: The Study of Protolanguages as an Aid to Glossogonic Research," in *Origins and Evolution of Language and Speech*, Stevan R. Hamad, Horst D. Steklis, and Jane Lancaster [Eds.], Annals of the New York Academy of Sciences, Vol. 280, 1976, p. 104.)

[6]Diringer, 1968, p. 161.

[7]Jensen, 1969, p. 255.

[8]Diringer, 1968, p. 161.

Diringer further points out that the innovative alphabet met the same resistance from conservative forces that other innovations have met throughout the ages, resulting in a lapse of centuries before the alphabet was established. Even then, he notes, it was used only in newly founded states; for older ones many centuries probably passed before an alphabetic system was adopted.

Childe, too, was impressed by the democratic potential of the alphabet. He says, "Thanks to the reduction of the number of characters and the elimination of the complexities introduced by ideograms and determinatives, reading and writing became as simple as they are today. Literacy ceased to be the mysterious privilege of a highly-specialized class. The small shopkeeper or pedlar could easily learn enough to at least sign his name and keep accounts."[9]

Thus, in addition to its virtues of simplicity and flexibility, the alphabet deserves respect for its accessibility as well. It has from its inception served not only as an instrument for written communications—other writing systems have done the same—but also as a key to unlock certain of the social, political, and economic fetters of multitudes.

---

[9]Gordon Childe, *What Happened in History*, Penguin Books, Baltimore, 1954, p. 182.

5

History of the English Alphabet

The origin of the hypothesized Proto-Semitic alphabet cannot yet be positively determined beyond general statements about the time and location of its first appearance. From that alphabet, however, several other alphabets, including the forerunner of our own, are believed to have been derived. Examples of such offshoots have been found in a number of archaeological discoveries. One discovery took place in the Syrian village Ras Shamrah, near the site of the ancient city Ugarit. Here, cuneiform alphabetic writing was found and dated to about the fourteenth century B.C.[1] This cuneiform alphabet is not considered to be a direct ancestor of our own.

Of our own ancestral script, the earliest examples so far discovered were found at the site of the ancient city Byblos (in modern Lebanon/ancient Phoenicia)—particularly the writings on a wall of the tomb of Ahiram, dating from the eleventh century B.C.[2] Although these Byblos writings are of major importance, other examples of the same alphabet have been found at different sites in that part of the world so that our alphabet's precise point of origin might have been anywhere in the wide Semitic region. In any case, the script represented by the Ahiram writings is believed to be the starting point for our present alphabet.[3]

THE NORTH SEMITIC ALPHABET

Scholars vary in the name they give this writing system. Some call it the North Semitic alphabet, while Gelb maintains that it is one of the West Semitic syllabaries.

---

[1]Ras Shamrah is also the site of the earliest musical writing system discovered so far.

[2]Gelb, 1963, pp. 131–132. Byblos was also noted for its papyrus industry. The papyrus was brought from Egypt by the merchants of Byblos, who became familiar with the Egyptian writing in the course of that commerce. The extent and nature of the relationship between the Egyptian and the Semitic writings is still not clear (Ogg, 1971, p. 75), but the fact of a relationship between the two is undisputed.

[3]Diringer, 1968, p. 160.

Despite differences about its name and about whether it was definitely an alphabet, there is a fair amount of agreement about the source of its characters. It is believed that the forms, but not the names, were derived from the Egyptian script, although the influence of Babylonian cuneiform and other contemporary scripts have been discerned in it as well.

Relation of the North Semitic to the Phoenician Alphabet

The earliest inscriptions written in this alphabet were found on soil inhabited by the Phoenicians. Though they probably did not invent it themselves, it has been linked to them for this reason and because they were so active in transmitting it to a great variety of other peoples and cultures. It was the Phoenicians, in fact, who were mainly responsible for transmitting it to the Greeks, the next people in the chain that connects the ancient alphabet to our own. Some authors even refer interchangeably to that earlier alphabet and to the later Phoenician alphabet, and certainly the description here of the system's characteristics applies fairly well to both of them.

Structure of the North Semitic (and Phoenician) Alphabet

In all, there were 22 characters in the North Semitic script. They generally corresponded in name, sound, sequence, and, to a lesser degree, in form, to the characters in such major alphabets derived from it as the Greek and the later Semitic Hebrew and Arabic alphabets.

The names of the characters were words beginning with the sounds that the characters represented. Thus, the Semitic word for "house"—*beth*—represented the phoneme /b/, while the Semitic word for "door"—*daleth*—represented the phoneme /d/. There is some question about whether the names or the sounds of some of the characters came first. The preponderance of evidence indicates that the sounds came first and the names were assigned at a later date.

Alphabetic Sequence

One aspect of our alphabet has changed remarkably little since the old North Semitic and Phoenician days. This is the listing of letters in a conventional order. Both the custom of such listing and the actual sequence itself have been found on artifacts dated as far back as the fourteenth century B.C. Throughout the long history of adding and dropping individual letters, the general outline has remained—even more in Semitic languages than our own.[4]

This persistence may result from the fact that letters of the alphabet have often been used as numbers so that the sequence was preserved in mathematical computations. Literary devices and various organizational procedures using alphabetiza-

---

[4]One notable exception was the Germanic runic alphabet or *futhark*, in which the sequence differed markedly from the Latin alphabet of its epoch. (See p. 46 n. 12 below.)

tion must have helped maintain it as well. One literary device that has come down to us is that of having each sentence or each word in a selection begin with the letters of the alphabet in sequence. The Bible, for example, includes a number of such selections in the ancient Hebrew—Psalm 111 and others. In our own time, the enormous reliance upon alphabetization in every scientific, economic, and cultural activity makes it inconceivable that the present sequence will be easily changed.

The basis for the original sequence is unknown. Guesses have been made that characters were grouped according to similarity of the sound of the name, the meaning of the name, the form of the name, or the form of the sign.[5] However, no acceptable evidence to prove any of these guesses has come down to us.

Semitic Characteristics of the North Semitic Alphabet

Two features of the North Semitic alphabet link it more closely to the later Semitic alphabets than to those that, like our own, were subsequently derived from the Greek. One feature is its directionality: It was uniformly written from right to left, as modern Arabic and Hebrew are. (Much later, during the flowering of interest in language and language history of the Renaissance—see pp. 108–109 below—Hebrew writing was observed to have the left-to-right Semitic direction. Since Hebrew was then believed to be the original language, the early philologists used the different directions as a reason to transpose letters within words in their efforts to find connections between Hebrew words and words in contemporary languages.)[6]

Secondly, like other Semitic written languages, the ancient characters represent only consonants, with no signs to represent vowel sounds. The reader of such a language figures out each word through a combination of the consonant symbols and the total context.

There has been much ado about this absence of vowel signs. Gelb asserts that without the vowel characters, all the Semitic systems are actually syllabic. Diringer and others insist that the North Semitic is a true alphabet but an imperfect one and that the lack of vowel characters is an indication of this imperfection rather than an indication that the system is syllabic. If Gelb is correct, then the Greek alphabet would be the first true one because of the vowel letters in it (see p. 36 below). Weighty as Gelb's opinion is, however, most scholars seem to agree with Diringer on this issue and consider the North Semitic a true alphabet.

Transmission of the Alphabet by the Phoenicians to the Greeks

The civilization of the Phoenicians flourished between 1200 B.C. and 876 B.C. Within that time, the Phoenicians became the outstanding sailors and merchants of the Mediterranean, visiting other groups who were settled on both sides of the sea as

---

[5]Moorhouse, 1953, p. 104.
[6]Otto Jespersen, *Language, Its Nature, Development and Origin*, George Allen & Unwin, London, 1922, p. 21.

far west as the tip of Spain. Among these groups were the Greeks, and one of the fortunate results of the Phoenician visits was that, early in the ninth century B.C., the Greeks learned the North Semitic–derived alphabetic writing that the Phoenicians used. The Greeks proceeded to alter that writing to fit their own needs.

THE GREEK ALPHABET

After the alphabet had been introduced into Greece, a number of changes were made—slowly, and somewhat differently in different parts of the country. First, a variety of local forms arose. Those were followed by a tendency toward greater and greater uniformity that resulted in two main types: the eastern and western Greek alphabets. Finally, in 403 B.C., the Ionic (an eastern) alphabet of Miletos was adopted officially in Athens. It became so influential that, within 50 years, all local ones gave way to it and the Ionic became the standard Greek alphabet. Gelb notes that the development of the full Greek alphabet was the final major step in the history of writing—nothing new has occurred in the inner structural development since then, only changes in appearance.[7]

Introduction of Vowels and Modification of Consonants

In taking over the alphabet from the Phoenicians, the Greeks adopted 19 characters without change. They retained the forms, the phonemes, and even the names of these 19,[8] although the meanings of the names were lost. All 19 were consonants since the Phoenicians had no vowel signs, and, in making up for this lack, the Greeks made their most important contribution to the development of the alphabet.

Instead of making up new signs for the vowels, however, the Greeks adopted existing consonant symbols from the Phoenician alphabet that were not useful for Greek speech and assigned vowel values to them. Thus, the Phoenician symbol *ayin*, which represented a guttural Semitic sound not used in Greek, was taken over in form, given a new name—*omicron*—and assigned a sound similar to one of our *o* sounds. In addition, some Phoenician signs were modified in sound value to represent similar Greek consonant sounds, and several new signs were added to represent Greek sounds not found in Phoenician. The final number of characters in the Greek alphabet was 24.

Changes in Letter Form

In time, the writing materials used by the Greeks affected the forms of the letters. One common practice was to use a stylus on a tablet with a wax surface. With the stylus, writing would be traced in the wax and a message would be scraped away when its use was over. Because of the pile-up of wax as a stylus moves, however,

---

[7]Gelb, 1963, p. 184.

[8]The names were somewhat modified so that Phoenician *aleph* became Greek *alpha*, *beth* became *beta*, and so on, but these were essentially minor changes.

the strokes were necessarily kept short, and so the written characters were composed of short, fairly straight strokes. That kind of writing was carried over into the writing done on other materials—papyrus and parchment, for example, and only later, from the third century B.C. on, did some freer, more curved writing develop.[9]

Direction of the Greek Alphabet

Another change made by the Greeks was in the direction of the writing. At first, they modified the right-to-left order of the Phoenicians and used the alternating *boustrophedón* (described on p. 10), at times starting at the bottom and going upward. As was customary when boustrophedón was used, the direction of individual letters was also changed to conform to the direction of each line. By 500 B.C., however, the strict left-to-right order that we know became standardized and has been used ever since in all alphabets derived from the Greeks. The direction of individual letters also became fixed as a result.

Spacing and Punctuation

Some of the characteristics of present writing that we take for granted were not available to the ancient Greeks. The simple device of putting a space between each word had still to be invented. Also, since neither punctuation nor the differentiation into capital and lowercase forms had evolved, there was no separation of sentences. To use Ogg's method of illustration, early Greek writing, as well as all other early writing, looked something like this to its readers:

> TOUSEOGGSMETHODOFILLUSTRATIONEARLY
> GREEKWRITINGASWELLASALLOTHEREARLY
> WRITINGLOOKEDSOMETHINGLIKETHISTOITS
> READERS[10]

In the history of alphabetic writing, the Greek alphabet is extremely important. Because of the changes and additions they made to the alphabet they had acquired from the Phoenicians, the Greeks were responsible for most of the one we use today. Furthermore, once the Greeks began to use their alphabet, its influence spread, and it took hold among various peoples, some of whom, like the Etruscans, were themselves of great influence.

THE LATIN ALPHABET

The Etruscans acquired the Greek alphabet during the early stages of its development. They picked it up probably during the eighth or ninth century B.C. The exact

---

[9]See pp. 43–45 below concerning curved forms.

[10]Ogg, 1971, p. 97. Sparse punctuation and lack of spacing was not confined to writings of such antiquity but continued for many years afterwards. It was not until the eighth century, during the reign of Charlemagne, that organized efforts were made to systematize spacing and punctuation. (See p. 46.)

time and location is a subject of debate, although Diringer states that the Etruscans were of eastern, probably Aegean, origin, and that they started using the alphabet before moving to the Italian peninsula.[11] It was there, in Italy, that the Etruscans acted as a link between the Greeks and the Romans, passing the alphabet from one to the other.

The Etruscans settled north of Rome some time before 800 B.C., started to spread southward from there, and managed by the sixth century B.C. to occupy a third of the Italian peninsula—including Rome—before their power declined in the fifth century B.C. It was during the Etruscan ascendancy, about 700 B.C., that the Romans started to use the Etruscan alphabet. That was relatively soon after the Greeks had themselves acquired the alphabet from the Phoenicians, so the Romans were actually developing and refining the Latin alphabet while the Greeks were still developing their own.

From the Greek-derived Etruscan system, the Romans adopted 21 characters, in this sequence: *A, B, C* (pronounced as "k"),[12] *D, E, F, Z, H, I, K, L, M, N, O, P, Q, R, S, T, V* (pronounced both as "v" and as the vowel "u"), and *X*. The forms of these letters were quite faithful to the original Semitic-Greek-Etruscan forms and remained so to a large extent. In time, however, several letters were added, and there was some shifting of the sequence. Thus, the letter *Z* was soon dropped from its position as the seventh letter since it was not needed in Latin. Then the letter *C*, which originally represented both the voiced and the unvoiced forms of the same speech sound, was separated into two letters: the unvoiced was still represented by *C*, but the voiced was represented by a new letter, *G*. The *G* was placed in the seventh position.

The last additions to be made resulted from the need to represent Greek words that were used after the Roman conquest of Greece in the first century B.C. At that time, the letters *Y* and *Z* were borrowed from the contemporary Greek writing system and added to the end of the alphabet. The final number of letters in the Latin alphabet then was 23—all of our present letters except for *J, U,* and *W*. These latter three were added within the last 1,000 years and are discussed below on pp. 39–41.

In addition to the new letters they incorporated, the Romans contributed another dimension to the alphabetic characters. They had a strong interest in the aesthetics of writing, and in their hands the letters became more rounded and beautiful. Since they were particularly concerned about the appearance of their many monuments and inscriptions, they devised techniques of chiseling the rounded forms onto stone, thus preserving them as models throughout the Roman Empire. Ogg, who stresses calligraphy in his book, states that, because of its harmony and proportions, the monument style of the Latin alphabet of the second century is still "thrilling" to look at.[13]

---

[11]Diringer, 1968, p. 388.

[12]Diringer, 1968, p. 419. Diringer notes that in the South Etruscan alphabet the three letters *C, K,* and *Q* were all used to represent the sound of our modern letter *K*. The *C*, however, was used before *E* and *I*, the *K* was used before *A*, and the *Q* was used before *V* (pronounced as modern "w"). Similar differentiation of the three letters among subsequent Latin-derived alphabets (with variation from alphabet to alphabet in the pronunciation of the *C*) may well stem from these ancient conventions.

[13]Ogg, 1971, p. 119. He refers to the letters inscribed on the pedestal of the column of Trajan in Rome (ca. A.D. 113) as the prime example of this style.

Names of the Letters

It was noted above (pp. 34 and 36) that the Phoenician/Greek names were Semitic words that started with the sound that the character represented. In Italy, however, the Greek names were dropped and replaced (among the Etruscans first, perhaps) by monosyllabic names. While the development of the Roman nomenclature for a number of the letters is not fully clear, it may be said that, from the fourth century, the vowel names were composed of a prolonged pronunciation of their sounds (*a* instead of *alpha*, for example). The consonants' monosyllabic names were composed of the phoneme followed by a vowel in the case of stops[14] (*be, de* instead of *beta, delta*) and by a vowel preceding the phoneme in the case of the continuants *F, L, M, N, R, S, X* (*el, es,* instead of *lambda, sigma*).[15] These names have come down to us in close to their Latin forms.

COMPLETION OF THE ALPHABET: *J, U,* AND *W*

The three characters *J, U,* and *W* were the last ones to be incorporated into the alphabet, and each evolved slowly.

The Letter *J*

The letter *J* was derived from the letter *I*. Upon adopting the alphabet from the Greeks, the Romans had taken the letter *I*, keeping the Greek pronunciation of Modern English long *e*, as the *i* in *machine*. Gradually, the Romans also began to use the letter *I* to represent a new consonantal sound—the sound of *i* in Modern English *onion*. That double use of the *I* was kept in Latin-derived languages, although the consonant pronunciation varied from language to language (for example, pronounced as *y* in *yes* in some languages and as *j* in *jump* in others).

With the Norman conquest of England in the eleventh century, the non-Latin Old English language acquired a consonantal *I* with a *j* sound, since that was the consonantal pronunciation of the *I* in the Old French spoken by the Norman conquerors. Both the consonant and the vowel pronunciations were kept for the same symbol from the eleventh through the seventeenth centuries. Because of its small size, scribes during those years often elongated the *I* at the beginnings and ends of words. In cursive writing, the prolongations tended to become curved, giving rise to *J*-like forms.

As an added complication, the letter *Y* was adopted as an alternative for *I* during the Middle English period so that for several centuries all three forms—*I, J,* and *Y*—alternated in English spelling. For much of that time, *Y* was used in final position in words. (This is the reason for our modern spelling patterns in which the final

---

[14]See p. 67 n. 13 below for the definition of *stop*.
[15]Arthur E. Gordon, "The Letter Names of the Latin Alphabet," *Visible Language*, Vol. 5, No. 3, Summer 1971, pp. 221–228.

Y is changed to *I* when an affix is added, as in *carry-carried, baby-babies,* and the like.) That left *J* to be used more or less exclusively in the final position in numerals, as in IIJ for *three* and VIJ for *seven.*[16]

The dot, which originated during the thirteenth century as a faint, slanting line over the *I*, was kept for the lower case *J*. Its purpose had been to identify the lower case *I* when it was adjacent to similarly stroked letters like *M, N,* and *U*, as well as to differentiate double *I* from *U*.[17]

Finally, in seventeenth century English (earlier in Spanish and French) the capital and lowercase *J*s were established as distinct letters and were assigned the values they currently have. Their close relationship was recognized for a long time after that, however—Noah Webster's 1806 dictionary may have been the first in which words that began with them were listed separately. Even in Samuel Johnson's landmark *Dictionary of the English Language* (1755) they were alphabetized as if they were the same letter.[18]

The Letter *U*

The letter *U* is derived from the Roman letter *V*. It first appeared in the third century A.D. as a rounded form of *V* and was used interchangeably with the pointed form until the seventeenth century. The *U/V* had both a consonant and a vowel sound, each of which could be represented by either *U* or *V*. (Again, similar to early *I/J* and modern *I/Y*.) Any differentiation was related to position in a word rather than to the sound represented, with *V* tending to be placed in initial positions and *U* placed in medial or final positions.

In the sixteenth and seventeenth centuries, the move toward our present mode of separating *U* and *V* began, gained momentum, and was formalized by 1700. Old habits die hard, however, and as with *I* and *J*, there were dictionaries as recently as the nineteenth century in which words starting with either letter were included in the same series.

The Letter *W*

The letter *W* has an unusually checkered history. It arose in the seventh century, when the Latin alphabet was used to write English. Since the Latin of that period did not contain the sound, a ligatured double *U* (*uu* or *W*) was introduced whenever the English "w" was required.

In the eighth century, however, this character was replaced by a runic character with the same sound, called a *wynn* (*wyn*) or *wen* and written *Ρ*.

---

[16]Thomas Pyles, *The Origins and Development of the English Language*, Harcourt Brace Jovanovich, New York, 1971, p. 61.

[17]Pyles, 1971.

[18]Mathews, 1966, p. 14. Mathews further notes that in Noah Webster's dictionary of 1806 "The I and J words were separated, possibly for the first time in a dictionary."

Fortunately, by that time, the ligature *uu/W* had passed to the continent and was used in France and Germany—kept in safe-keeping for several centuries, in a sense, for it was brought back to England in the eleventh century with the Norman conquest. At that point, *W* took firm hold in England, eventually superseding the *Þ*, so that the latter went out of use by the end of the thirteenth century.

6

Alternative Forms of Written English

Although I have continually referred to our current alphabet as if it had one form, there are, actually, four basic forms (called *hands* or *styles)* in modern use. First of all, there are the capital, uppercase, or majuscule letters employed at the beginnings of printed sentences. Secondly, there are the cursive[1] counterparts of these: the capital or majuscule cursive letters. Thirdly, there are small-letter, lowercase, or minuscule manuscript letters. And lastly, there are the lowercase or minuscule cursive letters. (Even within these four forms there are variations, such as the italicized print—actually related to cursive writing—and divergent writings of individual letters within each form.) Antecedents of these four forms have been in use at least since the time of the Romans.

The capital manuscript letters came first, and the other three forms were variants of them, derived over a long period of time, starting with modifications originated by the Romans. As long as writing was mainly confined to stone carvings and inscriptions, the capital manuscripts were the only letters used. Then, as new materials were developed and different purposes for writing emerged, other forms were gradually introduced. The capital manuscripts continued to be employed, however, for stone inscriptions and for formal literary writing.

EARLY CURSIVE FORMS: MAJUSCULE CURSIVE

The earliest variant form was majuscule cursive writing, which resulted from the rounding of the angular shapes of the original stone-oriented capital letters. This form was also characterized by the use of ligatures or couplings (such as æ and fi) and by a general scriptural flow.

---

[1]Originally goes back to the Latin *currere,* meaning "to run"; hence, moving, flowing writing.

The development at some point of cursive forms seems to be a tendency of all written languages. Examples of early writing systems in which this tendency was manifested are the Sumerian, Hittite, and Chinese, as well as the Egyptian. Thus, the Egyptian hieroglyphics developed a simplified cursive form called *hieratic*, which, for 3,000 years, was used concurrently with the classic, highly pictorial, hieroglyphic signs. Out of the hieratic emerged an even more abstract, cursive script called *demotic*, many of whose characters were ligatures of several hieratic forms, chained together much like modern English lowercase cursive writing. In time, the demotic came to be the "popular" script of Egypt, at least as important as the hieroglyphic.[2]

The development of cursive writing can be traced directly to the adoption of specific writing materials and implements: reed and then quill pens on papyrus, parchment, and vellum. As was noted above in the discussion of paleographic writing (p. 6), such materials permit a flowing script that requires less lifting of the writing tool than is called for by a process like chiseling on stone. As a result, writing can be accomplished with greater ease. The new ease is often accompanied by a widened spread of literacy, followed by a use of writing in many informal situations, all of which encourages the development of fluent writing with simplified shapes and various ligatures.

Although the exact date of the origin of Latin cursive writing is unknown, there are cursively written graffiti on the walls of Pompeii and Herculaneum—destroyed in A.D. 79—that bear witness to the everyday use of cursive writing by the first century. In addition, there is evidence that the Greeks had begun to use the cursive forms of their writing on papyrus manuscripts as early as the third century B.C.[3]

Informal cursive writing continued to be used in Italy but did not achieve literary status until the tenth century. From that time through the period of the Renaissance and beyond, it flourished as the Italian round hand or cursive. Then, in the sixteenth century, after the invention of the printing press (see pp. 117–120) a slanting form of it was adopted by a renowned Venetian printer named Aldus Manutius.[4] Aldus transferred the round hand into the printing type we know as italics—so named by the many non-Italians who admired and used it widely. This printed form preserved the cursive as a writing style and supported its adoption for handwriting as well.

Our present capital cursive forms, then, are derived directly from the Roman tradition through the Italian cursive writing. They did not undergo the international metamorphoses experienced by the lowercase alphabet forms that are discussed next.

DEVELOPMENT OF MINUSCULE OR LOWERCASE[5] FORMS

The same tendency toward rounding that was reflected in the informal cursive writing eventually influenced the formal capital writing also, although at a later date.

---

[2]Diringer, 1968, p. 36. Both writings, together with a Greek translation, were used for the inscription on the Rosetta Stone. First inscribed by Egyptian priests in 196 B.C., the stone was discovered in 1798, during Napoleon Bonaparte's expedition to Egypt. Scholars used the Greek translation to unlock the hitherto undeciphered Egyptian writing systems.

[3]Ogg, 1971, p. 99.

[4]Founder of the Aldine Press.

[5]First called *minuscule*, the term *lowercase* arose after the invention of the printing press, when printers kept the small letters in a separate case, below the case containing the capital, or uppercase, letters. (From Thompson, 1946, p. 21.)

Thus, a rounded type of formal script, called *uncial writing*, arose during the third century and became the most widely used literary form between the fourth and eighth centuries. It was characterized by such tendencies as, among others, the elimination or the extension of a part of a letter (as *b* from *B* or *q* from *Q*).[6]

Despite these innovations, uncial writing was still fairly close in appearance to the older capital writing. It did, however, pave the way for even more innovative alphabetic characters. Those evolved when uncial writing became influenced by the informal cursive, picking up such features as the connecting of letters and an even greater degree of rounding. As a result, a new form emerged—the *semi-uncial* (or, as some called it, the *half-uncial*) writing. It was the semi-uncial that became "the first approach to small-letter writing and the father of all small letters which were to come."[7] Diringer describes it as a half-and-half kind of writing, "easier than the uncials and more calligraphic than the cursive minuscule."[8]

Origins of the Caroline Minuscule

Because of the influence of the Romans, both the cursive and the semi-uncial Latin forms, alongside the classic majuscule writing, spread throughout western Europe. Then, with the diminishing of Roman power and the expansion of Christianity, new forces came into being and influenced the further development of alphabetic forms. Probably the greatest of those forces were the monasteries that were established as the repositories of literacy and learning. Almost in the way that the nonalphabetic written languages of ancient times were in the possession of elite, generally religious groups, so too, during the Dark Ages (from about 500 to 1000) in the peace of cloistered life, writing was prized and nourished.[9]

The alphabetic forms inherited from the Romans were gradually altered to a greater or lesser degree in each country. From the variant forms that arose, one

---

[6]Diringer, 1968, p. 421.

[7]Ogg, 1971, p. 156.

[8]Diringer, 1968, p. 424.

[9]The "cloistered life" here does not refer solely to that of monks engaged in preserving and fostering the writing heritage of the Christian Western world. Certainly, their work—of towering value—is well known.

What is not well known—and not mentioned in most of the twentieth century sources I consulted—was the widespread, continuous, and superb activity of nuns in the same enterprise. Only by chance, on Thanksgiving Day of 1975, while browsing through the private library of Maria and James Barnett, did I happen upon George H. Putnam's *Books and Their Makers During the Middle Ages* (2 vols., Putnam, New York, 1896), in which the contributions of both individual nuns and groups of nuns are glowingly related. Putnam says, for example, "The principal and most constant occupation of the learned Benedictine nuns was the transcription of manuscripts. It is difficult to estimate too highly the extent of the services rendered by these feminine hands to learning and to history throughout the Middle Ages. They brought to the work a dexterity, an elegance of attainment, and an assiduity which the monks themselves could not attain, and some of the most beautiful specimens of caligraphy which have been preserved from the Middle Ages are the work of nuns" (Vol. 1, pp. 52–53).

Putnam goes on to note that the employment of nuns as scribes dates from early Christian times, from the fourth century at least. He then lists, century by century, the illustrious accomplishments of nuns as scribes and scholars in various parts of western Europe.

More recently, in such works as *Beyond Their Sex: Learned Women of the European Past*, Patricia H. Labalme (Ed.), New York University Press, New York, 1980, efforts have been made to bring to light some of the overlooked instances of outstanding female achievement.

superseded the others and became the main form of western European book writing for several centuries. This was the Caroline minuscule, invented at the end of the eighth century, probably by Alcuin of York, abbot and founder of the school of Tours during the reign of Charlemagne.[10] (Diringer has some question about the exact time and the role of Alcuin and Charlemagne in its invention, although Ogg and others are unequivocal in their acceptance of Alcuin as the originator.)[11] It is this writing upon which our modern printed forms are based.

Apparently, Alcuin, himself English, was first influenced by a tradition of Anglo-Saxon writing derived from a lovely Irish semi-uncial script of the sixth century, the most famous of all the semi-uncials and called by Ogg "the most beautiful manuscript hand that has ever been seen."[12] Not only was the Caroline hand pleasing in appearance, but it was similar enough to prior alphabets to be readable and acceptable to Alcuin's contemporaries. The Caroline was also notable for the way it combined majuscules and minuscules in one alphabet much as we do today, influencing subsequent alphabets to do the same.[13] Thus, its minuscules were smaller than its majuscules and different from them in appearance, and majuscules were used at the beginnings of sentences. According to Ogg, moreover, it was Alcuin who first made divisions between sentences and paragraphs and who was the first to systematize the punctuation of manuscripts.[14] Above all, the Caroline minuscule is important because of its role in the history of printed forms, a role it began to play not long after Johann Gutenberg had perfected the printing press (see pp. 117–120 below).

From the Caroline to Roman Type

The Caroline minuscule was widely used from the ninth through the twelfth centuries. It slowly changed somewhat during that period but in the end was superseded by newer scripts that nevertheless retained the capital-minuscule and other conventions introduced by the Caroline. Noteworthy among these newer scripts was the Gothic black-letter, still used for German, which arose in the twelfth cen-

---

[10]Hence the name Caroline. This style is also referred to as the Carolingian hand.

[11]Diringer, 1968, p. 426. In the year 782 Charlemagne had invited Alcuin to head the school at Tours. (See p. 73 below for the background of Alcuin's scholarship.)

[12]Ogg, 1971, p. 156. The Anglo-Saxon script that developed from the beautiful Irish semi-uncial was used in England until the Norman invasion of 1066. In fact, it had been seventh century Irish missionaries who taught the Anglo-Saxons to write Latin, and the influence of the Irish on letter forms remained. Before the introduction of the Irish alphabet, the Anglo-Saxon tribes had used the runic alphabet (called *futhark*, from its first six letters or runes—from an old Scandinavian word meaning "secret"). The runes, according to Diringer (1968, p. 403) developed from a North Etruscan alphabet, probably not earlier than the second century B.C., and "can be considered the 'national' writing of the Teutons, especially of the North Germanic peoples" (p. 402). The runes were very different in appearance and sequence from the letters of the Latin alphabet, however, despite their cousinly origin. A modified Anglo-Saxon version of the runic alphabet was used in England for about five centuries, overlapping the introduction of the Latin alphabet. Holger Pedersen goes into a good deal of detail about *futhark*, and I suggest that readers curious about this interesting alphabet consult his work, *Linguistic Science in the Nineteenth Century*, John Webster Spargo (Trans.), Harvard University Press, Cambridge, 1931. Reprinted as paperback MB40, *The Discovery of Language*, Indiana University Press, Bloomington, 1959, pp. 229–239. Also, see Diringer, 1968, Ch. 21.

[13]Diringer, 1968, p. 426.

[14]Ogg, 1971, p. 174.

tury and was especially popular during the thirteenth and fourteenth centuries. Then, in the fourteenth century, the humanists[15] of Renaissance Italy rediscovered the Caroline and championed its use in that country.

At the end of the fifteenth century, Italy became a center for fine printing (see p. 119 below). Some of the foreign printers who settled in Venice noticed and admired a contemporary version of the Caroline minuscule and cast it into what became known as roman type. One of these printers, Nicholas Jenson, is especially associated with the development and printing of the roman type. Ogg tells us that Jenson "so perfected the roman small letters that his type forms became models not only for printers in his own day but for all since who have cared for the beautiful letter forms."[16] Gutenberg himself and the printers he taught had used the Gothic alphabet, and we might still be using it today if the roman forms had not been adopted. As it is, our current English books are printed in roman capital and small letters or in any of their hundreds of variations.

THE FOUR CORE STYLES OF TODAY

Down through the ages, different styles or hands of writing have developed for formal versus informal modes. The capital and cursive writing of Roman days and the scribal and popular hands before the invention of printing are examples of this. Similarly, after the invention of printing there were differences between the styles used for the alphabetic typefaces of printing and the hand-written styles, based on different previous models. By the end of the sixteenth century, two different traditions were well on their way to being established: that of the printer and that of the writing master—with surprisingly little influence brought to bear by either one upon the other. This was especially true in England and, soon after, in colonial North America. As time went on, hand-writing grew more and more flowery, embellished with frills and flourishes, while, if anything, printing grew sparer and sturdier. This was the situation through the nineteenth century.

The twentieth century saw a reaction to the earlier extremes of floral handwriting, and tamer styles, like the famous Palmer method, came into vogue. Despite this simplification, however, there is still so great a disparity between current printing and current cursive handwriting that we have, in effect, two different styles (or hands). To add to the complexity, the presence of both capital and lowercase forms in each style results in a total of four alphabetic styles. Although the four contain many similarities between them, there are still so many differences that learning to read and write any one of them does not easily result in learning to read and write any other. The connections within the lowercase cursive handwriting style, for example, give it an appearance entirely unlike any of the other three styles, while only after careful study will such forms as uppercase cursive *F*, *G*, *J*, or *Q* seem to bear any relation to their lowercase or printed counterparts.

---

[15]That is, those identified with the movement of the period that stressed secular, literary culture, grounded in ancient Greek and Roman writings.

[16]Ogg, 1971, p. 218. Jenson had originally been sent by the king of France to study printing with Gutenberg in Mainz. When the king died, Jenson decided to set up his own printing business in Venice (Putnam, 1896, passim).

Teachers and others responsible for school curricula have been aware that the existence of four different styles can be burdensome, particularly for young children just embarking on the road toward literacy. For this reason, it has been the practice in this country since the 1940s to postpone exposure to cursive writing for approximately 2 years after printed language has been introduced. Occasionally, cursive forms have been completely dropped from the curriculum.[17]

Most beginning reading programs, however, present both the upper- and lowercase forms either simultaneously or one very soon after the other and tend to play down the differences in form. Experience has shown this approach to be successful in reading print.[18] Fortunately, the ratio of capital to small letters in most written selections is so small that when meaningful material is presented early to beginning readers, the few capitals that occur are quickly assimilated.[19]

---

[17]Paul C. Burns, *Improving Handwriting Instruction in Elementary Schools*, Burgess, Minneapolis, 1968, p. 31.

[18]A divergence is the modern *i.t.a*, or *Initial Teaching Alphabet* of Sir James Pitman (see pp. 168–169 below), which has no capital forms. In places where capital forms are found in traditional English writing, such as at the start of a sentence, the i.t.a has an enlarged version of the letter. On the other hand, John R. Malone's UNIFON (see p. 168 n. 16) uses only capital forms, with the addition of certain new capital-like characters.

[19]This is true for the immediate present. The use of only capital forms in computer printouts has already begun to raise questions about the future of our written forms, however—including implications for the alphabet in which we teach children to read. It might be pointed out, though, that children have been able to deal with the capitalized forms in comics for years, even children who have some difficulty in reading.

7

English Punctuation Marks

By now, we have looked at all but one of the major characteristics of our writing system. This characteristic has had surprisingly little exploration in comparison to the meticulous appraisal given to each letter of the alphabet and to each style of print. I refer to the practice of using punctuation marks[1] to convey information. Such markings are not themselves pronounced. Instead, they give important clues about the verbal material—the words and sentences—they accompany. They often function as substitutes for the meaning messages carry by the phrasing, stress, and pitch of spoken language and thus add dimension to the flatness of written language.[2] (In modern linguistic models like that of Francis [pp. 7–8 above]), punctuation marks are graphemic representations of suprasegmental morphemes (see p. 199 below).

Although the use of various nonverbalized guide markings in written language is ancient and has been employed continuously for thousands of years—especially in nonalphabetic languages[3]—our own highly precise system of punctuation was set down in an organized fashion only at the end of the sixteenth century. Its roots, however, go back much further than that.

---

[1]There are actually only minor differences between the punctuation marks of written English and those of other European languages. As Gleason notes, "Because the punctuation system of all European languages has grown up through mutual interaction and on the basis of a common 'logical' grammar, all are basically similar" (1961, p. 432).

[2]These are the suprasegmental phonemes mentioned on p. 28.

[3]Gelb, 1963, p. 99. Grouping them all under the heading "auxiliary marks," Gelb says that there were classifiers, determinatives, semantic indicators, and punctuation marks present in Egyptian, Sumerian, Hittite, and Chinese. He later notes that there has been no systematic study of the auxiliary marks of these ancient languages (p. 113).

HISTORICAL OVERVIEW[4]

The modern punctuation marks with the earliest known history are the period, the colon, and the comma. At first, they were not punctuation marks, or even related to written language. Rather, the names were originally used in early Graeco-Roman rhetorical theory to identify rhythmical units of speech where the speaker could pause or take a breath. They were then called the *periodus*, the *kolon*, and the *komma*, and the length of the units they represented correspond to the roles played by their current namesakes.[5] Thus, the *periodus* was the longest unit of speech, the next shortest was the *kolon*, and the shortest of the three was the *komma*.

The first use of written punctuation points in the tradition leading to our own is credited to Aristophanes of Byzantium who, in the third century B.C., invented a regular system of such points for Greek in the schools of Alexandria. This practice spread and, by the fourth century, had been formalized in Latin writing tradition by the insertion of punctuation points between the conventional speech units just described.

Gradually, the points took on the names of the units they marked off: hence, period, colon, comma. The units themselves, however, were still set up to indicate pauses for breath and for rhythm. It was only in the seventh century that punctuation points began to be used more in the way they are today, namely, to set off units of meaning rather than just units of rhythm and breath. Isidore of Seville (early seventh century) is credited with being the first to suggest using punctuation in this way.[6] This new use was also carried over into the way other punctuation marks were used. Systematization of punctuation to a certain extent as well as of spacing started somewhat later, in Charlemagne's time (eighth century—see p. 46 above).

From Roman times through the Middle Ages, Latin was in the forefront of Western punctuation usage. New signs were generally invented and used first in Latin, then adopted for writing in other languages. Usage was always inconsistent and unorganized, however, even in Latin. It was only after the invention of the printing press that a decided movement toward uniformity began to take place. By the early sixteenth century, there had developed a rough but relatively consistent system of punctuation marks in Latin liturgical works. That led to greater systematization in other languages as well.

In English writing, the use of punctuation marks was rare through the fifteenth century. Their use was haphazard and frequently had no reference to the meaning of the text. In the late sixteenth and early seventeenth centuries, however, the influence of the Latin liturgical system spread to English writings, and an English system of punctuation slowly developed. Contributing to the development was an increase in education and an increase in the number of grammar books. The latter became a force in codifying and formalizing punctuation as well as other usage. The introduction of printing helped establish punctuation conventions, too.

The sixteenth century also saw the introduction of a new way to use punctuation: for such meaning and word-structure purposes as apostrophes for possessives

---

[4]Robert A. Peters, *A Linguistic History of English*, Houghton-Mifflin, Boston, 1968, Ch. 27, is the source for much of the material in this section.

[5]I can find no definite dates for this practice, but it certainly started before 300 B.C.

[6]Peters, 1968, p. 298.

and hyphens for compound words. From the sixteenth century on, English punctuation conventions continued to multiply until, in the writings from 1740–1770, our modern system can finally be discerned.[7] From that time through the end of the nineteenth century, the regularization and utilization of punctuation continued to grow, and numerous rules were set down by grammarians.

All of that was changed, with the start of the present century, when the trend toward more and more punctuation showed a marked reversal. A new emphasis on clarity in writing style—with shorter sentences requiring fewer markings—was mainly responsible for this decrease in punctuation. In addition, and perhaps proceeding from the same desire for greater simplicity in all artistic and creative areas, a simpler printing aesthetic came into being. This was reflected in trimmer-looking printed pages, with fewer markings and less clutter, and paralleled the movement toward less elaborate handwriting and printing styles that was characteristic of the same era (see p. 47). That trend is with us today.

ORIGINS OF SPECIFIC PUNCTUATION MARKS

In this section, the common punctuation marks will be listed in the approximate order of their invention, together with a brief summary of their origin and first appearance in English writing.

The Period, the Colon, and the Comma

It was noted earlier that the period, colon, and comma can be traced back to ancient Greek times. They were rarely used in English writings until the sixteenth century. Of all punctuation during the early days, the mark most often found is the period, although even its use was limited—and inconsistent to the point of chaos. The colon and the comma appear much less frequently and with equal inconsistency. They each had the same appearance they have today, and their functions are fairly parallel to their current ones, although until the end of the seventeenth century they still tended to mark off breathing rather than meaning units. After that time, these points followed the course of all English punctuation described at the end of the previous section.

The Semicolon

The semicolon is another punctuation point developed first in Latin. It can be found in writings beginning with the tenth century, when it was known as the *punctus elevatus* (elevated point). Campbell notes that it was the strongest stop in one system used in the late tenth and eleventh century English manuscripts, superseding the weaker period. At that time, too, an inverted semicolon was used to indicate a weak

---

[7]Peters, 1968, p. 304

stop. In the main, however, the semicolon was rarely used in English, and even then in characteristically unorganized and meaningless ways. Only during the sixteenth century was its function systematized, and it became commonly used by the end of that century.[8]

The Hyphen

The hyphen first appeared in English manuscripts at the end of the tenth century. At that time, its use was confined to words divided at the end of a line, much as we use it today. In some instances, an additional hyphen was used at the beginning of the next line to precede the final portion of the split word. By the end of the sixteenth century, it was also being used for marking compound words (*shoe-horne*, for example). During that century, it also appeared in the form of an equal sign (=) tilted upward.

The Question Mark

The question mark was first used in Latin at the end of the tenth century, when it was called the *punctus interrogativus*. It was first used in English in about 1520, appearing as an inverted form, hovering over the dot (~). By 1594, it was being written in the same direction that we give it today. It has always been given its customary function.

The Apostrophe

The word *apostrophe* was used in ancient rhetoric to indicate the absence of a person or thing and thus came to be used when a part of a word was absent. In the sixteenth century, it simply indicated missing letters (*turn'd*, *'tis*). By the late seventeenth century, its use had extended to the singular possessive case of nouns (*the king's house*). Actually, this use was an extension of the earlier one of denoting an absent letter because in Old and Middle English the possessive was written with an *es* (*kinges*). The apostrophe is therefore marking the absence of the *e*.

Finally, in the eighteenth century, the apostrophe was given the additional role of indicating the plural possessive (*kings'*).

Parentheses

Parentheses, also called *round brackets*, were in use, at least in printing, in the sixteenth century, where they set off (generally short) verbatim statements somewhat

---

[8]Ronald B. McKerrow, "Typographic Debut," in *Books and Printing*, Paul A. Bennett (Ed.), World Publishing Company, Cleveland, 1951, p. 81.

as quotation marks do today. They also seem to have been used to indicate emphasis. By 1771, if not before, parentheses had assumed their present function of setting off side comments. (Unfortunately, the terms *parentheses* and *brackets* were often used interchangeably by early sources, leading to present-day confusion about whether round or square brackets or both were meant.)

Square Brackets

Square brackets, also called *crochets* in the past, were in use in printing at least by 1603, serving the same function that parentheses do now. They were also occasionally used to set off a brief quotation. In the eighteenth century, brackets were described as enclosing a word or a sentence to explain what went before.[9]

Exclamation Point

The exclamation point seems to have originated in England at the beginning of the seventeenth century. It seems to have been first used to indicate admiration.[10]

Quotation Marks

Quotation marks were apparently in existence by the seventeenth century. Their use originally was to call attention to important passages, which often happened to be directly quoted statements. By the eighteenth century, they had become linked to verbatim quotations the way they are today. At first, the start of a quotation and the beginning of every line were marked. Only after the middle of the eighteenth century were the ends of quotations regularly indicated as in present-day writing.[11]

---

[9]*Oxford English Dictionary*, Vol. 1, p. 1045.
[10]Peters, 1968, p. 302. Quotation from Ben Jonson's *The English Grammar*, 1640.
[11]McKerrow, 1951, p. 82.

8

The Ancestry
of Spoken English

Indo-European Origins

Of the four historical processes we are examining, the one most familiar to non-specialists is probably the development of modern spoken English, mainly because of its major event: the combining of the Anglo-Saxon and the Norman French languages after the Norman invasion of England in 1066. While the importance of this event can hardly be overestimated, numerous other forces and interactions both long before and after 1066 shaped the language as well. These forces can be traced through a series of languages that began thousands of years ago and were first spoken in places far from England.[1] Gordon lists the languages chronologically, and we shall follow his sequence in reviewing this history:[2]

1. *Proto-* or *Primitive Indo-European* (undated, but probably before 3000 B.C.).

2. *Prow-* or *Primitive Germanic* (undated, but probably shortly before the beginning of the Christian era).

3. *West Germanic* (undated, but perhaps during the fourth century or earlier).

4. *Low West Germanic* (undated, but perhaps fifth to sixth century).[3]

5. *Old English,* formerly called *Anglo-Saxon* (late sixth century to about 1100).

6. *Middle English* (about 1100 to 1500).

---

[1]I must caution the reader that what was said earlier about the lack of certainty and the divergence of opinion on many points in the history of written language is at least as true about the history of spoken languages, perhaps even more so. Its primeval beginnings go back further, and its written remnants are suspect, since ancient records, even more than modern ones, often preserve a language different from everyday speech.

[2]James D. Gordon, *The English Language*, Crowell, New York, 1972, p. 87.

[3]Bloomfield, 1933, pp. 58–59. These possible dates for West Germanic and Low West Germanic were deduced from information appearing on these pages.

7. *Modern English* (about 1500 to the present). There are many dialects and regional variations of Modern English, just as there were of the older languages. Speaking historically, the term is used for the dialect spoken in England known as Received Standard (alternately, Received Standard Pronunciation or Received Pronunciation [abbreviated, RP]).

PROTO-INDO-EUROPEAN

Somewhat in the same way that a prototypic, prehistoric alphabet, the Proto-Semitic, has been hypothesized for our written language (see p. 30 above), a prototypic prehistoric mother tongue has been deduced for our spoken language. Now called *Proto-Indo-European*,[4] this ancient language was spoken by a small group of people who lived at least several thousand years before Christ.[5] Unfortunately, its speakers were illiterate, even though their Egyptian and Babylonian contemporaries were not. Therefore, there is no written record of Proto-Indo-European, and no living group still speaks it. The idea of its former existence was put forth, and some of its probable form was reconstructed, only after a comparison was made of the lexical, grammatical, and phonological features of the languages that appeared to have evolved from it.

Early Speakers of Proto-Indo-European

Most scholars agree on a European rather than an Asian origin of Proto-Indo-European. On the question of the precise original site, some authors leave open the possibility that it may have been in an area as far east as modern Lithuania. According to the most recent theory, however, the speakers of Proto-Indo-European first lived in the northern part of Europe, on the Baltic coast between the Elbe River (of modern Germany) and the Vistula (of modern Poland), a little earlier than 3000 B.C.[6] This location and time were so precisely arrived mainly after a careful analysis of a number of words relating to animal and plant life in the vocabularies of various Indo-European languages. Thus, for example, as one clue in determining the location, it was noted that the word for "salmon" appears in many forms in Indo-European languages that are spoken far from salmon-inhabited waters, while at the

---

[4]Gordon, 1972, p. 82. Gordon notes that the names *Indo-Germanic* and *Aryan* were formerly used. These have been replaced by *Proto-Indo-European*—derived from *Indo-European*, a term given to the languages presumed to have evolved from it.

[5]The concept of this prototypic spoken language differs from that of the prototypic alphabet in one important way, however: That alphabet is considered to be the original of all alphabets, while Proto-Indo-European appeared relatively recently in a total history of human speech that may be as long as a million years old. In fact, some scholars have even deduced an ancestor, Proto-Indo-Hittite, from which Proto-Indo-European may have been derived—a deduction that is still highly controversial, however. (Morton W. Bloomfield and Leonard Newmark, *A Linguistic Introduction to the History of English*, Knopf, New York, 1963, pp. 122 and 126. Also, Winfred P. Lehmann, *Historical Linguistics*, Holt, Rinehart and Winston, New York, 1973, p. 36, and Gordon, 1972, p. 87.)

[6]Paul Thieme, "The Indo-European Language," *Scientific American*, October 1958, pp. 72 and 74.

same time, the waters at the alleged ancient site are teeming with them.[7] Then, based on this location, the time was settled upon by such techniques as noting that the words for "goat" and probably "horse" are in the Indo-European vocabularies, and these animals were not domesticated in that area until a little before 3000 B.C.

At some point, groups of Proto-Indo-European speakers began to migrate to other areas of Europe and to western Asia. The separated groups incorporated minor differences of pronunciation, vocabulary, and other language characteristics into their speech so that, after a while, new dialects of Proto-Indo-European emerged.[8]

With the passing of time and a lack of the constant, direct communication we enjoy today, differences among the dialects grew, eventually becoming so great that the dialects developed into entirely new languages. Then, because groups of people continued to break off and migrate further and further apart from each other, the new languages themselves gave rise to new dialects that, in turn, developed into other new languages.[9]

During the thousands of years since Proto-Indo-European's existence, many new languages were generated from it in this fashion, and a large number of them are still spoken today. All have been grouped together and are considered to be one large branch—the largest, in fact—on the tree composed of all human languages.[10] This branch is further subdivided so that languages that have developed from the dialects of the same language are grouped together. Thus, the Romance group includes Italian, Spanish, and French, among others, while the Celtic group includes Gaelic, Breton, and Welsh. In all, 11 or 12 groups are believed to have developed from the ancient prototype and are called the *Indo-European* family.[11]

Initial Study of the Indo-European Family

A French Jesuit, Gaston Laurent Coeurdoux, in 1767, and an English orientalist, Sir William Jones, in 1786, are credited with being the first to conclude that such dispersed languages as Sanskrit, Latin, Greek, Gothic, Celtic, and Old Persian shared a

---

[7]The ancient word for salmon is still used practically in its original form. It is *laks-*, almost identical to the delicatessen *lox*, a kind of smoked salmon. The word *lox* was brought into the United States by Jewish émigrés from northeastern Europe. Also, a Swedish dish called *gravlaks*, made of marinated salmon, is popular in Scandinavia today.

[8]Dialects are forms or varieties of a language arising from regional or class peculiarities of vocabulary, pronunciation, or style. Two or more dialects are considered to be the same language as long as their speakers manage to understand each other's speech despite the differences. A dialect may develop into a new language when it acquires so many differences that its speakers and the speakers of the original language no longer understand each other.

Lehmann notes that on occasion dialects are called languages for reasons of national dignity. Thus, although Swedish and Norwegian are mutually understandable and, linguistically, true dialects, they are commonly referred to as separate languages (Lehmann, 1973, p. 33).

[9]Brook cautions against oversimplification of this complex process. There were overlappings and recurrent waves of migration, as well as various dialect differences, probably both in Proto-Indo-European and in the languages that succeeded it. All these precluded a neat, two-dimensional evolution. (G.L. Brook, *A History of the English Language*, Norton, New York, 1958, p. 33.)

[10]See p. 577 of *Thorndike Barnhart Advanced Dictionary* for a diagram of this tree.

[11]There is some variation in the manner of grouping Indo-European languages. Some scholars separate Indic and Iranian, for example, while others consider them to be one group. Similarly, Baltic and Slavic (or Slavonic) languages have been combined by some and separated by others. Also, some scholars include Hittite while others do not consider it to be a descendant of Indo-European. Rather, they believe it to be a parallel or sister branch that developed from a common ancestor—Proto-Indo-Hittite (see note 5). Some scholars include only language groups that are still being spoken and omit Hittite and Tocharian.

common ancestor. The story of how these and other scholars pulled together wide-spread clues to reach this conclusion is one of marvelous knowledge, insight, and ingenuity. Jones, especially, was influential in arousing interest in the concept of one original language. His is the often quoted statement that Sanskrit bears to Greek and Latin "a stronger affinity, both in the roots of verbs and in the forms of grammar, than could possibly have been produced by accident; so strong, indeed, that no philologer[12] could examine them all three without believing them to have sprung from some common source, which, perhaps, no longer exists; there is a similar reason, though not quite so forcible, for supposing that both the Gothick and the Celtick, though blended with a very different idiom, had the same origin with the Sanskrit."[13]

Interest in this possibility quickly caught on and, in 1816, a German scholar, Franz Bopp, published his treatise on the inflection of verbs in a number of the Indo-European languages. This event is said to mark the beginning of a systematic study of the Indo-European family. It is worthwhile noting that the work of Bopp was largely an application of the techniques used, long before, by Panini in his analysis of Sanskrit verbs.[14] Panini was a Hindu grammarian who, somewhere in the period around 400 B.C., codified the Sanskrit of his time in minutest, perfect detail.[15] His work was enormously influential in India. Knowledge of it and of Sanskrit started to reach Europe in the sixteenth century. As contact between India and Europe increased, scholars learned more about Panini's work, and it became a model for the study of individual languages as well as for comparative language study. Bopp was among those who strongly felt its influence.

This first work by Bopp appeared almost simultaneously with the work of Rasmus Rask, a Danish scholar, and Jacob Grimm (of fairy-tale fame, but an eminent linguist as well). In the second and third decades of the nineteenth century, both Rask and Grimm began to publish their discoveries of certain important phonological correspondences among Indo-European languages. The discoveries are known as Grimm's Law (rather unfairly, since Rask was the true discoverer, although Grimm presented it systematically) and are the cornerstone for understanding how the next ancestor of English, Proto-Germanic, was structured.

Since that time, many scholars have studied and compared the features shared by the families in each branch of the Indo-European family. They have arrived at general agreement about which specific features were inherited from the Proto-Indo-European ancestor.

---

[12]Linguist, that is. *Philology* was an earlier term for linguistics, mainly comparative and historical at that time.

[13]From a speech delivered in India before the Bengal Asiatic Society, partially quoted in Pedersen's book (1931, p. 18). Jones was altogether an extraordinary person. To mention just a few facts about him: he was a member of Samuel Johnson's circle who, before coming to India, had withdrawn as a candidate for Parliament just before election day because of his sympathy for the Colonies in the Revolutionary War and his opposition to the slave trade going on at that time (Pyles, 1971, pp. 85–86).

[14]Thieme, 1958, p. 66.

[15]Bloomfield, 1933, p. 11. Bloomfield states that Panini's grammar "is one of the greatest monuments of human intelligence." Furthermore, "No other language, to this day, has been so perfectly described."

Bloomfield dates Panini's treatise a bit later—between 350 and 250 B.C. The 400 B.C. date given above was obtained from a more recent source (Lehmann, 1973, p. 22).

The Heritage of Proto-Indo-European

The influence of Proto-Indo-European can be perceived in three aspects of the languages descended from it. Certain vocabulary words, grammatical forms, and a pronunciation change called *ablaut* have been traced back to this one original source.

Vocabulary

A large number of similar words are shared by languages in the Indo-European family. Scholars have concluded that these words were derived from an original Proto-Indo-European word and, in many instances, have deduced the forms of the original words by means of complex linguistic techniques. Reconstructed in this way are words for family members (*mother, father, brother, sister,* and so on), words for numbers (**oines, *dwo, *treies,* and others to 10, as well as the word for "hundred"),[16] words for body parts, some words for tools (*wheel, axle, yoke*), and words for many animals and plants.[17] Individual words, such as the word for God (**deivos*), and for down (**ni-*) are among the numerous others that have been listed.

Table 8.1 illustrates how the first three numbers are related within some languages of the Indo-European family.[18]

Table 8.1.   Relation of the first three numbers within some languages of the Proto-Indo-European family

PROTO-INDO-EUROPEAN	ENGLISH	LATIN	GREEK	WELSH	GOTHIC	DUTCH
*oinos	one	ūnus	oinē[1]	un	ains	een
*dwo	two	duo	dyo	dau	twai	twee
*treies	three	trēs	treis	tri	*threis	drie

[1]Actually, "one-spot on a die."

Grammatical Forms

Indo-European languages have retained elements of the grammar as well as a large number of individual words of Proto-Indo-European. This is especially true of Sanskrit, in which many of the original forms have survived and have eased the task of scholars seeking to reconstruct the earlier language.

All evidence points to a complex grammatical system that included the parts of speech found in Modern English: verbs, nouns, prepositions, adjectives, and so on. Because we are so familiar with this system, it is easy to assume that it is universal. On the contrary. According to Potter, responding to the question of whether the various parts of speech are applicable to all languages, "these word-classes apply to

---

[16]Conventionally, reconstructed words are indicated by a preceding asterisk.
[17]Pyles, 1971, pp. 91–92. Also, Thieme, 1958, among others.
[18]Pyles, 1971, p. 92 (adapted).

Indo-European languages alone."[19] Other scholars agree that, apart from verbs and nouns, which seem to be present in some form in all examined languages, none of the other parts of speech appear to be essential to the functioning of a language, and only Indo-European languages incorporate them all. Other languages have certain features, however, such as formality markers, that Indo-European languages lack.

Proto-Indo-European has also been characterized as an inflectional language, or one in which changes within the word itself are used to indicate different aspects of a word's grammatical function.[20] This took the form of expressing changes of tense, number, person, mood, gender, and so forth, by the addition of specific affixes and by changes in the vowels within words. Examples of this kind of change are, in current English, *run–running–ran–runs* and *book–books*, and in Romance languages like Spanish, verb conjugations such as *hablo–hablas–habla–hablamos*.[21]

Although Proto-Indo-European was highly inflectional (the most prominent example of such a language, according to Pedersen),[22] its descendants are considerably less so.

In the evolving new languages, many of the endings were dropped, to varying degrees within each language. Thus, Sanskrit retained many of them and, to a lesser degree, so did German. English, Spanish, and French, on the other hand, are among the languages that became less inflectional and dropped many of the endings. Modern English, in fact, has been classified as both isolating (as in *can go–will go–went*) and inflectional (as in *walk–walks–walking*).

Ablaut or Gradation

A feature of Proto-Indo-European that unites all its descendants relates to its extensive inflectional system. Its large number of suffixes resulted in many related polysyllabic words, and the pronounced accent or stress within such related words

---

[19]Simeon Potter, *Modern Linguistics*, Andre Deutsch, London, 1957, p. 99.

[20]Pedersen, 1931, p. 100.

[21]Linguists have identified four types of word structure according to which all languages of the world may be classified. These are: inflectional (described above), isolating (or analytic), agglutinative, and incorporating (or polysynthetic) types.

Isolating languages, like Chinese and, to a lesser extent, English, use a different word for each change of meaning, even with related words—as in the English group *is–am–were–are–was*.

Agglutinative languages, like Turkish and Modern Armenian, combine separate units of meaning (not necessarily words) to indicate meaning changes. Such languages differ from inflectional languages in that each such unit can stand on its own as well as in combination with other words. Examples in Modern English that are similar though not exactly the same are compound words like *cannot, into–onto, childlike–childbirth*. The units *can, not, in, to, child*, and so forth, are called *free forms*. (In inflectional languages, the units that are combined include many that cannot stand on their own but must always occur in combination with other units. Examples in English are affixes like *-ing, -ed, un-*, and so forth—called *bound forms*.)

Incorporating languages, like Old Irish, ancient Aztec, and that of modern Greenland, are actually extensions of inflectional languages. Here, even more meanings, including the objects of verbs, are conveyed by changes in the basic word. In such languages, subject, tense, object, indirect object, and so forth, are all included within the one verb form, which then becomes, essentially, a complete, one-word sentence consisting of bound forms. They can be lengthy and may end up looking like the famous English noun *antidisestablishmentarianism*. Bloomfield cites an example from the highly incorporating Eskimo language in which one long word meant "I am looking for something suitable for a fish-line" (1933, p. 207).

Rarely does any one type appear as the sole form of word structure in a given language. There is usually an overlap of more than one type so that the classification of any given language is relative.

[22]Pedersen, 1931, p. 100.

tended to shift from one syllable to another. This shifting occurs today in related words like *magnet–magnetic* and *adore–adoration*.[23] The change of stress affected the tone, quality, and duration of specific vowels within each word, somewhat as the vowel in the second syllable of *magnet* changes in *magnetic* and the one in the final syllable of *adore* changes in *adoration*.

In Proto-Indo-European, the vowels in related words changed in discernible patterns according to the degree of syllabic stress. By using certain comparative techniques, scholars have been able to identify the vowel variation patterns within a number of the ancient groups. Each vowel sound in these patterns has also been "graded" in comparison to the other vowels in its pattern and classified by such terms as normal grade, lengthened grade, weak grade, and zero or vanishing grade (in which the vowel sound disappears completely, as the second vowel sound has disappeared in the Modern English negative form *cannot–can't*).[24] Thus, the vowel sounds in the second syllables of *history*, *historic*, and *historian* might be graded as, respectively, weak or perhaps zero grade, normal grade, and lengthened grade.

This process of vowel variation was named *ablaut* by Jacob Grimm. Other terms used for it are *gradation* and *apophony*.

Awareness of the functioning of ablaut has been very helpful to scholars in seeking relationships among many words in different Indo-European languages.[25] During the ages in which offshoots of Proto-Indo-European grew into new languages, differing single forms of related words would be adopted by different languages. In time, the suffixes of the adopted forms would drop off or change, leaving the word's stem with the grade of the vowel that happened to be there.[26] When such a stage had been reached, it would be difficult to connect words with shortened or changed vowels from different languages without knowledge of the ancient ablaut patterns. With such knowledge, scholars have succeeded in tracing back to many probable Proto-Indo-European forms, and relationships between words in far-flung languages have become apparent. Gordon uses the word *knee* to give a fine example of how this worked: Proto-Indo-European has three forms: **geneu*, **goneu*, and **gneu*. These produced, respectively, Latin *genu*, Greek *gonu*, and English *knee* (*g* became *k* in all Germanic languages).[27]

---

[23]Gordon, 1972, p. 88. These examples and the examples in the following paragraph are based on Gordon's treatment of this topic.

[24]Potter (1957, p. 81) uses the modern English word *nest* as a classic example of zero grade. The word is derived from a Proto-Indo-European word meaning "place where a bird sits down" and originally sounded something like **ni-s'd-os*. The **ni-* meant "down," the **s'd* came from the same stem as the modern English word *sit*, and **os* meant "bird." The second syllable was unstressed, and its vowel had a weak grade—the unstressed schwa sound. This weak sound, in time, faded into zero grade (much as the second vowel in the word *different* has faded for many speakers) leaving **nisdos*. Then, through the ages, the last syllable dropped off, and the word evolved into *nest*.

[25]See p. 65 below for discussion of ablaut in relation to Germanic verb forms.

[26]The example of the evolution of the word *nest*, given in note 24 to illustrate zero grade, can be used to illustrate the process of ablaut as well.

[27]Gordon, 1972, p. 89.

9

The Germanic Heritage

Proceeding from Proto-Indo-European, the language next in the chain leading to Modern English is considered to be the forerunner of all languages of the Germanic branch of the Indo-European family. It is known as *Proto-Germanic, Primitive Germanic, Pre-Germanic*, or simply *Germanic*. It relates to such languages as English, German, Scandinavian, and Dutch in the way that Latin relates to Italian, Spanish, French, and other languages in the Romance branch of the Indo-European family.

Like Proto-Indo-European, Proto-Germanic has not left any direct evidence of its existence, either as a currently spoken language or in the form of written records.[1] It, too, has been reconstructed by scholars from characteristics that, although absent from languages belonging to other branches of the Indo-European family, are found in all languages believed to have descended from Proto-Germanic.

The period in which Proto-Germanic was spoken is thought to have been shortly before the Christian era, and its speakers probably lived in and around present-day Denmark. Because of the decided ways in which their language became differentiated, it is believed that they remained separated from other speakers of Indo-European for a long period of time.

The characteristics of Proto-Indo-European noted in the last chapter were common to all languages derived from it. As each branch of the Indo-European family evolved independently, however, each developed characteristics specific to itself. Why a certain feature became incorporated into any given language is unknown. One possibility is that as an Indo-European–speaking group moved into a new region and its language displaced the language there, some of the characteristics of the prior

---

[1]Lehmann, 1973, pp. 32–33. The earliest written records of any Germanic language to date are from the fourth century, mainly in the form of runic inscriptions in Norway and Denmark.

language became incorporated into the newly adopted Indo-European one. Such a possibility is only conjecture, however. All we can do is observe that, as groups of people were separated, their language changed in discernible patterns.

THE PROTO-GERMANIC LANGUAGE

Vocabulary

Despite the many words that have been borrowed from other languages (called loan words[2]) throughout the centuries, a large number of words that exist in Germanic languages do not have cognates (i.e., related words)[3] in any of the other Indo-European branches. Such words are presumed to be derived from Proto-Germanic. Examples in Modern English, Modern Swedish, and Modern German are: *rain–regn–Regen, drink–dricka–trinken, broad–bred–breit,* and *hold–hall–halten.*[4] Readers familiar with Romance languages will note that these examples are different from their Latinate synonyms. For example, "rain" is *pluie* in French and *lluvia* in Spanish while "to drink" is *boire* in French and *beber* in Spanish. (The root of the Modern English *beverage* is a borrowing from the Old French version.)

Grammatical Forms

In character with the language's highly inflectional nature, Proto-Germanic grammatical forms were numerous and complex. A noun system that rested on multiple inflectional endings showing number (singular and plural) and case was matched by a somewhat more elaborate adjective declension system. Personal pronouns were also fully inflected, as was the definite article (of which the word *the* is perhaps the sole survivor in Modern English).[5] All these were in line with the complexity inherited from Proto-Indo-European.

Only the verbs of Proto-Germanic moved toward simplification—dramatically, in fact. The number of tenses was reduced to two—the present and the absolute past (or preterite)—and most of the numerous inflectional endings were discarded. In place of these endings, the Germanic language adopted verb phrases[6] on the order of such Modern English forms as *will sing* or *had danced.* By contrast, other

---

[2]*Loan words* are exceedingly numerous in English, which is very open to new words and which has been spoken by groups of people who have been in contact with many foreign cultures. Any word not based on an original Germanic one is considered to have been borrowed.

[3]The term *cognates* is used to designate words in different languages that were derived from the same source. Thus, the English word *difficult* and the Spanish word *difícil* are cognates, derived from the same Latin root.

[4]Pyles, 1971, p. 110. These examples are based on Pyles's material.

[5]Alfred C. Baugh, *A History of the English Language,* Appleton-Century-Crofts, New York, 1957, pp. 64–67.

[6]Also called phrasal verbs or periphrastic (that is, roundabout) tenses (Gordon, 1972, p. 138).

Indo-European languages kept and, in some cases, even added to the older forms. Languages within the Romance branch, for example, contain many verb declensions, which can be easily observed in Latin and its descendants.

Another striking feature of Proto-Germanic verbs was the presence of two classes of verbs. For some unknown reason, a certain verb ending arose in Proto-Germanic that did not arise in any other branch of Indo-European. This was the form occurring in consonantal verbs (termed *weak verbs* by Jakob Grimm) that indicated the past tense by means of a dental suffix such as *d*, *t*, or *th*. Many Modern English verbs have similar endings: *bake–baked, sell–sold.*

These dental endings were used for the past tense of most Germanic verbs. Some verbs, however—*vocalic* or *strong verbs*—indicated changes in tense by means of internal vowel variations that related back to the old Proto-Indo-European ablaut (see pp. 60–61 above). In Proto-Indo-European, the changes in syllabic stress caused by the inflectional endings led to corresponding changes in the vowel sounds of the stem. When the endings dropped away, the vowel changes in the stem were kept and indicated the tense. Proto-Germanic strong verbs continued to utilize the internal vowel changes. In Modern English, the verbs *ride–rode, choose–chose, sing–sang,* and *stand–stood* are descendants of the older strong verbs.

EXERCISE

In the space provided below, write two Modern English verbs and their corresponding past tense forms that use internal vowel changes.

_____

_____

Pronunciation

As Vallins points out, "English is a language of strong stresses."[7] That characteristic first appeared in Proto-Germanic and had a powerful effect on its pronunciation.

---

[7]G.H. Vallins, *Spelling*, revised by D.G. Scragg, Andre Deutsch, London, 1965, p. 16.

Syllabic Stress

In contrast to syllabic accents in Proto-Indo-European—which seem to have been movable by rules—Proto-Germanic words were, with one important exception, uniformly stressed on the first syllable. In fact, Bloomfield and Newmark observe that English words with accents on other than the first syllable are generally borrowed (e.g., *photography, vocation*). In a number of instances, even borrowed words are stressed on the first syllable, having been changed through the years to conform to the English pattern. Thus, Italian *balcone*, which became English *balcóny*, is now English *bálcony*.[8]

The important exception to the initial-syllable stress pattern in Proto-Germanic was in the case of compound verbs like Modern English *begin* and *abide*. In those words, the *be-* and the *a-* had originally been separate prepositional adverbs. When they were absorbed into the verb to form a new compound, the stress remained on the original verb, that is, on the second syllable.

Vowel Changes

Certain vowel changes occurred in Proto-Germanic that did not occur in other branches of Indo-European. In one such change, Proto-Indo-European *short o* became Proto-Germanic *a*, as in *father*. Thus, the ancient **okto* for the number "eight" was *octo* in Latin and *ahtau* in Gothic, an old Germanic language.

Also, Proto-Indo-European *long a* became Proto-Germanic *long o*. For example, Latin, which retained the old vowel pronunciation, had *mater*, while Old English had *mōdor*.[9]

Consonant Shifts

It is a series of changes or shifts in the pronunciation of consonants, however, that is most noteworthy in Proto-Germanic. The changes are important both for the resulting differences in the pronunciation of many words and for the advance in historical linguistic theory that came about from the discovery of the patterns into which they fell. I refer to the patterns first perceived by Rask and Grimm (see p. 58) and known as *Grimm's Law*, or the *First Sound Shift*. Understanding the workings of shift was subsequently refined by those additional insights of Karl Verner known as *Verner's Law*.[10]

Even though the changes occurred gradually and over long periods of time, they functioned with great regularity. They are rather complicated for nonspecialists to digest, but awareness of some of them can help in understanding how words in other languages relate to many English words as well as provide a background for certain concepts we shall touch upon in this book.

---

[8]Bloomfield and Newmark, 1963, pp. 113–114.

[9]Pyles, 1971, p. 105.

[10]Verner first published his findings in an article called "An Exception to the First Consonant Shift" (translation of the original German title, "Eine Ausnahme der ersten Lautverschiebung," 1875) (Pedersen, 1931, p. 282).

Grimm's Law

The consonant sounds involved in Grimm's Law may be classified into three groups. One group consists of Proto-Indo-European initial voiced[11] aspirated[12] stops,[13] namely, the old forms of *b*, *d*, and *g*.

Although in Modern English the voiceless stops *p*, *t*, and *k* are more obviously aspirated than their voiced counterparts *b*, *d*, and *g*, in Proto-Indo-European the *b*, *d*, and *g* were also strongly aspirated as they are today in India and Ceylon.[14] This greater degree of aspiration is indicated by writing the three sounds as *bh*, *dh*, and *gh*.

These aspirated stops underwent a change in two shifts. In the first shift, the stops evolved into voiced fricatives[15] that were produced in the same part of the mouth that the original stops were, but now the air was permitted to move out rather than being closed off. It was as though, through the years, the pressure of the aspiration overcame the barrier caused by the closing of the mouthparts, and the sound of the escaping air was altered accordingly. The *bh* now sounded like what is currently known as *barred b*: That is, the *b* is pronounced with the lips only loosely in contact, so that the air slips through as if it were more like the voiced fricative *v*. The *dh* and *gh*, in like fashion, changed so that the air was permitted to stream out: the *dh* now sounded like Modern English voiced *th* while the *gh* changed to a guttural fricative, similar to the Greek *gamma*.

In the second and final shift, these three sounds changed into unaspirated voiced stops, much as we have them in Modern English. It was as though there was a reaction to the earlier increased emission of air—a reaction so strong that even the relatively small amount of air that had escaped during the aspirated stop period

---

[11]A voiced speech sound is produced as the vocal cords vibrate. One can generally recognize whether or not a speech sound is voiced by placing a hand on the throat while the sound is being produced.

The voiced speech sounds in present-day English include all the vowels and the consonants usually represented by the letters *b*, *d*, *g*, *j*, *l*, *m*, *n*, *r*, *v*, *w*, *y*, *z*, *ng* (as in *sing*), *th* (as in *that*), and *zh* as in *muzhik* (also found as the *z* in *azure* and the *s* in *pleasure*).

Speech sounds that are produced without the vocal cords vibrating are called *voiceless*. The voiceless speech sounds in current English are the consonants represented by the letters *f*, *h*, *k*, *p*, *s*, *t*, and the digraphs *ch* (as in *child*), *sh*, *th* (as in *think*), and *wh*.

[12]An aspirated speech sound is a consonant produced with a discernible puff of air, such as the *p* in *put*, the *t* in *take*, and the *c* in *coal*. The aspiration can be noted by placing a hand directly in front of the mouth to feel the puff of air as the sound is being made.

[13]A *stop* is a consonant produced in such a way that the air stream being exhaled is completely closed off by the pressing together of the mouthparts involved in its production. As a result, such sounds cannot be prolonged in the way that vowels and all other kinds of consonant sounds can. Another term used for stop is *plosive*.

Modern English stops are the sounds represented by the letters *p*, *b*, *t*, *d*, *k*, and *g* (as in *go*). Pronounce and compare these sounds with some nonstop consonants such as *s*, *f*, *l*, *m*, or with any of the vowels. Stops may be either voiced (*b*, *d*, *g*) or voiceless (*p*, *t*, *k*).

[14]William A. Smalley, *Manual of Articulatory Phonetics*, Practical Anthropology, Tarrytown, NY, 1963, p. 423.

[15]A *fricative* is a consonant sound in which the stoppage of air is not complete. Instead, one of the mouthparts involved in its production reaches so closely to the other that the air forces its way through in a stream, making a hissing or a buzzing sound (Smalley, 1963, p. 13). The term *spirant* has been used synonymously with fricative.

The fricatives found in Modern English are the sounds represented by the letters *f*, *v*, both *th*'s, *s*, *z*, *sh*, *zh*, and *h*.

Table 9.1.   Stages of consonant shifts for *b*, *d*, and *g*

STAGE I (PROTO-INDO-EUROPEAN)	TO	STAGE II (TRANSITION)	TO	STAGE III (PROTO-GERMANIC)
bh		ƀ		*b*
dh		*th (that)*		*d*
gh		guttural *g*		*g*

now seemed too great, and all air was stopped. As a result, we have modern unaspirated voiced stops *b*, *d*, and *g*. The stages of the shift in these three consonants may be charted as shown in Table 9.1.

The second group of consonant sounds included in Grimm's Law consists of Proto-Indo-European voiceless stops, which became Proto-Germanic voiceless fricatives. Here, too, the manner of articulating the consonants changed from a stiff to a looser control so that the air streamed out instead of being held in check. The consonants were *p*, *t*, and *k*, and (except when preceded by *s*) they evolved, respectively, into *f*, *th* (*thick*), and, in Modern English, to *h* in initial position. (This change occurred in only one shift for *p* and *t*, but in an intermediate stage *k* was pronounced as a guttural *ch* similar to the *ch* in modern German *nacht* [night]. Germanic languages other than English retained this guttural sound. See Table 9.2.)

The third group of consonants changed after the others. The Proto-Indo-European voiced stops *b*, *d*, and *g* changed into Proto-Germanic voiceless stops *p*, *t*, and *k*. See Table 9.3.

Words that illustrate the differences between the Germanic changes and the non-Germanic retention of the Proto-Indo-European consonants are: Greek canna*b*is–English hem*p*; Latin *d*uo–English *t*wo, and Latin a*g*er (field)–English a*c*re.

Verner's Law

While the three groups of changes in Grimm's Law accounted for a great number of similar words in different Indo-European languages, there were certain unexplained exceptions, notably, the appearance of voiced consonants where, according to Grimm's Law, voiceless ones belonged. It was Karl Verner who first accounted for the exceptions by pointing to the role played by syllabic stress. Pyles offers a useful example of how this works: Compare the sound of the *x* in *execute* and *exercise* with that in *exert* and *examine*.[16]

The intricacies of Verner's Law and how he demonstrated its development may be found elsewhere. Here, let us just note that by accounting for even minimal exceptions, Verner showed that every language sound change is a result of regularly operating laws and not "a mere whim of language."[17]

Moreover, Verner's work "forcefully brought to the attention of scholars the importance of accent in linguistic history."[18] Many times since then, syllabic stress has been observed to exert a powerful influence on other aspects of pronunciation.

---

[16]Pyles, 1971, p. 109.
[17]Pedersen, 1931, p. 283.
[18]Gordon, 1972, p. 90.

Table 9.2. Consonant shifts for *p*, *t*, and *k*

PROTO-INDO-EUROPEAN	TO	PROTO-GERMANIC
p		*f*
t		*th (thick)*
k	guttural *ch*	*h* in initial position

Table 9.3. Consonant shifts for *b*, *d*, and *g*

PROTO-INDO-EUROPEAN	TO	PROTO-GERMANIC
b		*p*
d		*t*
g		*k*

WEST GERMANIC

With the passage of time, Proto-Germanic was subdivided into two or three major language groups. There is some difference of opinion on this point: Most writers divide the newer languages into three groups: North Germanic, East Germanic, and West Germanic. Lehmann, however, states that the most recent linguistic evidence divides Proto-Germanic into two groups: West Germanic on the one hand and, on the other, a combination of what has been separately considered East Germanic and North Germanic.[19] In any case, it is from the West Germanic tradition that English stems.

The development of West Germanic from Proto-Germanic took place no later than the fourth century.

LOW WEST GERMANIC

West Germanic was itself soon subdivided into two major languages: High West Germanic and Low West Germanic. The separation is thought to have occurred during the fifth and sixth centuries.

The terms *High* and *Low* refer to the geographic regions in which the languages were first spoken. Speakers of High West Germanic lived in the mountainous southern part of Germany, while speakers of Low West Germanic lived in the northern coastal plain, near modern Schleswig-Holstein. High West Germanic evolved into the standard German of modern Austria and Germany. Low West Germanic is the ancestor of Modern Plattdeutsch (or Low German), Dutch, Flemish, Frisian, and English.

[19]Lehmann, 1973, p. 32.

Characteristics of Low West Germanic

Historically, the speakers of High West Germanic were "relatively isolated within the continent," while those of Low West Germanic and its descendants were "open to more influences that might bring change."[20] As a result, Low West Germanic and its descendants (especially English) grew much further away from the parent language, Proto-Germanic, than did High West Germanic.

Thus, Low West Germanic often adopted new words from other languages with practically no change, while High West Germanic traditionally replaced the meaning of a borrowed word with Germanic roots. The word *temporarily* can be used to illustrate how this worked: In Modern English, the Latin concept of using "time" as a basis for the idea of impermanence as well as the Latin word itself for time (*tempus*) were both adopted. In the Modern German word—*zeitweilig*—the concept was adopted but German roots were substituted for the Latin.

Because of these contrary methods of assimilating new words, foreign and foreign-sounding words proliferated far more in Low West Germanic languages, such as English, than in the High West Germanic ones.

Moreover, Low West Germanic and its descendants dropped many of the inflectional endings of case, number, gender, and so forth that High West Germanic retained. The decay of endings had been a long-time trend of the Germanic evolution from Proto-Indo-European, but it accelerated in Low West Germanic and continued to do so in the languages that evolved from it. This was particularly true of English.

While High West Germanic was generally more conservative than Low West Germanic, in one instance it was the more open to change: There was a regular shift in the pronunciation of dental consonants that occurred only in High West Germanic and remained with its descendants. Thus, *d* became *t* (Modern German *teuer* is Modern English *dear*), the old *t* became *ts* (spelled *z* or *tz*) or *s* (Modern German *zehn* is English *ten*, *Katz* is *cat*, while *suss* is *sweet*), and the *th* became *d* (Modern German *dick* is English *thick*).

A number of other consonants were shifted as well, though with less regularity. Often, however, *p* became *f* or *pf* (*fief* for *deep*, or *pfanne* for *pan*), *v* became *b* (*fiber* for *over*), and *k* became the well-known guttural *ch* (*machen* for *make*).

---

[20]Stuart Robertson, *The Development of Modern English*, revised by Frederic G. Cassidy, Prentice-Hall, Englewood Cliffs, NJ, 1954, p. 34.

10

Backgrounds of Old English

THE MIGRATION OF LOW WEST GERMANIC SPEAKERS TO THE BRITISH ISLES

Three groups of speakers of Low West Germanic—the Jutes, the Saxons, and the Angles—lived in the area bordering the North Sea that is now northern Germany/southern Denmark. Their location made it relatively convenient to travel to the British Isles—which lay directly to the west across the North Sea—and there is evidence that Germanic peoples arrived in Britain as early as the fourth century.[1] However, tradition has it that in the fifth century (449 is the date given),[2] they began a century-long invasion of Britain (the largest of the British Isles, that is, containing modern England, Scotland, and Wales). The three groups came in successive waves, probably in the order given above, and gradually overran the island. Finally, in all but a few outlying regions,[3] they displaced the Celtic people who had been living there.

---

[1] D.J.V. Fisher, *The Anglo-Saxon Age*, Longmans, London, 1973, p. 15.

[2] This date is based on the writings of the seventh and eighth century English historian, St. Bede (called the Venerable Bede). Bede stated that the three Germanic groups were initially invited by Vortigern, king of the Britons, to come help him against the Picts, who were attacking him from the north. (The Picts lived in what is now modern Scotland. See p. 73 for some further details about them.) The invitation was accepted and the "guests" indeed helped vanquish the northern enemies. Then, however, instead of peacefully settling down, or perhaps returning to the continent, they sent word home to their warlike relatives to join them in the fertile, vulnerable land. And join them they did, in great numbers. In time, according to Bede, the Germanic groups allied themselves with the Picts and proceeded to devastate most of Britain by a "heathenish" slaughter and conquest of the land.

Although no one can attest to the complete accuracy of it, modern authors generally agree that much of what Bede wrote is probably true. A Modern English translation of Bede's original work can be found in Bede, *A History of the English Church and People* (dated 731), Leo Sherley-Price (Trans.), Penguin Books, Harmondsworth, England, 1955.

[3] Wales was one of the areas that retained its Celtic character, including its language. The Welsh tongue in use today is a descendant of the non-Germanic tongue spoken by the early Celtic inhabitants. Cornwall, the other major Celtic refuge, kept its Cornish language for a somewhat shorter time—the last known speaker died in the eighteenth century.

The invaders naturally brought their Low West Germanic language with them, and it eventually became the standard language of the country. It was not to remain intact, however. In the new environment and over the course of the two centuries that followed the first invasion, it evolved into a new language, *Old English* (also called *Anglo-Saxon*). Among the circumstances effecting this evolution was the existence of the earlier inhabitants of Britain, who had long lived with a colonial presence—the Romans—on British soil. The backgrounds of both the Celts and the Romans were very different from the backgrounds of the Germanic groups and, to a limited extent, this also affected how the language changed.

The Celts

The Celts in Britain were the descendants of an Indo-European–speaking people who had themselves come as invaders. Many centuries earlier, in prehistoric times, they had replaced "multi-racial" inhabitants, about whom very little is known today.[4] Although the date of the arrival of the first Celts in Britain is not established, we know they were a branch of a widespread, Celtic-speaking population that apparently emerged in Central Europe north of the Alps and then moved out over a large area of Europe, especially during the 500 years before Christ. They reached as far east as Ankara and westward to Spain, northern Italy, Gaul (or modern France), Britain, and Ireland, until they were overcome by the Romans under the leadership of Julius Caesar. They were the "Gauls" of Roman histories, and, after their conquest by the Romans, their Celtic language gradually gave way to Latin. By the early part of the Christian era, in fact, Celtic had practically disappeared from the continent. It continued to exist in the British Isles, however, the last region where Celtic was the dominant tongue.

The original Celtic language was most closely related to early Italic—more so than Latin is to Greek, as a matter of fact. It is not classified as a Romance language, however. Rather, Celtic and the languages stemming from it comprise a separate branch of the Indo-European family. The later Celtic languages and their speakers have been divided by linguists into two groups, depending on how a certain Proto-Indo-European speech sound was pronounced. The sound k^w, was like k pronounced with rounded lips. Celtic languages in which the k^w became an unrounded velar, guttural sound are called *q-Celtic* or *Goidelic* (related to the term *Gaelic*) and their speakers are Goidelic Celts. Those languages in which the lip-rounding led to a *p* pronunciation are known as *p-Celtic* or *Brythonic*[5] (related to the terms *Briton* and *Britain*) and their speakers are Brythonic Celts. In the British Isles, most of the Goidelic Celts lived in Ireland, although the Scotch-Irish of northern Britain and the

---

[4]The first inhabitants of whom there is any trace came by land from Europe when Britain was still part of the continent—before the most recent Ice Age, that is. Much later, after the Ice Age and after the flooding that separated Britain from the mainland, the so-called Iberians are believed to have settled gradually. Many of these were apparently Mediterranean and Alpine peoples. They were the constructors of Stonehenge, in about 1600 B.C., although they had lived in Britain for thousands of years before that date. (G.M. Trevelyan, *History of England*, Longmans, Green, New York, 1945, pp. 2–7. Also, R.M. Rayner, *England in Early and Medieval Times*, Longmans, Green, New York, 1931, pp. 1–9.)

[5]*Cymric* is a term also used to refer to this group. *Brythonic*, according to the Oxford English Dictionary, was coined from a Welsh word for Briton, while *Cymric* has long been in use from the Welsh word for "Welsh." Both terms exclude the Gaelic/Scotch-Irish Celts.

people of the Isle of Man were also Goidelic. Celts living in other parts of the British Isles were generally Brythonic.[6]

The Goidelic Celts of the British Isles remained separate from the Brythonic for many centuries and were independent even during the periods of Roman and Germanic domination of Britain. They managed to preserve their Celtic tongue to modern times, although in the fifth century they adopted Christianity and, with equal eagerness, became engrossed in the secular culture of classical Greece and Rome. Through their efforts, they assisted both traditions to flourish in places far from their Irish land.

The contributions of the Irish toward the enhancement and spread of writing in early times have already been touched upon (see p. 46). On an even more comprehensive scale, they assumed leadership in the preservation of tradition and learning—classical as well as Christian—from the seventh to the tenth centuries. Their involvement reached deeply into the European midcontinent, where Irish and Irish-influenced scholars were associated with outstanding centers of cultures in the Alps and northern Italy. They also exerted a strong influence closer to home, in the establishment of outposts of learning in northern England.[7] All during this time, they were able to maintain much of their Celtic individuality.

The Brythonic Celts, on the other hand, were far more heavily pressured by other peoples. Even before the Germanic groups came, the power of Rome had reached Britain and had affected the Brythonic culture.

The Romans in Britain

The Romans played a circumscribed role in Britain's early history. Although Britain was a Roman colony for almost four centuries, only some of the Latin culture was absorbed into the Celtic language and customs. Roman officials ruled the British natives but did not actually assimilate with them. When Christianity was adopted by the Romans, however, it was adopted by the British as well—probably the most important effect of the Roman occupation.

The first contact with Rome occurred in 54 B.C., when Julius Caesar led Roman soldiers in an invasion of southeastern "Britannia," conquering the Celtic inhabitants. The Romans did not settle there at that time, though, because the Celts paid them to go away. The Romans departed, not to return until almost a century later, in A.D. 43.

This time the Romans stayed, spreading out over the Celtic parts of Britain. They stopped short of the northern area inhabited by the Picts, who remained steadfast in what is now modern Scotland.[8] Nor did the Romans cross the narrow sea to Ireland. They retained Britain as a colony for nearly 400 years, until the power of Rome itself began to decline in the fifth century. When it became necessary to use every resource against enemies close to home, the Romans voluntarily withdrew

---

[6]Gordon notes that the two groups came to the British Isles in two separate waves—first the Goidelic and then the Brythonic Celts. The dates of the migration are not known, as they occurred in prehistoric times (Gordon, 1972, p. 94).

[7]It was at one of these outposts, the school of York, that Alcuin was nurtured (see p. 46).

[8]The origins of the Picts are uncertain. Morris notes that though there were six different groups of varying antiquity and origin among them, these have been confused with each other *(continued on p. 74)*

from Britain and left its former colony without a powerful protector. Shortly after this the Germanic groups began to arrive. They found the inhabitants of Britain to be products of their history—namely, Christians who spoke a Brythonic Celtic tongue with a sprinkling of Latin words.

BRITAIN IN THE FIFTH AND SIXTH CENTURIES

Generally speaking, the three groups of Germanic invaders settled in three different parts of England: the smallest group, the Jutes, settled in the small southeastern peninsula of Kent; the Saxons in a larger southern region; and the much larger group of Angles in a much larger area in the Midlands and in the north.[9]

After conquering Britain, the new Germanic settlers adopted neither the language nor the religion of their new home. Rather, after destroying most organized Christianity in Britain, they continued to worship the gods led by Woden and Thunor. During this period, Rome-nurtured Celtic Christians escaped to Wales and Cornwall and there established a monastic religious movement with a strong missionary component. From that base, St. Patrick is said to have gone to Ireland in the fifth century and to have helped found the great Irish tradition of scholarship.

This was a time of tumultuous settling in for the German groups in Britain. Blair stresses that despite the enormous changes that took place, a remarkable lack of recorded information is available so that all statements regarding the period are conjectural. He states, "These changes, whose magnitude is unsurpassed in the later history of Britain, were accompanied by a breakdown in those processes of recording history which are the normal accompaniment of literate civilization in less turbulent ages."[10]

The Tradition of King Arthur

During this period, in the sixth century, King Arthur is said to have lived. Though Arthur's existence is undisputed and he was certainly famous in his time, we know very little about him that is factual or that even dates from his era. Both Morris[11] and

---

because the Romans grouped all together under one term, *Pied*—meaning "painted people," since their bodies were customarily painted. (John Morris, *The Age of Arthur*, Scribner, New York, 1973, p. 186.)

The Picts retained power in the north of Britain until 846. In that year, they were conquered by the Scots, a Goidelic group that had originally come from Ireland in the fifth century and settled in the northeast near the territory of the Picts. Any information we have about them is based on sources from groups other than the Picts. As Stenton points out, "The internal history of the Pictish nation is utterly obscure." (F.M. Stenton, *Anglo-Saxon England*, Oxford University Press, London, 1971, p. 87.)

[9]Gordon, 1972, p. 95. This neat characterization of the settlement of the three groups is based to a considerable extent on St. Bede's history. Blair, however, questions what Gordon accepts, voicing strong doubts about any clear-cut separation of the groups and about the relative numbers of settlers from each group—despite his respect for Bede, the source for much of the conventionally accepted information about this period. (Peter Hunter Blair, *An Introduction to Anglo-Saxon England*, 2nd ed., Cambridge University Press, London, 1977, pp. 10–11.) Stenton, too, minimizes the validity of Bede's characterization. He points out, however, that Bede based it largely on common traditions of his and of earlier eras, traditions that were probably fundamentally correct (Stenton, 1971, pp. 10–11).

[10]Blair, 1977, p. 2.

[11]John Morris, 1973, p. 141. Morris notes that "even the barest outline of who he was and what he did must be inferred from dubious uncertain hints."

Miller[12] underscore the paucity of verified information about him. It was as late as 600 years after he lived that his reputation was embellished with tales of his Round Table, his Merlin, and his knights. Miller attributes many of our current conceptions about Arthur and his times to the twelfth century writings of Geoffrey of Monmouth. She notes that Geoffrey's widely circulated *History of the Kings of Britain* (written in 1136–1138) is open to serious question and was doubted even in his own day, and quotes the harsh statement by English historian William of Malmesbury, who lived at about the same time: "Everything this man wrote about Arthur and his successors . . . was made up, partly by himself and partly by others, either from an inordinate love of lying, or for the sake of pleasing the Britons."[13]

Later authors, both English and French, continued to embroider the stories with details whose attractiveness accounts for the cyclical popularity the Arthurian legends have enjoyed for hundreds of years.[14]

From Low West Germanic to Old English

Despite the lack of authenticated written records, evidence provided by archaeological findings, place-names, and later tradition indicates that this period was a time of strife among chieftains of the various groups of settlers, punctuated by the establishment and the merging of a number of small kingdoms. It was also the period in which much of the evolution from Low West Germanic to Old English occurred.

While the Germanic settlers did not adopt the language they found in Celtic Britain, neither did they have much contact with the continental mainland from which they came. As a result, changes began to take place in their language fairly soon after their arrival. First, new dialects of the original Low West Germanic arose, with each region of Germanic settlers developing a somewhat different dialect—regional differences, incidentally, that have lasted to modern times. It has not been established whether those differences were due to the different continental origins of the three groups of speakers or to their geographic separation after they settled down on English soil.[15] As noted above (p. 74 n. 9), Blair feels strongly that the division of geographic regions according to three distinct groups of Germanic settlers cannot be substantiated, and he would therefore ascribe current dialect differences to conditions on British soil rather than to continental origins.

Those dialects—and, thus, the language itself—then continued to change until speakers from the mainland were no longer able to understand it. By the end of the sixth century, the Low West Germanic of Britain had evolved into Old English.[16]

---

[12]Helen Hill Miller, *The Realms of Arthur*, Scribner, New York, 1969.

[13]Miller, 1969, p. 129. This same William of Malmesbury is cited as the author of the earliest existing comment on the English language. In his book, *History of the Popes* (1125), he blames Danish and Norman influences for what he perceived as the corruption of the English language of his day (Bloomfield and Newmark, 1963, p. 302).

[14]The first great book of English poems printed by William Caxton in 1485 was Sir Thomas Malory's *Morte d'Arthur*. Malory's version became the source book for subsequent authors of Arthurian stories.

[15]Gordon, 1972, p. 96.

[16]Gordon, 1972, p. 87. Gordon notes that, although the earliest writings recorded in Old English date from the late seventh century, the language of these written texts had undoubtedly been a spoken tongue during the prior century.

After becoming a distinct new language, Old English continued to exist, with only gradual changes, for 500 years. During that time, it was subject to a sequence of historical events that first so encouraged its development that it became the main language of Britain, then enabled it to survive close contact with the language of a new group of invaders—the Scandinavians—and finally led to its union with the language of yet another group of invaders—the Normans. Let us look at these events as a background to the description of Old English that will follow.

THE ANGLO-SAXON HEPTARCHY (600–830)

The years of strife among the Anglo-Saxon chieftains[17] culminated in the emergence by the year 600 of what some historians call the Anglo-Saxon Heptarchy: a group of seven separate kingdoms that were ruled by descendants of the Germanic newcomers rather than by Celtic leaders. The seven kingdoms were Northumbria, Mercia, East Anglia, Kent, Essex (or East Saxon), Sussex (or South Saxon), and Wessex (or West Saxon). During the years 600 through 830, Anglo-Saxon Britain was dominated by one or another of these kingdoms—particularly by Northumbria, then Mercia, and then Wessex.

The year 600 is given as the start of the Heptarchy because just before that date a monk named Augustine was sent from Rome by Pope Gregory the Great to convert the "Angli" heathens to Christianity.[18] In 597, Augustine and the group of missionaries he led landed on the Isle of Thanet, in the kingdom of Kent. They were cordially received by King Aethelberht, who—perhaps fortunately for the missionaries—had a Christian wife. Augustine converted and baptized Aethelberht and helped to build a church in Kent—the first church at Canterbury. Pope Gregory then appointed Augustine to be the first archbishop of Canterbury and the head of Roman Christianity in Britain.

The reintroduction of Christianity from Rome led to a series of clashes between the Roman churchmen and the Celtic Christians of the Irish and Welsh tradition. Celtic Christianity had been isolated from the Roman church for the century and a half since the departure of the Romans from Britain and had independently developed many traditions, including an organization very different from that on the continent. In the end, Roman Christianity prevailed, however, and the two factions combined. Christianity spread throughout Britain, bringing with it a gradual calming down and a relative orderliness that has been associated with the era of the Heptarchy.

---

[17]The term *Anglo-Saxon* was first used by continental Latin sources to differentiate the British Saxons from the mainland Saxon groups. The term was less often used in Britain, although it appeared there in tenth century writings (Blair, 1977, pp. 12–13).

[18]There is a tale—current as early as the seventh century and repeated by Bede with some questionable modifications—that in Rome, before he became pope, Gregory had seen some young Anglo-Saxons with fair skin and hair. He was very much impressed with their appearance and by the fact that they came from a heathenish people. He attempted to go to Britain personally to preach about Christianity but was stopped by the Roman citizens. His later efforts to have the Anglo-Saxons converted were said to have been rooted in this experience. Stenton believes that Gregory's great statesmanship also gave impetus to his efforts because of the political advantage of drawing this lost province back into the Roman circle (Stenton, 1971, pp. 103–104).

Along with the increase in order came a proliferation of learning and culture, and a number of excellent schools and monastic centers were founded. These centers grew to be the most outstanding in Western Europe, nourishing great scholars like the Venerable Bede (ca. 671–753) and Alcuin (ca. 732–804) and serving as models for similar centers in other countries. The monasteries at Jarrow, Wearmouth, and York were among the most prominent of these centers, featuring rich libraries that provided British scholars with immediate access to important scholarly works.

The Heptarchy is considered to have ended in the year 830. Just prior to that year, in 825, King Egbert of Wessex managed to wrest the overlordship of the seven kingdoms for himself and for Wessex. During his reign, the kingdoms of Anglo-Saxon Britain became united into a more integrated complex. The supremacy of Wessex was solidified by Egbert and his successors, notably Alfred the Great, who reigned from 871 to 899.[19]

King Alfred was particularly remarkable because of his stature both as a military leader and as an author. His translations of important Latin works into Old English are the major sources for our knowledge of Old English. In fact, because of Alfred's unique efforts, only writings in the West Saxon dialect of Old English are available to us in any quantity.

THE SCANDINAVIAN INVASIONS

For about two centuries following the Heptarchy—between the years 830 and 1017—kings from the house of Wessex reigned in Anglo-Saxon Britain. Throughout that period, they were plagued by pagan invaders from the continental mainland—from regions that are now modern Norway and Denmark. The invaders were part of an aggressive movement of Scandinavian peoples into widespread areas of Europe, a movement reminiscent of the movement of Celtic conquest throughout Europe that had led to the earlier invasions of Britain by the Celts.

Scandinavian operations in the British Isles began during the eighth century, when small raiding parties from Norway attacked, plundered, and then departed from various coastal spots in northern Britain and Scotland. In time, these small raids grew in size and were augmented by similar raids by Danes in southern Britain.

Then, in the middle of the ninth century, powerful Scandinavian armies arrived from the continent and proceeded to conquer much of Anglo-Saxon Britain. All of Britain might have been taken over by the Scandinavians if Alfred the Great had not managed to stop them by his superb leadership of the English armies. As a result, a treaty was drawn up in the year 886 between Alfred and King Guthrum of the East

---

[19]It should be noted that during Anglo-Saxon times, questions of accession to the throne, as well as many other questions related to royal governance, were generally reviewed by the king's council, or *witan*—a group of distinguished political, church, and noble leaders selected by the king. It was customary for the *witan* to select a successor upon the death of a king—generally, although not always, from the king's family. The right of the eldest (primogeniture) was not established in England until after the Norman Conquest, and Anglo-Saxon kings would be selected for one or more of a variety of reasons, including royal blood, competence, and political expedience. Much of the later discord during the Anglo-Saxon and the Anglo-Saxon/Danish control of England was fostered by the lack of explicit rules of succession. The quarrels leading up to the Norman Conquest were also provoked by this lack (see pp. 88–90).

Anglican Danes. The treaty gave the northern areas to the Danes,[20] areas that came to be called *Danelaw*. Control of the rest of Saxon Britain was to remain in Anglo-Saxon hands, and so it did: Kings of the house of Wessex continued to rule until the early part of the eleventh century.

* * * * *

Against the foregoing background let us pause to view the English language at this stage of its development.

---

[20]The Anglo-Saxons called all the Scandinavians in Britain *Danes*, although the invaders were actually a mixture of Norwegian, Danish, and Swedish groups. The terms *Vikings* and *Norsemen* have often been applied to the Scandinavians of those times as well, also without differentiating among the groups. *Vikings* has been used to designate Scandinavian sea pirates, while *Danes* and *Norsemen* have referred more to geographic origins than to characteristic behavior.

11

Old English Pronunciation

At the start of the Old English period, the language was practically all Germanic, stemming from Low West Germanic, although it contained individual words of both Celtic and Latin origin. Later, Norse words entered because of the close contact with the Scandinavian groups and, in great quantity, additional Latin words came in as well.

Like its forerunners, Proto-Indo-European and the older Germanic languages, Old English was primarily an inflectional language[1] and, although the process of simplification that had started with Proto-Germanic continued, the English language at that stage was considerably more complex than it is today. Thus, there was still an intricate system of noun inflections, including three genders, with equally intricate matching systems of adjectives and definite articles.

In addition, the language was still characterized by a number of different dialects.

OLD ENGLISH DIALECTS

The major Old English dialects, in which some writings have come down to us, were the Northumbrian, Mercian, Kentish, and West Saxon dialects. Of the writings that have come down, the largest number by far are in the West Saxon dialect, which was spoken south and west of the Thames River, down to the coast and over to the border of Cornwall. The preeminence of West Saxon writings is a result of the achievements of Alfred the Great (ca. 848–899).[2] He not only provided an unparalleled cli-

---

[1]See p. 60 for further information on inflectional languages and on the inflectional nature of Proto-Indo-European.

[2]See p. 77.

79

mate of learning and scholarship in Wessex but, together with a coterie of learned clergymen, translated many Latin works into West Saxon.

For that reason, the characteristics of Old English that are described later in this chapter have been primarily derived from West Saxon texts. Fortunately, the dialects varied only slightly from each other, and statements based on the West Saxon dialect are in all likelihood true of the other dialects as well. (It is not from the West Saxon but from the Mercian dialect that our standard Modern English is directly descended, however. West Saxon holds a lesser position in the evolution of the spoken language; it is outstanding for its literature rather than for its role in the subsequent course of the language.)

OLD ENGLISH PRONUNCIATION

Unlike its forerunners, Old English has come down to us in written form. Therefore, its pronunciation patterns can be related to the phonics of its written language— highly useful for tracing pronunciation and spelling relationships with the languages that evolved from it: Middle and Modern English.

Syllabic Stress

The pattern of syllabic stress in Old English was very similar to the stress pattern of Low West Germanic. That is, in polysyllabic words the stress fell on the first syllable, except when the first syllable had originally been a prefix. In such words, the stress was on the first syllable of the root as in the verbs *genémned* (named) and *bewéddod* (wedded).[3]

This emphasis on the initial syllable in almost all words gradually led to a reduction in the duration of the vowel sounds in final syllables. The resulting brevity of the final sounds then often made it difficult to distinguish between what had originally been different sounds so that *a*, *e*, *o*, and *u* sounded alike in such positions. This confusion affected the spelling of words at times, since scribes occasionally interchanged altered vowel letters, although they tended generally to adhere to traditional spelling.[4] Pyles notes that this reduction of the vowel sound in the final syllable first appeared in the tenth century, an indication of the rate at which the process took place.[5]

---

[3]This pattern was not limited to verbs, although it was more common among them.

[4]In Modern English, this similarity in pronunciation can be observed in the final syllables of *hangar, eager, nadir, tailor, augur,* and *satyr.* For spelling, a similar confusion exists nowadays with these and other parallel endings in unaccented syllables like *-ary/-ery* or *-ance/-ence.* The unaccented vowel sounds in such words are often difficult for children who are just learning to spell and for individuals who tend to rely on phonics clues rather than on visual recall in spelling. Although unaccented syllables containing a neutral vowel sound (or schwa) are never easy for phonics-oriented spellers, this parallel kind of ending seems to cause excessive difficulty.

[5]Pyles, 1971, p. 122. That is, the initial syllable stress had to have begun well back in Old English times in order to have affected the unstressed syllable even before the Middle English period. Moore states that by the year 1100, almost all unstressed vowels except *i* had changed to schwa (Samuel Moore, *Historical Outlines of English Sounds and Inflections,* revised by Albert H. Marckwardt, George Wahr, Ann Arbor, MI, 1951, p. 72).

Compound words were also stressed on the first syllable. In addition, the second word in the compound received a secondary stress, as it still does in Modern English. (Compare *schoolhouse* with *scholar* and *grandmother* with *excellent*.)

Vowels

In its written form, Old English contained 10 characters for vowel sounds: 7 monophthongs and 3 diphthongs.[6]

The pronunciation patterns of those characters were much less complex—that is, much more structured and consistent—than are the pronunciation patterns of the Modern English vowel symbols.

The pronunciation of five of the seven Old English monophthongs—*a*, *e*, *i*, *o*, and *u*—generally corresponded to their pronunciations in present-day continental European languages. A sixth monophthong, *y*, was pronounced as Modern French *u* or Modern German *ü*, articulated by saying *oo* while the lips are kept rounded and tense. In time, the rounded quality of that pronunciation was lost in Old English, and the *y* pronunciations were merged with those of *i*. The seventh monophthong was the ligature æ, pronounced as Modern English *short a* as in *ax*.

The three diphthongs were *ea*, *eo*, and *ie*.[7] Their pronunciations are given below in the list of Old English vowel pronunciations.

Short and Long Vowel Pairs

Just as each of the Modern English vowel characters currently represents more than one pronunciation, each Old English vowel character represented more than one pronunciation, but in a highly organized way: each of the 10 characters had two perfectly matched pronunciations. One, called *short*, was of regular duration; while the other, called *long*, was of more prolonged duration. Aside from the length of time, the pronunciations in each pair were practically identical.[8] Each of the two lengths was a different phoneme; that is, each was treated as an entirely different vowel rather than merely as a variation of the longer or shorter member of the pair.

In written Old English, the lengthened vowel was occasionally indicated by an accent mark over the long vowel. In addition, and more reliably, lengthening was at

---

[6]A *diphthong* is "two vowels or vowel-like sounds combined in a single syllable" (Bolinger, 1975, p. 42). Examples are the *ou* in *house* and the *u* in *use*.

A *monophthong* is made up of a single vowel sound, such as the *a* in *ax* and *e* in *egg*. Both terms refer only to spoken language and not to any written characters or combinations of characters. A given monophthong or diphthong can be represented by any number of different written characters, as the monophthong represented by the *o* in *come*, the *ou* in *touch*, the *u* in *up*, or the *a* in *a* as well as the diphthong represented by the *ou* in *house*, the *ow* in *now*, and the *au* in *Mau Mau*.

[7]See Table 11.1, note 2.

[8]A. Campbell, *Old English Grammar*, Oxford University Press, London, 1959, p. 14. Although he notes that "our knowledge of the sounds of a dead language can never be more than approximate," Campbell stresses that "It is fundamental to the history of English vowels that the long and short vowels were practically identical in quality till about 1200" (1959, p. 14 n. 2).

times indicated in early Old English manuscripts by *gemination,* or doubling of the vowel letter[9] (so that *long a* would be written as *aa* or *long i* as *ii*).

This meaning of the terms long and short vowels should be of special interest to teachers of reading, who have traditionally used these terms to identify certain pronunciations of Modern English vowel letters ("long" as in *ate, eke, ice, ode,* and *use* or *rude,* and "short" as in *ax, egg, it, ox,* and *up*). Due to language changes over the centuries, however, these modern long and short pronunciations are not differentiated by duration, nor are the sounds in each pair matched in the way they are produced, as the Old English pairs had been.[10] For example, Modern English *long a* and *long i* are actually diphthongs, with very different sounds from *short a* and *short i,* both of which are simple monophthongs. Also, as an illustration of the relation of the terms long and short to the actual duration of these vowel sounds in casually uttered Modern English, the *short a* in *band* actually takes longer to pronounce than does the *long a* in *bake.* The other Modern English vowel pairs have similar inconsistencies.

Furthermore, each Modern English vowel letter has more—some, many more—than two pronunciations, each phonemically different. Consider the *a* in *back, balk, bake, balm,* and *balloon,* or any of the *e*'s in *the, they, them, these,* and *there.*

Because of the intricacies of the Modern English vowel system, thoughtful teachers of reading who are not familiar with this historical background have tended to believe that there is no logic to calling the Modern English vowel sounds *short* and *long* other than as a time-hallowed mnemonic device when teaching the deadly vowels. The fact is that our modern short and long vowels are, for the most part, descended from the Old English ones and, therefore, when used today, these terms are still related, although very distantly, to the Old English ones. The specific pronunciation may be different, but many a Modern English word with a currently termed long or short vowel sound is derived from a word that had the corresponding long or short sound in Old English. Thus, the *long i* in the Old English word *pipe* was pronounced as the *i* in *machine.* In Modern English, though the *i* in *pipe* has an entirely different pronunciation, it is still termed *long i.* See Table 11.1.

Umlaut in Early Old English

An important process in vowel pronunciation took place early in Old English times, even before the existing Old English writings were set down, in fact. This process is known as *umlaut,* or *vowel mutation,* and refers to a vowel assimilating or adopting the sound of the vowel in an adjacent syllable. In Old English, umlaut occurred frequently in the case of two-syllable words that had a back vowel sound in the first syllable and a front vowel[11] sound in the second syllable. In such words, the back

---

[9]Randolph Quirk and C.L. Wrenn, *An Old English Grammar,* Holt, Rinehart and Winston, New York, 1957, pp. 9–10. Also, Campbell, 1959, pp. 12–13.

[10]"Long" and "short" vowel sounds exist in Greek, too, like the sounds of *omega* (literally, large *o*) and *omicron* (literally, small *o*).

[11]A back vowel is produced with a backward arching of the tongue as it is pronounced. A front vowel is made with an opposite, frontward arching of the tongue. Back and front vowel movements may be compared by alternating *short o* with *short e* or *short i*. In addition, there are central vowels, pronounced with the tongue arching in the center of the mouth.

Table 11.1. Old English vowels[1]

Monophthongs

SPELLING	SHORT PRONUNCIATION	LONG PRONUNCIATION
a	*a*lms	*a*lms (prolonged duration)
e	*e*gg	th*e*re (prolonged duration without diphthongization)
i	*i*t	mar*i*ne (without diphthongization to a "y" sound at the end)
o	b*o*rn	g*o*ld (without diphthongization to a "w" sound at the end)
u	p*u*ll	r*u*de
y	Modern German *ü*	*ü* (prolonged duration)
æ	*a*x	*a*x (prolonged duration)

Diphthongs

SPELLING	SHORT PRONUNCIATION[2]	LONG PRONUNCIATION
ea[3]	Old Eng. *short* æ + ə	Old Eng. *long* æ + ə
eo	Old Eng. *short e* + Old Eng. *short o*	Old Eng. *long e* + Old Eng. *short o*
ie[4]	Old Eng. *short i* + ə	Old Eng. *long i* + ə

[1]Based upon Moore's listing of the vowels of the Mercian dialect, from which Standard Modern English is derived, rather than from the more frequently examined West Saxon dialect. (Moore, 1951, pp. 65–66.) Also, all examples are given with their Modern English pronunciations unless otherwise indicated.

[2]There is some question about whether the short form of the diphthongs were truly diphthongs or whether the second character was added before and after certain consonants by Anglo-Saxon scholars (Moore, 1951, p. 19). Also, Pyles has questions and references on this point (1971, p. 123).

[3]The *ea*'s of Old English were very different from the Modern English *ea* both in pronunciation and in historical development. The older ones disappeared early by being smoothed out to monophthongs in pronunciation and by changes in spelling to conform to their new pronunciations. The later *ea* arose as a new pattern devised by the spelling reformers of the sixteenth century.

[4]Found in the West Saxon dialect, not in the Mercian.

vowel sound in the first syllable became fronted. This particular pattern of vowel mutation is called *i-umlaut* because, also prehistorically, in words where the unstressed syllable contained *i* (or *j*, which was interchanged with *i* in Old English), the unstressed syllable dropped off, leaving only the stressed syllable with its newly acquired fronted vowel sound.

It was the mutated, one-syllable form that was set down in Old English writings because the umlaut process was completed by the time scholars were recording in Old English. The earlier, two-syllable form had to be reconstructed by linguists, using methods of comparative linguistic analysis, (especially to Gothic, which shows the cognate earlier forms in written documents).[12] Examples of the reconstructed

---

[12]Harvey Minkoff, personal communication.

forms and their Modern English forms are: **bankiz–bench, *fodjan–feed*, and **fotiz–feet*.

The forms and pronunciations of many Modern English words, particularly certain unusual plurals, can be traced back to the Old English i-umlaut.[13] *Feet, teeth,* and *geese* are examples of such unusual plurals. Their old two-syllable forms were subject to umlaut, hence lost the last syllable, and changed the vowel. The one-syllable singular forms were not mutated: **fot–foot, *toth–tooth, *gos–goose.*

Lengthening of Vowel Sounds

In late Old English, short vowel sounds lengthened when they preceded consonant clusters *-ld, -mb, -nd, -ng, -rd, -rl, -rn, -rs,* and *-rth*. This accounts for the long vowel sounds in Modern English words like *climb* and *told*.[14]

EXERCISE

In the space provided below, write two Modern English words, each starting with a consonant cluster that is followed by a long vowel sound.

_____

_____

The Old English consonant sounds were much closer to their Modern English counterparts than were the Old English vowels. In the appendix, the Modern English consonant characters are listed together with the sounds they represented in Old English. The few obsolete Old English consonant characters are described as well.

Doubling of Consonants

In Old English, geminate (or doubled) consonants indicated prolonged pronunciation, perhaps somewhat in the way that trilled Modern Spanish *rr* is prolonged in contrast to untrilled Modern Spanish single *r*. (Compare Modern Spanish *perro* [dog] with *pero* [but].) All our current consonants had geminate forms in Old En-

---

[13]Bloomfield and Newmark note that the Modern English word *pretty* is an example of the i-umlaut in process. The pronunciation of the stressed *e* is an assimilation of the vowel sound of the last syllable (1963, p. 334).

[14]Pyles, 1971, pp. 141–142, 164. When a third consonant followed, however, the vowel remained short, as in *child–children*. (See p. 104 n. 14 below for the further development of this process in Middle English.)

glish except *j*, *k*, *q*, *v*, *w*, *y*, and *z* (each of which either did not exist or, for reasons noted in the next section,[15] was not yet firmly established).

The doubling dates back to older Germanic traditions, when it occurred to consonants (except for the *r*) in certain medial positions, such as those following a short vowel and preceding an *r* or an *l* (as in *æpple–apple*, *foddor–fodder*). In a number of Old English words, inflectional endings dropped off, leaving the doubled consonant in final position. Starting from the eleventh century, many doubled consonants began to be simplified to single consonants when they occurred at the ends of words and syllables, particularly unstressed syllables. During Old English times, the pronunciation of geminate consonants was apparently still prolonged, even where the written form had been reduced to a single letter. Only later—sometime between the twelfth and fifteenth centuries—did the single and double consonant pronunciations fall together.

Old English Consonant Clusters

The Old English consonant clusters were remarkably like those of Modern English. Most of the older ones have been retained, supplemented by newer ones found in foreign words or in names that have kept their original spellings (e.g., "gw" as in *guava*, or "shn" as in *schnauzer*). Old English consonant clusters that have been lost are *fn-*, *gn-*, *hl-*, *hn-*, *hr-*, *kn-*, *wl-*, and *wr-*. All of these lost their initial consonant sounds and spellings in Middle English times (although *gn-*, *kn-*, and *wr-* kept their original spellings).[16]

EXERCISE

In the space provided below, write one Modern English word each for the consonant clusters *gn-*, *kn-*, and *wr-*.

_____

_____

• • • • •

Much of the Old English language and pronunciation was drastically changed by the events depicted in the next chapter.

---

[15]See Appendix, Old English Consonants.

[16]Robert D. Stevick, *English and Its History*, Allyn & Bacon, Boston, 1968, Ch. 5, contains comprehensive listings of consonant clusters from early through modern times, together with detailed discussions of cluster patterns.

12

Backgrounds of Middle English

The Norman Conquest

Anglo-Saxon kings continued to reign over Saxon Britain from the time of the 886 treaty between Alfred and Guthrum (pp. 77–78 above) through the start of the eleventh century. Their power gradually lessened, however, because of additional invasions from the Scandinavian mainland as well as continuous Danish unrest on British soil.

AETHELRED II OF WESSEX

Saxon power eroded most seriously during the oppressive and inept 38-year reign of Aethelred II of Wessex, who ascended the throne of England[1] in the year 979. A clue to the low esteem in which he was held can be seen in the pun of his nickname, Unraed or the Unready—since *Aethelred* means "noble counsel" and *Unraed* means "no counsel."

An act of grim cruelty by Aethelred was responsible for a major invasion that led to the collapse of Anglo-Saxon control. In the year 1002, because he feared a Danish plot against himself, he ordered that all Danish men in England be killed on November 13. The massacre of the Danes was remembered for a long time afterward. Unfortunately for Aethelred and Anglo-Saxon leadership of England, among those massacred was the sister of Swein Forkbeard, king of Denmark. To avenge her death, Swein invaded England in 1003, starting a series of attacks by continental Danes that resulted in an expansion of the Danish domain on English soil. Fi-

---

[1]Regular use of the term *England* (at first Englaland) began at about this time. It was derived from the Old English *Engle* or Latin *Angli*, referring to the Germanic group, the Angles. Blair, who believes that the Angles were neither more numerous nor more important than the other groups, states that the reason for adopting this term is obscure. The term *Britannia* (or *Brittania)* had been used in formal Latin writings for many years before this (Blair, 1977, pp. 11–12).

nally, all ruling power came into Danish hands in the year 1016, when the *witan* offered the English crown to Swein's younger son Cnut (or Canute).

KING CNUT

For 18 years, Cnut ruled England with a benevolent, though strong and military, hand, and he was recalled with admiration in later years. During his reign, his elder brother died, so Cnut acquired the crown of Denmark as well. Moreover, as the result of an intensive political and military campaign, he also became king of Norway. While Cnut ruled, therefore, England and much of Scandinavia were combined under one reign, but this merger did not last long. The complete conquest of England by the Normans followed only 30 years after Cnut's death.

EDWARD THE CONFESSOR

Cnut died in 1035. For 5 years after that a series of complex, blood-stained struggles for the throne was waged among various English and Danish factions, culminating in the accession in 1042 of Cnut's stepson, Edward, who had been raised abroad by his uncle, Richard II, duke of Normandy.[2]

Edward, called the Confessor because of his asceticism and piety,[3] reigned until January 1066. Historians disagree about Edward's real stature, although Stenton believes that he has probably been underestimated.[4] There is little doubt, however, that Edward's Norman affiliation was apparent throughout his reign. During the quarter-century of his regime, the Norman tastes and customs with which he had been raised were introduced and supported throughout England. In addition, he assigned Norman adherents to powerful positions in the church and in his court. All this, finally, produced a condition in England that led Trevelyan to say about Edward: "His rôle in English history was to prepare the way for the Norman Conquest."[5] Moreover, the aesceticism that prevented him from leaving any immediate heirs was partially responsible for the disastrous struggle for the crown that followed his death.

CLAIMANTS TO THE THRONE OF ENGLAND

When Edward the Confessor died in January 1066, there were four major claimants to the throne of England. One of them was Edgar the Atheling, a descendant of Aethelred the Unready by his first wife. Another was Harald Hardraada, king of Norway, who claimed the throne on the basis of the union of the Scandinavian countries

---

[2]See p. 91 for further information about Richard of Normandy.
[3]The name was given to him by the pope who beatified him a century later. One of Edward's notable achievements was the construction of Westminster Abbey.
[4]Stenton, 1971, p. 424.
[5]Trevelyan, 1945, p. 107.

with England under King Cnut. A third claimant was Harold, son of Godwine, the earl of Wessex and the brother-in-law of Edward the Confessor. Harold had relatively little royal blood but was extremely powerful and able. In addition, he had assumed many governmental responsibilities during the later years of Edward's life, when the king had become increasingly immersed in religious matters.

And the fourth claimant was William, Duke of Normandy. William based his claim on Edward's openly naming him as his choice in 1051 as well as on an oath taken by Harold Godwineson of Wessex in about the year 1064. The story of Harold's oath, in which he promised to do all in his power to obtain the throne for William, provides an insight into some of the customs and thinking of the time. According to the Bayeux tapestry,[6] as well as to contemporary Norman writers, Edward had sent Harold to the mainland on an expedition. Heavy winds forced Harold's ship to land at Ponthieu, where he was made prisoner by the count of Ponthieu. William rescued him, and Harold took an oath to support William's aspirations to the English throne.[7]

Despite the promises made to William, Edward's successor was selected even before the king's death. The *witan* met and unanimously decided upon Harold of Wessex as an Englishman who had demonstrated the leadership necessary in a time of great external and internal pressures. Immediately upon Edward's death, within 24 hours, in fact, Harold was crowned, but he was destined to be king for only 9 months. Almost from the moment of his accession his rivals moved to take the throne from him and, in the end, he was crushed as he attempted to defend himself in military battles on three separate fronts within the space of a few days.

The Final Struggles

As soon as he heard of Harold's coronation, William sent a representative to question Harold's acceptance of what had been promised to him, William, and learned that Harold would not give up the throne without a fight. William then appealed to the pope, presenting his claim on the basis of Harold's oath. The pope judged in favor of the Norman duke, even sending a banner to support a great military expedition to win the crown of England. Not only did William thus gain sympathy for his

---

[6]The famous Bayeux tapestry is an extraordinary and reliable source of information about the Norman Conquest and the events leading up to it. This magnificently designed, richly colored work of art is said to have been commissioned by the half-brother of William the Conqueror, Bishop Odo of Bayeux, within 20 years after the battle of Hastings.

The tapestry is a 231-foot-long history, embroidered in wool on linen. It depicts scene after scene of the dramatic story both pictorially and with accompanying text. An important source on the tapestry is Sir Frank Stenton (Ed.), *The Bayeux Tapestry: A Comprehensive Survey*, Phaidon, New York, 1957. Also, excellent photographs of the entire tapestry, together with a description of its origins and the history surrounding it, may be found in Kenneth M. Setton's article, "900 Years Ago: The Norman Conquest," *National Geographic Magazine*, Vol. 130, No. 2, August 1966, pp. 206–251.

[7]The question of William's right to the throne, and therefore of the justice of the Norman invasion, has aroused such strong emotional reactions that it is hard to obtain a dispassionate view. Matthew gives much greater weight to William's case than do a number of other, more traditional historians—perhaps because he included many Norman as well as English sources in his research. I have tended to rely on Matthew's opinions because of the balance of his arguments as well as the esteem in which he is held. (D.J.A. Matthew, *The Norman Conquest*, Schocken, New York, 1966.)

cause on the continent, but he also had great riches at his disposal. He was therefore able to attract experienced, well-trained fighting men from all over Europe to enlist in his service.

By the fall of 1066, William felt prepared for battle and, at St. Valery-sur-Somme, stationed his army and a fleet to transport them across the English Channel. He waited there for favorable winds to arise. King Harold was well aware of the presence of the Norman army and of William's intentions. Therefore, throughout the summer and early fall, he positioned his own forces at key points along the coast.

Harold's early preparations were of no help in the long run, however. When the invasion finally came, he and his forces were a long distance away in the north, where he had rushed to fend off (successfully) two major assaults by Harald Hardraada.

The Battle of Hastings

On September 27, 1066, while Harold was still far up north, favorable winds arose on the continent, and William set sail that night, arriving at Pevensey the next morning. Finding no English defenders to meet him, William had time to survey the area and eventually to dig in at a more strategic location a bit further north, at Hastings. There he waited.

About 2 days after William's arrival, word of it reached King Harold, who was still north at York. He dashed off to the south to stop the invaders. Under the travel conditions of the time, however, it took nearly 2 weeks to reach the Normans, and only half of Harold's semidispersed army was able to join him. Harold arrived at Hastings on October 14, where he was surprised with an immediate onslaught by the alerted William.

After an intense battle, lasting from 9 in the morning of the 14th on into the night, the Normans were victorious. Harold himself was killed by an arrow, and no comparable English leader was available to take his place. In the days that followed, some of the English made a few abortive attempts to continue their resistance, but by then the acceptance of Norman control was inevitable and was made official on Christmas Day, 1066, with the crowning of William at Westminster Abbey.

ORIGINS OF THE NORMANS

The Norman conquerors of England came from a section of northern France that had been invaded by Scandinavians in the eighth, ninth, and tenth centuries much in the same way that Scandinavians had invaded England in those times: slowly at first, but gradually gaining momentum and purpose. Then, in the year 911, one of the most famous Scandinavian leaders, Rollo (or Hrolfr), planned to attack Paris itself. Charles the Simple, king of France, learned of the plan and offered Rollo a large region of northern France in exchange for allegiance to himself and conversion to Christianity. Rollo agreed to the terms, changed his name to Robert, and became the first duke of what was later to become Normandy (from a root meaning "north").

Rollo managed during his lifetime to extend his power to areas of France beyond those originally granted to him and laid the foundation for a familial ruling group that controlled northern France for several centuries, pretty much independently of the French kings. While they were fewer in number than the native Franks, the Scandinavians in northern France retained the top political power there. At the same time, they completely adopted the French language and culture.

Little of the early internal Norman history has come down to us directly. Only in the eleventh century did they make any attempt to record their prior history, and even that was merely a commissioned legendary book, not even written by a Norman. We do know, however, that for most of the tenth century they were quietly settling in and gradually intermarrying. Then, in the year 996, Richard II became duke of what was by then called Normandy, incidentally bringing with him strong ties to the English throne: He was the brother-in-law of Aethelred and of Cnut, as well as the uncle of Edward the Confessor.[8] During Richard's reign (996–1025) there was a change from the relative passivity of the tenth century. The now-combined group, the Normans, emerged as a vigorous, aggressive people. Their energy flowered under Richard's leadership and continued to develop even further when William I, later the conqueror of England, took power in 1047.[9]

The Normans' most outstanding talents—the talents that enabled them to expand and to influence both neighboring and far-off peoples—lay in their military ability and in their skill at building castles. They were especially adept at the military equestrian arts, producing many knights well trained to fight on horseback. Their architectural acumen included the speedy construction of churches, dwellings, and massive fortresses. This combination of an excellent fighting force and an ability to build valuable structures enabled the Norman army to reach a level of power and efficiency that contributed greatly to their victories in England and elsewhere. Their successful military expeditions resulted in the establishment of a Norman commonwealth with strong loyalties to the Normandy homeland in Sicily, southern Italy (especially Naples), and Antioch, Palestine, as well as in England and various sections of France. Thus, as with the Celtic and the earlier Scandinavian invasions there, the invasion of Britain by the Normans was not an isolated event but part of a much wider expansionist movement of a suddenly aggressive people.

THE ANGLO-NORMAN PERIOD

After the Conquest, many of those who had served in William's army remained in England. They were joined by thousands of others who, throughout the eleventh and twelfth centuries, came to serve in the foreign forces that were needed to sustain Norman power during that time. These newcomers mingled and intermarried

---

[8]Richard's sister, Emma of Normandy, was the reason for these ties. Emma was married first to Aethelred and then to Cnut and played an important role in the maneuvers to secure the English throne.

[9]William, the illegitimate son of Robert I, duke of Normandy, had actually gained the title in 1035, when he was a child of 7, but was forced to spend a stormy childhood under a variety of scheming guardians. He became duke in fact at the age of 20, when he successfully defended himself against a plot to supplant him.

with the native English so that by the end of the twelfth century it was "scarcely possible . . . to tell who is English, who of Norman race."[10]

In addition to these humbler newcomers, a new group of landowners and church leaders arrived to take over positions of power in England. The lands and possessions of English noblemen who had been killed at Hastings and during subsequent sporadic revolts against William were given to these Normans and other elite foreigners. William was an exceedingly meticulous administrator and directed a carefully allocated redistribution of all these lands as they became available, confiscating only the property of those who opposed him or who were gone and giving the total property of each to a thoughtfully chosen successor.

Churchly power, too, was soon transferred from English hands. As high church positions became available, they were filled with appointees from the continent rather than with Englishmen. Also, when a number of new monastic centers were established, monks were brought over from the monasteries of the mainland to staff them, while Norman scribes often replaced the Anglo-Saxon scribes who had handed down the Old English scribal traditions for many generations (see p. 116 for further discussion on this point).

Up until the thirteenth century, these powerful Anglo-Normans maintained a dual allegiance to the king of France as well as to the king of England, who still kept the title and domains of the duke of Normandy. In fact, during that time, the king of England controlled more French territory than did the king of France—some of it in the southwestern as well as in the northern part of France. The Anglo-Norman landowners also controlled large areas in both England and France.

THE SEPARATION FROM FRANCE

The dual allegiances caused relatively little conflict as long as the English king was more powerful than the king of France. The latter was in no position to assert himself or to make demands. The picture changed, however, by the beginning of the thirteenth century, when the French king's power increased, as did rivalry between the two monarchies. Matters were brought to a head when the ill-conceived actions of King John of England (brother of Richard the Lion-Hearted) antagonized King Philip II of France and some of the powerful French nobles. As a result, in the year 1204 King Philip confiscated the large Norman properties of several owners of dual estates and decreed that French estates of other Anglo-Normans were to be given up or divided within families.

The process of carrying out these divisions struggled along until about 1244, when Louis IX of France and Henry III of England decreed jointly that a choice must be made between them. King Louis is quoted as having put the matter very clearly: "As it is impossible that any man living in my kingdom, and having possessions in England, can competently serve two masters, he must either inseparably attach himself to me or to the king of England."[11]

---

[10]Baugh (1957, p. 142) quotes from a passage written in the year 1177.

[11]Baugh, 1957, p. 153. (Quoted from the works of Matthew Paris, a thirteenth century monastic chronicler.)

Despite the unified voice of both monarchs in issuing the decree, the problem of dual allegiance continued to cause friction for many decades. This friction was aggravated by a reaction in England to all things foreign, particularly French (due in large part to resentment at privileges granted to foreign favorites during the long reign of Henry III [1216–1272] and his wife, Eleanor of Provence). The antiforeign feeling was coupled with an acceleration of interest in and appreciation for the pre-Conquest English heritage, an appreciation that had awakened during the twelfth century.[12]

Finally, in the year 1337, open warfare broke out between the two countries and continued on and off for another century. These hostilities, known as the Hundred Years' War (1337–1453), ended with the total separation of England and France.

---

[12]It was during the twelfth century revival of interest in early English times that Geoffrey of Monmouth wrote his *History of the Kings of Britain*, containing the tales of King Arthur. (See p. 75)

13

From Old to Middle English

For the more than 500 years of Anglo-Saxon domination, Old English remained the language of most of Britain. The victory of the Normans in 1066 started a process of dramatic change within the language that affected all aspects of it. By about the year 1100, the language became so different from Old English (though retaining enough still to be English) that it has been distinguished from the earlier stage and called *Middle English*.[1]

For several generations, Middle English was the spoken tongue of the ordinary population while the educated upper classes spoke Norman French and wrote in French and Latin. The English language could not help but be affected by the proximity of so many speakers of French during those years and by the fact that so many of those who spoke English also spoke French. Consequently, from the time of the Conquest, the Norman language added enormously to the English vocabulary and left indelible markings on the English language in other ways as well.

THE LANGUAGE OF THE NORMANS

It was noted above (p. 91) that the Scandinavians in Normandy soon adopted the French language. They adopted it so completely that, aside from some names, there were few traces of Old Norse in their speech by the time the invasion of England took place. The French language that they learned was, like all Romance languages other than Latin itself, an offshoot of the Vulgar Latin dialect (or the everyday, common people's dialect) rather than of Classical Latin. In Vulgar Latin, certain words were different and the grammar was simpler than in the artificial Classical Latin, with fewer inflected forms. Classical Latin was used for formal literary purposes

---

[1]Obviously, the bridge between Old and Modern English.

and not for the relaxed communication of daily living. In the parts of Europe that the Romans conquered, therefore, it was the Vulgar Latin speech that was picked up and modified—differently in each area, as can be seen from the variety of Romance languages that have come down to us.

Norman French on English Soil

At the time of the Conquest of England, there were four main French dialects: Norman, Picard, Burgundian, and the Central French of the region around Paris (also called *Ile-de-France*). Of those, Norman was predominant among the invading troops, although there were also men from other parts of France. Following the Conquest and through the twelfth century, Norman French remained the language of the new rulers of England as well as of all who were associated with the upper echelons there. Even kings—Henry II, for example, who reigned from 1154 to 1189—did not speak English (although Henry II understood it). His wife, Eleanor of Aquitaine, did not even understand it, but used an interpreter when conversing with English-speaking subjects. Until the end of the twelfth century, Old English was relegated solely to the Anglo-Saxon commoners, many of whom spoke only English during that time.

In addition to those who spoke only French and those, more numerous, who spoke only English, there were many who were bilingual and many who spoke one of the languages but understood the other as well. While at first a speaker's language depended on his nationality, intermarriage and the mingling of native Englishmen and Normans soon caused the differentiation to depend more upon social than upon ethnic factors. Those who could make use of both languages might therefore be thought of as belonging to a middle class, in touch with both extremes of society, and they grew in number from the thirteenth century on.

One important result of this mingling was the flow into the English language of a large number of French words—more than 10,000, in fact, of which about 75% are still in use today. (Other borrowings, though fewer, still numbered in the thousands, and came from Latin and the Germanic languages—Dutch, Flemish, and Low Germanic.)

Rejection of French in England

When the separation of England and France occurred during the thirteenth and fourteenth centuries, the parallel rise of patriotic feeling within England brought with it a reversal in attitude toward the English language. From being denigrated, it rose to a higher status than Norman French and became the language of the upper classes. The reaction against Norman French was so strong that the upper-class English preferred the Parisian French dialect to it, and Norman French even became an object of derision.

By the beginning of the fourteenth century, English was once more known to everybody; by the second half of that century, it had been accepted by all classes as their spoken tongue. At the same time, knowledge of French declined to such an extent that by the fifteenth century many members of the aristocracy could not speak it.

ATTITUDES TOWARD WRITTEN ENGLISH

The preceding discussion of changing attitudes toward English and French refers to spoken rather than to written language. Attitudes toward written communication did not vary significantly from those toward speech, however.

From the time of the Norman Conquest until the middle of the thirteenth century, practically all official and private writing—aside from certain monastic writings—was done in French or Latin. Popular literature in English was created and transmitted orally.[2] Then, for about a century (ca. 1250–1350), there occurred what Baugh calls the "Period of Religious and Secular Literature in English,"[3] which included English versions of French writings—reflecting the transition from French to English current at the time. That was followed by 50 years of a magnificent flowering of English literature (1350–1400), which Baugh refers to as a "Period of Great Individual Writers." Geoffrey Chaucer (1350–1400) was the most outstanding of those writers, although a number of others produced literary works of great quality and impact. William Langland's *The Visions of William Concerning Piers the Plowman* (ca. 1362) and *Sir Gawain and the Green Knight* (author unknown)[4] are but two examples of such masterpieces.

English started to take over as the language of choice for all written communication only during the reign of Henry V (1413–1422); there were few private or semi-official letters written in English before 1400. The year 1425 is given as the approximate date of its adoption for all writing purposes.[5] Before that time, English was spoken uninhibitedly, without the control of scribes and scholars—who tend to act as preservers of language—or of personal writing, which forces attention on a language's precise forms.[6] Consequently, certain features of the language developed freely and unchecked, serving both to enrich it on the one hand and to move it toward greater simplicity on the other. The process of grammatical simplification that had begun in Old English continued and was accelerated during the Middle English period. As a consequence, the structure of English in Chaucer's time had evolved into a form very close to that of Modern English.

MIDDLE ENGLISH DIALECTS

In the same way that there were a number of regional or local dialects of Old English, there were a number of Middle English dialects also. They corresponded more or less to the major Old English regional dialects. (See pp. 79–80 above.) Thus, the

---

[2]See M.T. Clanchy, *From Memory to Written Record (England, 1066–1307)*, Harvard University Press, Cambridge, MA, 1979, for a comprehensive treatment of spoken and written language in post-Conquest England.

[3]Baugh, 1957, p. 186.

[4]Yet another instance of the appeal of the Arthurian stories, preceding Malory's *Morte d'Arthur* (1469).

[5]Baugh, 1957, p. 184. Also, see p. 121 n. 15 for discussion of the Chancery scribes.

[6]Nowadays, obvious examples of how the control of written language can help to preserve spoken language are style guides for editors, authors, and students, as well as the use of dictionaries to confirm "correct" pronunciation and word meaning in addition to their control of spelling.

Middle English Northern dialect developed from the old Northumbrian, the Middle English Midlands dialects (East and West) developed from Mercian, and the Middle English Southern dialect developed from West Saxon. Old Kentish developed into what is considered a subdivision of the Southern dialect.

With Old English, however, the writings that came down were largely in the West Saxon dialect so that linguists have been able to focus on the one dialect in studying the structure of Old English. Middle English presents a problem in this respect. For most of the period during which Middle English writings were set down (until the latter part of the fifteenth century), each author used his local dialect, and in each dialect there are writings of outstanding significance. Linguists and others studying the language of that period must learn several dialects to explore the literature of the time.

Standard Modern English, including the English spoken in the United States, eventually developed from the dialect used in the writings of Chaucer. That was a London variety of the East Midland dialect, spoken in the court and by a stratum of active, energetic individuals focused in and about the London area. It was not until about the middle of the sixteenth century that it was universally accepted as the standard of educated English. Since then, it has become known as the *Received Standard* (see p. 56 above), a term used more in Great Britain than in the United States. Actually, it is only the written form of the London Standard that has been universally adopted. Regional dialects and local variations of spoken English still abound all over the world.

14

Middle English Pronunciation

Following the lead of Moore[1] and others, I have chosen the late fourteenth century pronunciations and spelling of Chaucer to represent the Middle English period in the lists and discussions presented in this chapter. It is not possible to present "standard" pronunciations for Middle English phonemes because there was no standard Middle English dialect, and pronunciations are more susceptible to dialect variations than are vocabulary and grammatical forms.

The four-century span of the Middle English period was marked by a great number of language changes, with wide variations in pronunciation emerging during that time, particularly in the case of long vowels. English consonants have not changed much throughout the ages, and short vowels not much more. Short vowels were mostly shortened or lengthened in certain positions, rather than themselves changed in quality. Therefore, Chaucer was chosen because he lived and wrote at a time when most of the Middle English patterns had settled into the language and because his writings preceded the high point of the Great Vowel Shift (see pp. 107–108)—with its final enormous impact on long vowel pronunciation—and the consequent metamorphosis into Modern English. Furthermore, his London dialect turned out to be the forerunner of standard Modern English.[2]

---

[1]Moore, 1951, p. 36.

[2]According to Baugh, however, Chaucer's English was modified by certain Southern dialect features, although it was still close to the most direct forerunner of Modern English, namely, the English found in official documents and other writings of the "men of affairs" who lived in the London area. Baugh also points out that the subsequent adoption of the London dialect by the early printers of the fifteenth century was of crucial importance in establishing it as the standard. (Baugh, 1957, pp. 233–235. Also, see pp. 121–122 below on Caxton's choice of spelling patterns.)

SYLLABIC STRESS

It was pointed out above[3] that Old English continued the Germanic trend toward stress of the initial syllable in polysyllabic words, with the consequent reduction of the vowel in the final syllable to the schwa sound. This process continued in force throughout the Middle English period, with dramatic consequences. Pyles states that "the most significant of all developments in [the structure of] the language occurred with the Middle English falling together of *a*, *o*, and *u* with *e* in unstressed syllables, all ultimately becoming [ə]"[4] (and written with an *e*). Thus, old English *lama* became Middle English *lame*, Old English *feallath* became Middle English *falleth*, Old English *nacod* became Middle English *naked*, and so forth.

The great significance of this change is that it led to the minimizing and then to the dropping of word endings. As a consequence, inflectional endings were dropped as well, and English was altered from an inflectional to an isolating or analytic language.[5]

Syllabic stress shifted in borrowed words as well as in native English words, although foreign words were not affected until some time after they had been adopted. There was generally a transition during which a word might be accented either way. Such shifts can be detected in Middle English poetry, where, for example, a frequently used French loan word like *contree* (Modern English *country*) appears in carefully scanned lines in the works of Chaucer. Sometimes the accent is obviously on the first syllable; at others it is just as obviously on the second.[6]

LETTER–SOUND CORRESPONDENCE

During the Middle English period, correspondence between the spoken phonemes and the written alphabetic letters became increasingly incomplete, foreshadowing the incomplete correspondence we find today. This was strikingly different from the relative regularity of Old English spelling (see p. 115 below) and was mainly a by-product of the Norman Conquest. At that time, the influx of French words, which were based on a different system of phonemes, brought different speech sounds and different speech sound combinations. Also, the constantly increasing number of persons who spoke both English and French helped to mingle the phonemes of both languages.[7] Those phonemes then had to be represented in written communication between individuals who varied considerably in their familiarity with English and French. Since at the same time the earlier alphabetic characters were used to represent various phonemes in different ways by different individuals—many of whom were not well educated—a great many inconsistencies inevitably arose. The

---

[3]See p. 65 above.
[4]Pyles, 1971, p. 165.
[5]See note 21 in Chapter 8 for discussion of inflectional and isolating languages.
[6]Gordon, 1972, pp. 118–119. Some Modern English words are undergoing a change in syllabic stress even today—the word *acclimate*, for example.

[7]The French language was also affected by the bilingualism and, in fact, the French Anglo-Norman dialect came to be looked down upon because of the variations it developed.

bulk of the Middle English period is notable for the wide variety of uncontrolled spellings that appear in manuscripts of the time. Mainly from the thirteenth century on, Norman scribes made some effort to alter spellings toward greater sound–letter correspondence to make manuscripts easier to read. Those changes were much more limited in scope than the major spelling reforms of the sixteenth century, however (see pp. 122–124 below). Moreover, while the latter changes were made to conform to theories about word origins,[8] the Middle English spelling reforms were solely attempts to match speech and writing in a language that was undergoing extremely rapid change.

Campbell points out that the spelling changes in early Middle English were made in response to pronunciation changes and dialect differences.[9] Within the Middle English period, however, such flexibility diminished and spelling became more and more fixed even though there continued to be pronunciation changes. As a result, although early Middle English writing reflects the spoken language of the time more accurately than does late Middle English writing, the later period shows much less confusion about the spelling of each individual word.

MIDDLE ENGLISH VOWELS

Chaucer's fourteenth century English contained seven long and five short vowel phonemes. The long vowels kept the Old English pronunciations of the letters *a, e, i, o,* and *u*[10] (*y* had been absorbed into *i* this time), and the letters *a* and *o* had each acquired an additional long vowel phoneme. The short vowel sounds were very similar both to Old English and to Modern English short vowel sounds. The exceptions are noted in the list of Middle English vowels in Table 14.1. Also, as in Modern English, unstressed short vowels had the schwa sound—especially in prefixes and suffixes—as did the *final e* in those instances where it was still pronounced. (See pp. 104–106 below on silent *final e.*)

There were also approximately seven different diphthongs during the Middle English period. Although linguists differ on some of these, I have again followed Moore's lead and used his classification.[11]

Long and Short Vowel Pairs

Long and short vowels were no longer paired as neatly as they had been in Old English. Changes were mainly in the long vowel pronunciations. The only short vowel changes were the development of neutral vowel sounds for *e* and *i* in unaccented syllables, as in Modern English supplement and beautiful, and the loss of *short* æ. In written English, the doubled *aa, ee,* and *oo* were adopted in some words to indi-

---

[8]Richard L. Venezky, "A Study of English Spelling-to-Sound Correspondences on Historical Principles," unpublished doctoral dissertation, Stanford University, 1965, p. 208.

[9]Campbell, 1959, p. 19.

[10]See pp. 81–84 above for Old English vowel pronunciations.

[11]Moore, 1951, pp. 36, 66.

Table 14.1.   Middle English vowels[1]

Monophthongs

SPELLING	SHORT PRONUNCIATION	LONG PRONUNCIATION
a	*a*lms	*a*lms (prolonged duration)
aa		*a*lms (prolonged duration)
e	1) *e*bb 2) schwa (suppl*e*ment)	
e, ee		1) *a*te (prolonged duration without diphthongization) 2) *a*x (prolonged duration)[2]
i[3]	1) *i*t 2) beaut*i*ful	mach*i*ne (without diphthongization)
o	b*o*rn	
o, oo		1) b*o*rn (prolonged duration) 2) g*o*ld (prolonged duration without diphthongization)
u, o	1) p*u*ll 2) *o* before or after *m* or *n* (therefore, m*o*ther, c*o*me, t*o*ngue)	
ou, ow		r*u*de (prolonged duration without diphthongization)
y	Under French influence, words that had been pronounced with the Old English *short* or *long* rounded *y* were changed to the *short* or *long u* pronunciation and spelled with *u*. The written letter *y* then began to be used as an alternate for *i*, first in words where it replaced final Old English *ie* and then in other words as well. The alternation in spelling of *i* and *y* remained until far into the Middle English period and was used for both the consonantal and the vowel pronunciations.	

(continued)

[1]Based mainly on Moore, 1951, pp. 36, 66–67.

[2]Although spelled with *e*, this was a *long a* pronunciation that was derived from the Old English *long* æ pronunciation.

[3]Used alternately with the letter *y*, acquiring a consonantal in addition to the vowel pronunciations during this period. See information relating to *y* on pp. 39–40 and 225–226.

cate long pronunciations of those vowels. The single, *a*, *e*, and *o* were kept for the long vowel pronunciations as well, however, contributing to the increasing inconsistency of Middle English letter–sound correspondence.

Diphthongs were no longer paired at all and were especially varied in spelling because of the confusions that resulted from the separation of the written *i* and *y* and the introduction of the *w* and other French spelling conventions. (See pp. 39–41 for discussion of the derivation of these characters.)

Table 14.1.   *(continued)*

Diphthongs

SPELLING[4]	PRONUNCIATION
au, aw	s*au*erkr*au*t
ai, ay, ei, ey	As *a* in *ax* + *short i.* (Does not occur in Modern English.)
eu, ew	*Short e* + Middle English *short u* (Does not occur in Modern English.)
u, eu, ew	c*u*te, f*eu*d, f*ew*[5]
oi, oy	1) *oi*l, b*oy* (Mainly from French borrowed words.) 2) As in New York dialect "m*oi*der" (murder)
ou, ow, o	*o* as in b*o*rn + *u* as in p*u*ll
ou, ow	*o* as in b*o*rn (prolonged) + *u* as in p*u*ll

[4]It can be seen that much of the variation in the spelling of diphthongs during this period was due to the interchange of either *i* and *y* or *u* and *w*. With these diphthongs, the *w* was employed to differentiate the *u* from the *v* before vowels. (Hence, the name "double u.") The *y* was employed next to stroke letters (*m*, *n*, for example) because the little single stroke letter *i* might get lost in such a position. (See pp. 39–41 above.) Both *y* and *w* were used in the final position.
   The assigning of more than one pronunciation to the same spelling probably relates to the influx of foreign words with different phonemic systems.
[5]We also find the two pronunciations of *u*, *eu*, and *ew* in Modern English *long u*: r*u*de–c*u*be, rheumatism–f*eu*d, and dr*ew*–f*ew*.

SMOOTHING OF OLD ENGLISH DIPHTHONGS

In addition to the formation of new diphthongs, the Middle English period saw the "smoothing out" or reduction to simple monophthongs of the Old English diphthongs. The spelling of words containing these former diphthongs was changed, often to conform with the spellings of similar Middle English sounds that had been derived from other historical sources, either French or Old English (see Table 14.2).

Middle English Vowels in Closed and Open Syllables

An important innovation of the Middle English period was the alteration of vowel pronunciations according to whether they occurred in open or in closed syllables.[12] One alteration was the lengthening of *short a*, *short e*, and *short o* so that, for example, the short vowels in the open syllables of the following Old English words were lengthened: *nama* (meaning "name") became Middle English *na:me*, *stelen* (meaning "to steal") became Middle English *ste:len*, and *throte* (meaning "throat") became Middle English *thro:te*.[13] (By Modern English times, the *a* was added in *steal* and *throat* to indicate that the first vowel was long.)

---

[12]See p. 24 for the definition of open and closed syllable.
[13]These examples, as well as those in the succeeding paragraphs, are taken from Pyles, 1971, pp. 163–164.

Table 14.2.   Smoothing of Old English diphthongs

OLD ENGLISH DIPHTHONG SPELLING	MIDDLE ENGLISH PRONUNCIATION	MIDDLE ENGLISH SPELLING
Long ea	*a* in *ax* (prolonged)	streem
Short ea	*a* in *arm*	*a*rm
Long eo	*a* in *ate* (prolonged)	deep
Short eo	*e* in *ebb*	herte

The same lengthening of short vowels in open syllables happened to *short i/y* and *short u*, although these vowels changed in pronunciation as well as duration. Thus, *short i* and *short y* became *long e* so that Old English *wicu* (meaning "week") became Middle English *weke*, and Old English *yvel* (meaning "evil") became Middle English *evel*. Also, *short u* became *long o* so that Old English *wudu* (meaning "wood") became Middle English *wode*.

Along with the lengthening of short vowels in open syllables, there was a shortening of many, though not all, long vowels that had hitherto been in closed syllables. Thus, the *long i* in *wisdom* became the same *short i* it has remained in Modern English, and the *long e* in Old English *twentig* became the *short e* in Modern English *twenty*.[14] (In words with three or more syllables, the shortening occurred even more consistently than in two-syllable words, as *clean–cleanliness*.)

Final E

Closely associated with Middle English times (although it actually began earlier and ended later) is a development that should be of special interest to teachers of reading. This was the emergence of the silent *final e*, a particularly useful signal in reading when it indicates that the preceding vowel is long (as in *gate*, *supreme*, *hope*, and innumerable others).

Although they all look and are pronounced alike, in any given word the silent *final e* may be one of three types, each with a different historical background. These are: 1) organic, etymological, or inflectional *final e*; 2) inorganic *final e*; and 3) scribal or orthographic *final e*.

---

[14]This shortening affected a number of those vowels that, in Old English, had been lengthened before *mb*, *nd*, *rd*, and others listed on p. 84. With this shortening of long forms in closed syllables, a number of the vowels that had been lengthened because they came before these clusters reverted to their short forms. Those that remained long were vowels preceding *-ld* (*wild*, *old*), *long i* before *-mb* and *-nd* (*climb*, *find*), *long o* before *-mb* (*comb*), and *long u* before *-nd* (*found*) (Pyles, 1971). These same patterns exist today.

EXERCISE

In the space provided below, write two additional words ending in the silent *final e* that indicate a preceding long vowel.

_____

Organic, Etymological, or Inflectional Final E

This type of *final e* arose first—as far back as the tenth century. It was a vestige of the vowels of Old English inflectional or other word endings that had existed in earlier times but were lost through vowel changes and the dropping of stressed endings. Although the original word endings might have contained any one of a number of vowel sounds, toward the end of the dropping-off process, the final vowels were reduced to the schwa sound and written with an *e*.

Ultimately, some time between the years 1350 and 1500, even the schwa pronunciation disappeared. In many instances, particularly where it was preceded by a long vowel, the *e* remained solely as a written symbol. (In other instances, the *e* was dropped in both spelling and pronunciation.)

Examples of Modern English words with this type of *final e* are *time*, *stake*, and *before*.

Inorganic Final E

Early Middle English times saw the rise of another type of *final e*.[15] This new one, called *inorganic*, appeared in words that had never undergone the process of language change or vowel reduction that resulted in the organic *final e*. Linguists can attribute its presence only to some form of analogy.[16] Once it was accepted in a word, inorganic *final e* received the same treatment as organic *final e*; namely, it was pronounced as schwa at first but lost all pronunciation between the years 1350 and 1500. After its pronunciation had disappeared, inorganic *final e* was kept in the spelling of some words and dropped from others, in the same way that organic *final e* was kept or dropped.

---

[15]Moore, 1951, p. 62.

[16]Analogy is a linguistic term referring to the tendency to apply an existing language pattern in situations where the pattern did not develop historically. While an analogy usually stems from a lack of knowledge, there are innumerable instances of the eventual assimilation of such changes into standard spoken or written language. An example of a common use of analogy is the way a young child will follow the pattern of *walk–walked* or *help–helped* and say *throw–throwed* (Gordon, 1972, p. 55). Minkoff points out that *helped*, now totally standard English, was itself derived by such an analogy. The earlier forms were *healp* (singular) and *hulp* (plural) (personal communication).

Examples of Modern English words with inorganic *final e* are *bride* (from Old English *bryd*) and *home* (from Old English *ham*).

Scribal or Orthographic Final E

Last to develop was the scribal or orthographic *final e*. It stems from the late Middle English and early Modern English times, after both the organic and the inorganic *final e* had lost their pronunciations. Scribal *final e* was never pronounced.

At first, it was added thoughtlessly by some of the scribes to certain words as an analogy to similar words with organic or inorganic *final e*. Later, it was added purposefully to other words as a guide to their pronunciation. Thus, Mulcaster, an important sixteenth century teacher and advocate of spelling reform, suggested the use of silent *final e* to indicate that the vowel in the preceding syllable was long (e.g., *cap–cape*).[17]

Other examples of the use of silent *final e* as a pronunciation guide include its occurrence after *final c* or *final g* to indicate that they are soft (e.g., *franc–France*, *rag–rage*), and after words in which *final s* was part of the original root to indicate that the *s* did not indicate plurality (e.g., *els–else* or *fals–false*).[18]

MIDDLE ENGLISH CONSONANTS

Not surprisingly, since English consonants have seldom changed much, Middle English consonants showed comparatively few changes from their Old English counterparts. There were some losses of individual allophones in certain positions, and a number of pronunciation changes that had been foreshadowed in Old English were more fully realized. (See Appendix, *Middle English Consonants*.)

---

[17]Richard Mulcaster, *The First Part of the Elementarie...*, Thomas Vautroullier, London, 1582. Reproduced by Scolar Press, Menston, England, 1970, pp. 111–112. Mulcaster (the teacher of Edmund Spenser) is especially noted for this work, in which he presented numerous suggestions for spelling reform. (See pp. 123 below.)
[18]Venezky, 1965, p. 116.

15

The Transition from Middle to Modern English

A number of major trends and processes during the fifteenth and sixteenth centuries led to the standardization of spoken and written English in forms very close to their present ones. These processes included the Great Vowel Shift, the Renaissance, the opening of the world to European exploration, a scholarly interest in the study of language, the invention and initial use of printing with movable type, and a rising preoccupation with English spelling.

Although all these had their greatest impact on the language during these two centuries, their sources are to be found in earlier years, and most of them continued to function for a long time afterward. Moreover, there was a great deal of interaction between them. In this chapter, the processes relating to spoken English are discussed individually, and a number of interactions are pointed out. Written English—including spelling patterns and the invention of printing—is discussed in Chapter 16.

THE GREAT VOWEL SHIFT

At the end of Chaucer's time, near the close of the fourteenth and the beginning of the fifteenth century, an important series of related changes in the pronunciation of the long vowels began to take place: The long vowel in each word began to be pronounced with a tongue position higher[1] than had been used in the pronunciation of

---

[1]The terms *high*, *low*, and *mid*, with their accompanying verbs *raising* and *lowering* refer to the degree of elevation of the part of the tongue that is raised in the production of a vowel sound. Thus, there are high, mid, and low back vowels; high, low, and mid central vowels; and high, mid, and low front vowels.

the vowel up to then. Those vowels that were already in the highest position became diphthongs. In the case of the letters *e* and *o*, more than one different vowel sound developed from the original single long vowel. This change is known as the *Great Vowel Shift*,[2] and, as a result of it, most of the long vowel and diphthong pronunciations of Modern English were established.

The shifts in pronunciation all started at about the same time but took place in an irregular fashion so that some sound alterations were completed before others. Most had taken place by the sixteenth century, although a small number occurred as late as the end of the seventeenth century. As had been observed before with respect to other pronunciation changes, there is no apparent reason for these new pronunciations to have developed; they simply happened, and only afterward did scholars perceive the clear-cut patterns.

It is important to note that the Great Vowel Shift took place after English spelling was more or less established. Therefore, the spoken changes were not reflected in the written vowel letters. That circumstance, together with the factors discussed below under *English Spelling*, accounts for many of our Modern English spelling "irregularities."[3]

The sequence of change from the Middle English long vowels to their Modern English counterparts can be outlined as shown in Table 15.1.

Table 15.1.   Change from Middle English long vowels to Modern English counterparts

EARLY MIDDLE ENGLISH SPELLING	CHAUCER'S MIDDLE ENGLISH PRONUNCIATIONS TO MODERN ENGLISH PRONUNCIATIONS
a:	*a*lms – to *a*x – to *e*bb – to *a*te
e:	1) *a*te – to f*ee*t
	2) *a*x – to *e*bb or *ea*t – to gr*ea*t or *ea*t
i:	mar*i*ne – to *əy* – to *I*, m*y*
o:	1) b*o*rn – to g*o*
	2) g*o*ld – to b*oo*t or b*oo*k or bl*oo*d
u:	r*u*de – to *əu* – to *ou*t

THE RENAISSANCE

During the late fourteenth and fifteenth centuries, a powerful new influence that helped to transform Middle English into Modern English was being shaped. This was the Renaissance—an intellectual and cultural movement based on a renewal of interest in ancient pre-Christian literature and culture, principally the Greek. It flourished in Italy during the fifteenth century and swept on to other European countries, reaching England in the sixteenth century.

---

[2]The name was given by Otto Jespersen.
[3]That is, words whose written forms do not completely match certain conventionally accepted spelling patterns. There are those who see a large number of such words as "regular." See Chapters 22–27 below for discussions of divergent views of English spelling patterns.

Greek Influence on the Renaissance

The Renaissance originated with the opening of commerce between Italy and the then-Christian Near East during the fourteenth century. That opening fostered contact between the Italians and the followers of the Greek Orthodox tradition, who had maintained ties with the ancient Greek language and literature. Then, the Moslem conquest of Constantinople in 1453 gave added stimulus to the new-born interest through the influx of Greek-Christian scholars who found refuge in the West. Such scholars were a valuable source of information to eager Western scholars, especially in subjects that had languished in the West during the centuries since the decline of the secular classical tradition.

Although the Renaissance touched every aspect of European living, of special importance here is the development of a concern with the scholarly study of language. That concern was kindled because one of the subjects the Greeks found especially intriguing was that of human language—its origin and history as well as its structure. The scholars of the Renaissance tended to channel their newfound interest into the study of contemporary languages (see p. 111 below), but they were greatly influenced by the Greek writings. Many of the ideas about language that had been set down by the Greeks were incorporated into the new linguistic studies and then passed on to the linguistic scholars who came after. Because of this chain, Bloomfield attributes great influence on our modern linguistics to the ancient Greeks, stating that, "Our traditional lore about language is due largely to them."[4]

SCHOLARLY INTEREST IN THE STUDY OF LANGUAGE

Effects of World Exploration on Languages

Another consequence of the fall of Constantinople was the closing to European travel of the Near Eastern routes to the Far East. It therefore became necessary to search for new routes—and the world opened up to European exploration. Expeditions to seek out and trace new routes ended up in little-known areas, where unfamiliar peoples spoke strange languages and followed exotic systems of living. Not only did the Europeans visit the new areas, but many of them eventually settled in and colonized the places they found especially appealing.

Borrowings from New Languages

One result of this contact with different civilizations was the borrowing of words from entirely new language sources, many of the words reflecting the objects and natural history of remote parts of the earth. All the languages of European countries with traditions of exploration absorbed numerous new words of this kind. The exact words varied according to chance and according to the area that was traded

---

[4]Bloomfield, 1933, p. 4.

with or colonized by a given country. Then, in the course of commercial or cultural interchange, many of these words were transmitted to other European languages that had not had the initial direct contact. Most European languages consequently contain a stock of such borrowed words. In English, for example, *mongoose* entered directly from the word *mangus* of the Marathi language of western India. On the other hand, the word *gingham*, from the Malaysian word *ginggan*, meaning "striped," entered by way of the French adaptation, *guingan*. Sixteenth century English, in fact, contained words borrowed from more than 50 other languages.[5] (It is also true, of course, that the reverse occurred and that European words entered the newly contacted languages.)

Modification of European Languages in Far-Off Places

Another by-product of the opening of the world to European commerce and colonization was the exportation of European languages to other countries. In each area were pockets of settlers who were native speakers of a European language. There were also individual members of the indigenous population who soon learned enough of the European language to communicate in it. It is not surprising, therefore, that their interaction led to modifications in the European language.

Languages were altered by the addition of new words and expressions as well as by the changes in pronunciation—in some cases giving rise to new dialects. The modifications varied according to the type of settler (occupation, specific region of the European country of origin, class of society, and so on) and the nature of the settled area (wildlife and geographic features, customs and accoutrements of the indigenous people, phonemes and other characteristics of the indigenous language, presence of speakers of other European languages, and so on) as well as by the mysterious, unaccountable element that is present in almost every language change. The result of this process can be seen in the current differences between Standard British English and the English of the United States or Australia, between Parisian French and the French of Canada or of Martinique, and between Castilian Spanish and the Spanish of Mexico or of Argentina. (See pp. 140–143 below for discussion of the effects of colonization on the English language.)

RISE OF INTEREST IN THE FORMAL STUDY OF LANGUAGE

Contact with Non–Indo-European Languages

Both the early expeditions and the settlements that followed were often marked by the presence of missionaries. These missionaries added a scholarly dimension to the treatment by Europeans of the indigenous cultures—including their languages. Languages were of prime importance then, as they are today, in the efforts of missionaries to establish themselves in new areas, and certain missionaries were particularly interested in working with the unfamiliar tongues, generally non–Indo-European. These missionaries set about translating basic religious texts from the

---

[5]Baugh, 1957, p. 273.

original Latin and compiling information about the words and other features of the new languages. The various translations and compilations they produced were disseminated among other scholars, feeding into the characteristic Renaissance preoccupation with all language.

The interest of religious scholars in the study of non–Indo-European languages was supplemented by the interest of a new class of secular scholars. The intellectual horizons of the Renaissance had been expanded by the extension of learning to a larger number of the upper classes. Education was no longer an exclusively ecclesiastical responsibility, as it had been when only those going into religious life or those in a select group of aristocrats needed to read and write. (In England, especially, the development of secular learning and secular teachers was a complete innovation.)

Study of Vernacular Languages

Of all the linguistic trends of the Renaissance, perhaps the most important for English was the rise of a scholarly concern with contemporary Western languages (see pp. 113–114 below for the effects on English). Throughout the earlier centuries, only Latin had been studied and, to some extent, systematized. Vernacular[6] languages had been deprecated as being unorganized, everyday jargon, with Latin alone considered a language worthy of serious examination or of use in learned writing.

That attitude changed during the Renaissance, and vernacular languages rose in status—the English language as well as the vernacular tongues of such countries as France, Italy, Germany, and Spain. Those languages had similar histories and similar problems and, for like reasons, each met with resistance from scholars before it gained their support. Insufficient vocabulary, lack of spelling uniformity, and, in some cases, multiple dialects were among the reasons given for not accepting the vernacular languages. Also, there were advantages seen in keeping a single familiar language—Latin—for international communication among the learned and religious groups in each country.

Baugh has an excellent discussion of the arguments for and against vernacular languages that were put forward in the fifteenth and sixteenth centuries.[7] He concludes that the eventual triumph of the vernacular languages was based on one overriding factor: the extraordinary appeal of the Renaissance itself, particularly to a new constellation of persons who were centered in government and business. These men were neither ecclesiasts nor academicians, but they were sophisticated and educated enough to be aware of the ideas and information contained in books. They were also persons of some power and influence, and, as they pressed for easier access to the treasures of classical knowledge, more and more translations (as well as newer writings) were produced in the vernacular languages they readily understood.[8]

---

[6]Originally, the word *vernacular* was derived from the Latin root *verna*, meaning "home-born slave." It referred to the everyday languages used by the indigenous populations in places colonized by Rome. Eventually, the meaning was extended to refer to a language spoken by persons in a culture that also used a literary, learned language—such as Italian in contrast to Latin.

[7]Baugh, 1957, pp. 243–250.

[8]See pp. 30–31 above and Childe, 1954, p. 182. The rise of a commercial class had accompanied the invention of the alphabet, which had also been a means of spreading knowledge originally sequestered with an elite group.

THE RENAISSANCE IN ENGLAND

While the Renaissance was in full flower in other European countries, most of English energy during the fifteenth century was put into foreign and civil wars, with little left for the nourishment of arts and letters that so distinguished England in the prior and succeeding centuries.

England in the Fifteenth and Sixteenth Centuries

The Hundred Years' War between England and France (see p. 93 above) raged until 1453.[9] Only 2 years later, this time within the borders of Britain, another lengthy series of debilitating battles began, the Wars of the Roses. Called a "murderous mêlée" by Trevelyan,[10] this new turmoil was essentially nothing more than a struggle between two parties of powerful nobles (under the banners of the red-rosed York and the white-rosed Lancaster) for the possession of the English crown. The Wars of the Roses dragged on until August 22, 1485, when the Lancastrian Henry Tudor, Earl of Richmond, managed to capture the crown from the Yorkist Richard III[11] and begin to rule firmly for 24 years as Henry VII.

In the year 1509, the crowning of Henry's son, Henry VIII (1491–1547), saw a new burst of creative and scholarly talents. Henry VIII's life-loving temperament as well as an economic recovery from the struggles of the previous century provided a hospitable environment for the Renaissance that had held aloof from England until then.

The Elizabethan Age

Building on the successes of Henry's reign, his daughter Elizabeth I (1533–1603) went on to promote a Golden Age of near-Athenian grandeur in the 45 years of her inspired guidance. William Shakespeare alone—the quintessential Elizabethan—was enough to illuminate any age. Add to his name the names of Edmund Spenser, Ben Jonson, and Christopher Marlowe among the many poets and dramatists of soaring excellence who incorporated the classical heritage as well as the riches of the European Renaissance into the special English-French culture that had evolved in the past few centuries. Literary works of great quality of every type were abundant, while the other arts flourished as well, all adding to the ferment of ideas and creative accomplishment.

The Reformation

During the Renaissance, a major religious upheaval took place first in Europe and then in England—the Reformation or Protestant Revolt of the sixteenth century. Baugh,

---

[9]In that year, the French finally forced the last of the English from French soil, except for Calais, which remained in English hands until 1558.

[10]Trevelyan, 1945, p. 264.

[11]Notorious as the suspected murderer of the young princes in the Tower, a suspicion now generally discredited.

like others, perceives the Reformation as "a phase of the Renaissance,"[12] and mentions two noteworthy ways that the Reformation influenced the English language.

One way was by the "almost unbelievable" number of theological writings produced in English rather than in Latin to convince lay readers of the validity of the Protestant beliefs. Those writings helped both their authors and their readers to become increasingly familiar with written English.

The other was the initiation (ca. 1566) of the study of Old English so that old manuscripts could be consulted for proof that the English church had continued through the years as an institution independent of Rome. Access to Old English writings was also needed to ascertain the sources of such doctrines as the divine right of kings (which the Protestants hoped to discredit) and for learning about English traditions of government in the days before the supremacy of the Roman church.[13]

RENAISSANCE INFLUENCES ON THE ENGLISH LANGUAGE

Inkhorn Terms

The English scholars who responded to the desire for translations of foreign books often found it difficult to translate from Latin or other foreign languages because they could not find contemporary English words to convey the original texts with precision. Therefore, a number of translators deliberately introduced foreign words into English (chiefly from Latin, although many from French as well as from Greek and other languages). This practice was extended to original English writings by authors who felt that certain foreign words could express their ideas more precisely than any English words they knew. Foreign words that were borrowed in this deliberate fashion (rather than incidentally by way of oral language, as had predominantly occurred in the past) were known as *inkhorn terms*.

Inkhorn terms (called this in derision) provoked a great deal of controversy, and for much of the sixteenth century arguments approving or opposing such borrowing appeared in many writings.[14] Eventually, the opposition diminished, and by the seventeenth century, criticism of inkhorn terms was directed to the ostentatious overuse of such borrowings rather than to the borrowing itself. During the sixteenth and seventeenth centuries, inkhorn terms entered English by the thousands, adding richness and grace and an enormous capacity to express fine shades of meaning.

Effects of the Foreign Borrowings

Aside from the great enrichment of the English lexicon, the inkhorn borrowings left two important legacies. One resulted from the unusually rapid accumulation of new, frequently complex, and polysyllabic words. Their cumbersome presence helped

---

[12]Baugh, 1957, p. 247.
[13]Baugh, 1957, pp. 344–345n.
[14]Sir Thomas Elyot and Sir Thomas More were responsible for many new inkhorn words. Thomas Wilson is one who spoke out against them, especially in his widely read book, *Arte of Rhetoric* (1553).

inspire the compilation of dictionaries—starting on a small scale in the sixteenth century but expanding into a significant movement when the full flower of the English Renaissance was followed by an epoch with a far more structured and formal intellectual climate (see Chapter 17).

The other legacy of the inkhorn borrowings was a large body of English words that kept their original foreign spellings. Because such words were borrowed after the basic English spelling patterns had been set[15] and often were not fully assimilated into English until many years had passed, their spellings were seldom changed. As a result, Modern English has many words with foreign spelling patterns whose existence lends support to those who perceive our written language as one filled with irregularities (see Chapters 22–25).[16]

-----

[15]By about 1650. See p. 123 below.

[16]On this point, Venezky notes: "More irregular spellings in English are due to borrowings than to any other cause." (His own view, however, is that "such borrowings cannot be classed as entirely irregular since their spellings mark their foreign identity.") Venezky, 1965, p. 216.

16

Backgrounds of English Spelling

We come now to the last of the four historical processes we are studying, the development of the spelling patterns of written English. Some of these patterns have been noted in the discussions and tables of Old and Middle English. Here we will try to present a broad overview of what occurred.

PRE-NORMAN SPELLING: THE SCRIBAL TRADITION

The first written forms of spoken English were set down in the runic *futhark* in pre-Christian England. The Latin alphabet was introduced by those Irish missionaries who converted the Anglo-Saxons to Christianity in the seventh century. Although there was not a perfect one-to-one phoneme–letter match, the Latin alphabet spelling of the English of that time was essentially phonemic[1] so that the written forms corresponded to a large extent to the pronunciations of the words. Marckwardt and Rosier note that Old English was set down in "an alphabet considerably more consistent and regular than ours."[2]

As time passed, however, and the pronunciation of spoken English changed, the Anglo-Saxon scribes did not alter the written forms of the words very much. Instead, they tended to keep the spellings of the obsolete pronunciations as part of a scribal tradition, choosing to preserve original spellings rather than to accommodate new pronunciations as they arose. Such a course was natural since, as noted later in this chapter (p. 121), scribes were intended to be copyists, and accurate transcription was of principal importance in setting down the holy books that were

---

[1]Stevick, 1968, p. 276.

[2]Albert H. Marckwardt and James L. Rosier, *Old English*, Norton, New York, 1972, p. 4. Among the variations that kept the early alphabetic spelling from being strictly phonemic was a lack of separate characters to distinguish the long from the short vowels.

their chief responsibility. That scribal tradition set a precedent for the subsequent English practice of adhering to historic rather than to phonemic spellings.

English Spelling During the Norman Period

In the upheaval and transfer of power that followed the Norman Conquest, Normans frequently supplanted the Anglo-Saxon scribes (see p. 92 above). The Norman scribes were not familiar with the traditional English spellings and tried instead to write the English language by matching spelling with speech sounds. In many cases, the same Norman symbols and spelling patterns used for the French and Latin loan words that were flooding the language were adopted for setting down native English words.[3] In that manner, the letters *g*, *q*, *w*, and *z* as well as such patterns as the *ch* in *child* and the *gu* before *e* in *guest* or *tongue* were incorporated into English spelling.

THE MIDDLE ENGLISH SCRIBAL TRADITION

The spelling patterns of Middle English developed more or less haphazardly during the two centuries (mid-eleventh to mid-thirteenth) that Norman French and Latin reigned as the prestige languages in England. The spelling in the manuscripts of Middle English is based in part on Old English spelling traditions and in part on French or Latin spelling habits,[4] with efforts at sound–spelling correspondence introduced by the scribes who often spoke dialects different from that of the texts they copied.

With the elevation in status of English during the thirteenth century, a new spelling tradition began, one that tended to be established after the end of the fourteenth century. This new Middle English scribal tradition, which included forms passed from scribe to scribe as in the old Anglo-Saxon scribal tradition, was handed down through the fifteenth century. Although there continued to be considerable change in spelling, there was a norm that preserved a number of spelling patterns that were not changed in accordance with the pronunciation changes of those years.

Etymological or Historical Spellings

The influence of the scribal tradition can be seen in a curious practice that affected a number of English words at the end of the Middle English period—chiefly during the fifteenth century, though before and after as well. This was the effort by certain classical scholars to alter the spelling of various phonemically spelled words to make them conform to their historical origins (and by thus highlighting the elegance

---

[3]Vallins, 1965, p. 13.
[4]Fernand Mossé, *A Handbook of Middle English*, Johns Hopkins University Press, Baltimore, 1968, p. 8.

of its origins also to "elevate" the English language). For example, the Old English word *sealm* was traced back to the Latin *psalmus* or Greek *psalmos*. Consequently, its spelling was changed to *psalm*, although the *p* was never pronounced in spoken English. The English word *dette* was traced back to the Latin *debitum* and therefore changed in spelling to *debt*, although the *b* was never pronounced, since by the time the word entered English from the original French, the "b" pronunciation had already disappeared.

Among the etymological spellings established at a later date was the alteration of the word *receit* by Samuel Johnson in the eighteenth century. The word had entered English by way of the French *recette*, but could be traced back to the Latin word *receptum*. Johnson changed the English spelling to *receipt*, although the *p* remained silent.

False Etymological Spellings

In some cases, word histories were traced back erroneously. Consequently, certain Modern English words are spelled neither fully phonemically nor fully historically. The process of analogy (see p. 105 n. 16) was often responsible for these mistakes. Thus, the word *island*, which actually comes from the native English word *iegland*, acquired the silent *s* because it was incorrectly believed to have come from the French word *isle* (from the Latin *insula*) combined with the word *land*.

The letters *gh* were also often added with little historical accuracy. For example, the words *delight* (from the French *delite*) and *spright* (originally *sprite*, and now used in Modern English *sprightly*) were mistakenly changed to conform to the word *light*. The *gh* in *light*, however, is a legitimate reminder of the voiceless palatal or velar fricative *h* in the earlier form *liht*. Furthermore, the word *hiccup* was inaccurately believed to be related to the word *cough* and was therefore altered to *hiccough*.

THE PRINTING TRADITION

An entirely new force upon English spelling was created by the appearance in 1450 of Johann Gutenberg's movable type. This invention, with its immeasurable impact on every aspect of life, affected our writing in many ways.

Origins of Printing

Although the name Gutenberg is rightly associated with the creation of the printing press as we know it, he was not the first to conceive of the idea of marking a surface by pressing a form onto it. Thousands of years ago, Egyptians and Babylonians, as well as others living in the lands bordering the eastern Mediterranean, had pressed carved forms on such surfaces as clay or wax. Egyptian scarabs, Babylonian cuneiform, and various forms of ancient seals are familiar examples of their skills. A long time afterward, in the second century, another printing tradition emerged in China.

Early Chinese Printing

Soon after they had invented paper,[5] the Chinese began to make designs and pictures by pressing inked blocks of wood on paper. The method they used is called *block-printing*, a technique in which the basic units are wooden or metal blocks upon which whole compositions of pictures, designs, writing, or combinations of them are set down. (The counterpart to block-printing is *type-printing*, in which the basic units are individually written characters that are temporarily bound together to comprise a desired text, but that can be moved apart and then reused for the assembling of another text. Modern books, newspapers, and the like are printed by such movable type. Examples of modern block-printing are etchings and lithographs.) By the seventh century, the Chinese had extended their block-printing from solely pictorial representations to writing and were printing characters on scrolls.

The Chinese continued to evolve their printing processes and finally developed a movable type with which they were able to print books. A well-known example of old Chinese type-printing is a book produced in Korea in 1337, currently housed in the British Museum. Despite its long history, however, no idea of this invention appears to have reached Western Europe, where movable type was independently invented and reached a far more advanced stage.

Johann Gutenberg (ca. 1398–1468)

There is evidence that as early as the twelfth century some manner of printing was being done in Europe, in Germany and elsewhere: cloth-printing, maps, stamping letters, and, by the early 1400s, the printing of characters cut on wood blocks. Nevertheless, it was not until the mid-1400s, in the Alsatian city of Strasbourg, that "a towering genius"[6] named Johann Gutenberg first devised a machine for making impressions on large sheets from movable, molded, metal forms. His method made it possible to publish whole books with infinitely greater ease than had ever been known before.

Little information about Gutenberg's life is available to us today. He was born in Mainz, Germany, and moved to Strasbourg where, in the 1430s and 1440s, he began his efforts to produce a satisfactory printing press. He worked on such a machine for a number of years, finally perfecting it in Mainz, to which he had returned some time in the late 1440s. The historical date for the completion of the printing press is given as August 22, 1450.[7] By then, Gutenberg had brought his machine to a superb level of functioning: his solutions to some of the knotty problems he faced

---

[5]Paper has been used in China since A.D. 105, when word of its invention was brought to the Chinese emperor by a government official named Tsai Lun. In the eighth century, Arabs in Samarkand discovered and adopted the use of paper, which then reached Europe in the twelfth century, during the Moorish occupation of Spain. Until that time, Europeans had written on parchment made from animal skins.

[6]George D. Painter, *William Caxton*, Putnam, New York, 1976, p. 53.

[7]On that date Gutenberg signed a contract to borrow 800 gold gulden (at 6% interest), which he pledged to use to print books (Putnam, 1896, Vol. 1, p. 360).

have not been surpassed to this day. Thus, his alloy of lead, tin, and antimony is still considered the finest metal for type, while his choice of oil-based paint has turned out to be the finest kind of printer's ink.

Gutenberg's contribution to the new art of printing did not end with his inventing the printing press. He went on to use his invention to publish books of extraordinary beauty. An exalted standard for the early printers was set by such works as Gutenberg's first published book, his Latin Bible, which Painter calls "perhaps the most beautiful and technically perfect book ever printed."[8]

This level of quality cost time and money that led Gutenberg into a life of persistent financial difficulties. Despite his struggles with debts and lawsuits, however, Gutenberg "was recognised by all as a man of knowledge and character, and as a born leader, whose integrity of purpose and whose nobility of aim were acknowledged by all with whom he had to do."[9]

Not only did Gutenberg perfect a great machine and produce exemplary works with it, but he freely taught others how to use his invention. This generous sharing gave impetus to the adoption of printing by his contemporaries and thus speeded up its worldwide acceptance.

Spread of Printing

Because Mainz was the major city in the Rhine region at that time, Gutenberg was able to attract a number of earnest students of printing—many of them former scribes—and Mainz became the first center of the new art. In 1462, however, Mainz was sacked during a religious war, and many of its inhabitants scattered, the newly established printers among them. The result of the printers' dispersal was a spread of the new art, which slowly picked up momentum. Starting in Strasbourg and then Cologne, new centers of printing were established in Germany, then in Italy via Switzerland, then in Paris, and, in 1476, in London. By the end of the fifteenth century, printing had spread to most of Europe.[10]

Effects of the Printing Press

The fruits of Gutenberg's machine are, of course, beyond measure. Among them were a number of dramatic effects on European communication.

Most directly, literacy was encouraged, since the newer, cheaper process permitted many more individuals to own the books that Gutenberg and succeeding printers produced. In turn, the possession of books and the greatly expanded opportunity to read activated the spread of literacy and of a general cultural enrichment to larger numbers of the population—with a resultant demand for more books.

Because of the broadened market and because books became much easier to produce, there was now incentive as well as time to print books of lesser impor-

---

[8]Painter, 1976, p. 53.

[9]Putnam, 1896, Vol. 1, p. 364.

[10]The first printer in the Americas was Juan Pablos, Mexico City, 1539. Stephen Daye was the first in what is now the United States. He built and then, in 1639, set up the first printing press in the home of the president of Harvard College, Reverend Henry Dunster. (Isaiah Thomas, *The History of Printing in America*, 1st edition, 1810, 2nd edition, 1874. Edition of 1970, Marcus A. McCorison [Ed.], Crown, New York, pp. 50, 288.)

tance, often in the vernacular rather than in Latin. In this way, the introduction of printing raised the status of the vernacular in each country and stimulated the publication and dissemination of great numbers of writings.

The great new invention also resulted in the printing of writings in such less accessible languages as Old Gothic and Hebrew. Consequently, scholars found it easy to learn and to compare more languages, thereby enriching their linguistic studies and leading them to heretofore little explored aspects of communication.

The Printing Press in England: William Caxton

Just as the printing press had an immense effect on all continental Europe, England and the English language were deeply touched by it. The person responsible for establishing printing in England and furthering its use there was William Caxton (ca. 1422–1491), called "the father of English printing."[11] In the year 1476, even before the full impact of the Renaissance had reached England, Caxton set up the first printing press in Westminster Abbey and thus brought about what Trevelyan calls "perhaps the greatest English event of the century."[12]

Caxton was a prominent cloth merchant who fit the description of the sophisticated nonacademic Renaissance person given above (p. 111). His enterprises took him to the continent for many years—chiefly to Germany and the Low Countries, with his headquarters in Bruges. There he took on the roles of semiofficial ambassador and leader of English merchants. In 1471, for reasons that are still obscure, Caxton moved to Cologne, Germany, one of the centers of the new printing industry. While there, Caxton became acquainted and enchanted with the new process. So enchanted in fact, that he studied under one of the master printers, probably Johann Veldener,[13] for several years and then returned to Bruges for a short time. In Bruges, he set up his own press to publish the first printed book in English. Fittingly, in light of the Renaissance emphasis on classical Greek culture, this was Caxton's own translation of French stories based on the history of Troy—called *The Recuyell* (or Collection) *of the Historyes of Troye.*

In the year 1476, Caxton returned to England and set up the first English printing press in Westminster, where he published the first book printed on English soil: *The Dictes and Sayings of the Philosophers.* Caxton then went on to print many outstanding works—not only translations from ancient and contemporary languages, but native English writings such as *The Canterbury Tales* (Chaucer) and, in 1485, Sir Thomas Malory's *Morte d'Arthur.*

Printing and the Standardization of English Spelling

Caxton's work had vast consequences. The same effects that the printing press had on the continent appeared in England as well: greater literacy for a new population

---

[11]Ogg, 1971, p. 225.
[12]Trevelyan, 1945, p. 265.
[13]Painter, 1976, pp. 56–57.

of readers, an intensified demand for books—especially marked in England—and a broader, more profound, scholarly activity. (See pp. 119–120 above.)

The increased visibility of the vernacular English language in written form was another factor that helped raise it to a more prestigious level and caused it to be included in the evolving study of language. Since the scholars of the day tended toward questioning and systematizing as well as toward describing, one effect of their scrutiny was a movement to standardize English spelling to replace the prevailing inconsistent spellings of individual writers. This movement fit in with the practical needs of the printers, who had the same kind of decision-making responsibility that had earlier rested with the scribes. Both scribes and printers were primarily copyists—rather than scholars—whose role was to render with great accuracy what others had written instead of interpreting or originating the text on their own. In fact, the very first printers either were scribes themselves or, as Gutenberg had done, employed former scribes for the layout of the texts.

Printing was especially influential in helping to standardize English spelling because of the simple fact that the individual copies of each edition were identical. It gave wide exposure and much weight to those spellings that were selected.[14] Of paramount importance were the spellings chosen by Caxton, who set the course of the printing trade for many years.

Caxton's Choice

Whether he was conscious of them or not, Caxton lived at a time when a number of powerful forces were pulling the spoken and written forms of English in various directions. These forces included the Great Vowel Shift, the efforts to link English to classical word derivations, the venerable scribal tradition of preserving old spelling forms that were often based on obsolete pronunciations, and a wide variety of regional and class dialects.

Caxton's problem was whether to set down his printed writings according to the spellings of the old scribal tradition or whether to use spellings that corresponded to the pronunciation of the spoken language of his day. Not surprisingly, in view of his perspective as a printer/copyist, Caxton chose a conservative route and utilized nonphonemic historical forms.[15] By doing so, he determined the basic prin-

---

[14]The direct effect of printing on spelling standardization is underscored by the fact that while spelling was being standardized in printed texts, individuals who wrote by hand continued to spell inconsistently—often according to the way words sounded to the particular writer.

Such unstandardized writings became very useful to scholars seeking to determine the pronunciation of spoken English in periods when printed spellings were no longer accurate reflections of the pronunciation of the time—notably during Shakespeare's time and even later. (Sir James Pitman and John St. John, *Alphabets and Reading*, Pitman, New York, 1969, p. 65.)

[15]More specifically, according to Fischer, Caxton was influenced by the scribes of the Chancery—the bureaucracy of clerk-scribes charged with writing down official proclamations and parliamentary records. Starting in 1420, these scribes began to write in English and during the next four decades developed Chancery Standard or Chancery English, containing forms of handwriting, grammar, vocabulary, and spelling that grew to be uniform in official documents throughout the country, while not identified with any one of the many regional or social varieties of the "civic English" of the day. For spelling, Chancery English tended to preserve the older, nonphonemic forms.

Fischer points out that when Caxton returned to England in 1476, he set up his printing press in Westminster "under the shadow" of the government offices where Chancery Standard (*continued on p. 122*)

ciples of all future English spelling. Over and above the superficial variations and the numerous attempts at greater sound–spelling correspondence during the years since Caxton's time, English spelling has always been geared toward standard, uniform patterns rather than toward actual pronunciations. Neither is it surprising that the printers who came after Caxton also followed a conservative route—not only looking to established usage for their choices of written forms, but resisting deliberate efforts at alphabet reform (see p. 176 n. 17 below).

The practical value of saving effort and space in the process of setting down type has influenced spelling forms as well. The shortening of such words as *catalogue* and *programme* has been spurred by the brevity of the shorter forms, and the advantage of saving space was given by George Bernard Shaw as an added reason for using the new alphabet he advocated. (See pp. 167–168 below.)

REACTIONS TO NONPHONEMIC SPELLINGS

The impact of Caxton's decision was not felt immediately. Almost 100 years passed before the accumulated effects of overlooking changes in pronunciation was felt. By the last half of the sixteenth century, however, the discrepancies between spoken and written English were obvious and, for many, uncomfortable. By then, the increase in literacy had brought with it an increase in reading and writing instruction. Gordon notes that schoolchildren and foreigners (who now wished to learn the English vernacular) were populations that required not only such instruction but elementary schoolbooks as well.[16] These needs converged with the scholarly interest in vernacular languages and in the study of language in general, resulting in a detailed examination of all aspects of the English language. Dunkel characterizes the years between 1511 and 1658 in this way: "Never before or since have language teaching and language learning been so important as they then were, and never have so many first-rate minds given major attention to them."[17]

English spelling and what was conceived as its inconsistencies were particularly well scrutinized, and zealous efforts were made to deal with them. It was then that a number of spelling reformers began to emerge.

---

was used. Fischer links this proximity with Caxton's printed English forms and views the Chancery contributions to English language forms in this way:

"The dominance of the scribal tradition lasted only till the advent of printing. By the end of the fifteenth century, printers and educators had begun to assume dominant roles in codifying the approved forms and idiom of written English.... But during the crucial period between 1420 and 1460...the essential characteristics of Modern Written English were determined by the *practice* of the clerks in Chancery, and communicated throughout England by professional scribes writing in Chancery script, under the influence of Chancery idiom.... Modern English is not Chancery English. In its style, in its forms, and particularly in its capitalization and punctuation, it has continued to evolve. But Chancery English of the early fifteenth century is the starting point for this evolution, and has left an indelible impression upon the spelling, grammar, and idiom of Modern English." (John H. Fischer, "Chancery and the Emergence of Standard Written English in the Fifteenth Century," *Speculum*, 1977, pp. 898–899.) I am grateful to Richard Venezky for referring me to this article.

[16]Gordon, 1972, p. 250.

[17]Harold B. Dunkel, "Language Teaching in an Old Key," *Modern Language Journal*, May 1963, pp. 203–204. (Also quoted in Mathews, 1966, p. 24.)

English Spelling Reform: The Orthoepists

On the whole, the spelling reformers tended to be teachers of reading and writing who tried to steer English spelling toward sound–spelling correspondence and away from the scribal-historical direction of the past. Because of their concern with pronunciation, these men have often been called *orthoepists*, forerunners of future phoneticians and phonologists.[18] In their heyday—the latter part of the sixteenth and the first part of the seventeenth century—the spelling reformers managed to institute many orthographic changes, many of which have lasted until today. Baugh states that English spelling was "fairly settled" between the years 1500 and 1650.[19]

Each spelling reformer presented proposals for achieving greater uniformity in spelling—proposals that fell into three approaches. One approach was to devise an augmented alphabet—one with added symbols to stand for the phonemes that had no characters of their own in the English alphabet. John Hart, author of *An Orthographie . . .* (1569), was one of those who offered this solution and whose work was a model for similar efforts.[20]

A second approach was to utilize the existing alphabet but to change the spellings of words to conform to speech and, often, to use some sort of dot, line, or other diacritical mark to indicate a variation of the sound of a specific letter (as $\breve{a}$ for the *a* in *ax* and $\bar{a}$ for the *a* in *ate*). William Bullokar, author of *A Booke at Large* (1580) developed one of the many diacritical marking systems that did not last.[21]

The third group of reformers wished to keep the nonphonemic spellings but to strive for consistency among certain spelling patterns. Thus, Richard Mulcaster, author of the famous *The First Part of the Elementarie* (1582),[22] believed that changing the old nonphonemic patterns would be extremely disruptive to the literate and hard to institute. He chose, rather, to describe a number of specific alterations, such as using the final *silent e* to show that the preceding vowel is long and using *-er* instead of *-re* (as, *theater* instead of *theatre)*. (See p. 174 below for Noah Webster's concern with *-er/-re.*) It is not clear whether Mulcaster was directly responsible for the invention of many of his suggestions or whether they were already part of a developing spelling tradition. His work was held in great respect, however, and was picked up by the authors of school spelling manuals.

---

[18]The term *orthoepist* means "one who is concerned with correct speech" and is best applied to a group of late eighteenth century writers on pronunciation. Dobson points out that the spelling reformers of the sixteenth and seventeenth centuries were not primarily interested in correct speech. Rather, except for certain authors of grammars for foreigners, their concern with pronunciation stemmed from their main interest—reading and spelling. (E.J. Dobson, *English Pronunciation 1500–1700*, Oxford University Press, London, 1968, pp. 193–194.)

[19]Baugh, 1957, p. 257. Even at this point, however, there was still a considerable degree of flexibility. It was not until the eighteenth century, with the acceptance of dictionary spellings, that spelling forms were fixed in the modern way, where the aim is for each word to have an unyieldingly consistent form.

[20]Pitman and St. John (1969) give detailed descriptions of many augmented alphabets and diacritical marking systems from early times to the present, with samples and tables of the characters of the systems they discuss.

[21]Also counted in this second group should be the very first English spelling reformer, the monk Orm, author of a set of moralistic verses called *The Ormulum* (1200). Like the spelling reformers of subsequent centuries, Orm sought to arrange spelling to conform consistently to pronunciation, demonstrating his suggested changes in the spelling of the Ormulum. None of his creative ideas were picked up directly by subsequent spelling reformers (although his consistency in following his own rules has been of great help to scholars in determining the pronunciation of the English of his day).

[22]Mulcaster, 1970.

Early Spelling Manuals

Even before the spelling reformers began to focus on English spelling patterns, simple spelling books meant for school use began to appear. One of them, the *Abc for chyldren* (early 1560s, published by John King, author unknown) is noteworthy as the earliest speller extant but is a confused work of poor quality.

Among the later, more sophisticated works is Edmund Coote's two-volume *The English Schoole-Maister* (1596).[23] The first volume of this highly influential spelling manual for teachers contains nonsense syllables to be used to form words; in the second volume, Coote discusses syllabication, characteristics of vowels and consonants, and grammar.

Although Coote never admitted it, his work is based on Mulcaster's ideas and spelling rules. In any case, *The English Schoole-Maister* was extremely popular—its fifty-fourth edition was published in 1737—and authors of subsequent spelling books, both in England and later on in North America, looked to it for its format as well as looking to Mulcaster for his theories on spelling rules and patterns. Through the schools, therefore, both Mulcaster and Coote affected the course of English spelling.

---

[23]Edmund Coote, *The English Schoole-Maister,* First Edition. At London. Printed by the Widow Orwin, for Ralph Jackson and Robert Dextar, 1596.

17

Seventeenth and Eighteenth Century Authoritarianism

Backgrounds of the English Dictionary

After the long reign of Elizabeth I (1533–1603), the start of the seventeenth century in England marked the beginning of a shift from what Baugh terms the "adventurous individualism" of the Renaissance "to a desire for system and regularity."[1] This desire was manifested in a concern with orderliness that permeated English cultural and artistic life at a time when the relative peace of the Renaissance era was replaced by political turbulence.

THE POLITICAL UPHEAVALS OF SEVENTEENTH CENTURY ENGLAND

The turbulence began when the death of Queen Elizabeth initiated a struggle between the newly rising—often Puritanical—middle classes and the autocratic, royalist nobility headed by the unpopular Stuart kings. The struggle, highlighted by an outright civil war and the beheading of Charles I (1649), lasted for most of the seventeenth century.

Civic calm and political ease returned to England after 1689, when William and Mary of Orange were jointly crowned king and queen—by an act of Parliament rather than on the basis of a hereditary or a divine right.[2] Despite external difficulties (notably, a 50-year war with France), William and Mary were able to retain the

---

[1]Baugh, 1957, p. 306.
[2]All subsequent English monarchs have been crowned by similar acts of Parliament.

confidence of the great majority of the English people so that their reign (1689–1702) ushered in an internal order that has lasted ever since.

Little of English political history needs to be added beyond this point. The events of the eighteenth century and after are well enough known for our purposes, and the changes in language since that time can be related to familiar historical settings and events.

THE ENGLISH LANGUAGE DURING THE SEVENTEENTH AND EIGHTEENTH CENTURIES

It was noted earlier that the basic forms of English pronunciation and grammar had been fairly well established by the end of the sixteenth century, and, certainly when compared with the rate of linguistic change in previous centuries, relatively little has been added since then. Most changes have been changes in vocabulary—through the addition of new words, the dropping of old ones, and changes in the meanings of existing words. While such vocabulary changes have occurred freely, changes in other aspects of language have taken place slowly and have often met with strong resistance.

The stability of spoken as well as of written English stems in part from the cessation of such invasions of Britain as those of the Germanic, Scandinavian, and Norman groups, in which the foreign tongue brought by each invading people altered the existing language forms. Another restraining influence—on spelling—was the printing press, discussed in Chapter 16. English was even more decidedly fixed, however, especially in its written form, by the events and scholarship of the seventeenth and eighteenth centuries.

New Spirit of Rationalism and Order

Against a background of political upheaval and innovation, the intellectual spirit of the seventeenth century replaced the easy independence of the Renaissance with a heightened respect for order, authority, and human reason. These newer values grew in importance as the century wore on so that, by the eighteenth century, all who were engaged in scholarship became concerned with some sort of logical regulation of their disciplines. The scholars who concentrated on the study of language were no exception. They set about organizing and trying to fix various aspects of spoken and written English.

Rise of the Middle Classes

Another force that stimulated the desire for regulation of the language was the rise to power of the middle classes. One frequent price of upward social mobility is an insecurity about the speech and manners identified with the prestigious social levels. The middle classes of the seventeenth and eighteenth centuries were caught up in such insecurity and looked for guidelines to upper-class behavior and to language patterns that were not natural to them. Great emphasis came to be placed on "correct" forms, which then were prescribed for all who wanted to appear well bred.

Language was particularly focused upon, and regulatory processes were devised that succeeded in preserving many language forms of that day. Moreover, a belief in the existence of an authoritative "correctness" in all matters of spoken and written language was established—a belief that even the least literate member of English-speaking society has come to take for granted ever since.

Efforts to Establish Language Prescriptions

One of the seventeenth century plans to produce authoritative decisions about the English language was a long-term, hotly argued, but never-realized attempt to establish an English (or British) Academy along the lines of the already functioning French and Italian Academies to set down rules about English grammar and vocabulary. Many eminent authors and scholars—including Joseph Addison, Daniel Defoe, John Dryden, and Jonathan Swift—were strongly in favor of some sort of organization to produce an authoritative picture of the language in its contemporary form as well as to decide on the acceptability of any changes.

While plans for an academy never bore fruit, the arguments of its supporters helped to delineate seventeenth and eighteenth century concerns about the English language. For these concerns, a number of solutions were tried.

One solution, dealing with syntax and form, was the eighteenth century production of rule books on grammar and rhetoric. Outstanding among these were Robert Lowth's *A Short Introduction to English Grammar with Critical Notes* (1762) and Lindley Murray's *English Grammar Adapted to Different Classes of Learning* (1795). Lowth's book laid the foundation for the tradition of English grammatical rules that governs us even today—a tradition of rules based on "logic" rather than on contemporary usage. Murray's book, reissued many times, was an enormously popular vehicle for Lowth's prescriptive grammar throughout the nineteenth century and has had a great effect on the grammar of today.[3]

Another solution was the compilation of English dictionaries—ultimately a towering force in the standardization and maintenance of our language. The evolution of dictionaries from centuries-old pedagogic practices to the carefully conceived and often monumental reference works of recent times was an outgrowth of the eighteenth century yearning for authoritative prescriptions.

THE ENGLISH DICTIONARY: EARLY COMPILATIONS[4]

The first English dictionaries were simply listings of selected words and their meanings. Gradually, they acquired their present major functions of defining a great

---

[3]A basic source on the formulation of rules for English usage is Sterling A. Leonard's *The Doctrine of Correctness in English Usage, 1700–1800*, University of Wisconsin Studies in Language and Literature, No. 25, Madison, 1929.

[4]The major source for this topic is De Witt T. Starnes and Gertrude E. Noyes, *The English Dictionary from Cawdrey to Johnson 1604–1755*, University of North Carolina Press, Chapel Hill, 1946.

range of words as well as of recording specific spellings, pronunciations, and etymologies (that is, word derivations).[5] Dictionaries also grew to include various lists, tables, and illustrations for historical and other background information.

What occurred, essentially, was a coalescence of four simple study tools. These were glossaries, vocabularies, foreign language teaching manuals, and English–Latin or Latin–English and other interlingual dictionaries. While the interlingual dictionaries contributed the most, each of the four tools evolved characteristics that were assimilated into the ultimate dictionary format. Throughout the gradual process, almost every author built directly on a preceding author's work and, perhaps of special interest to readers of this book, practically all the works were devised by teachers trying to facilitate their students' learning.

Glossaries

Glossaries, which antedate the other study tools, were alphabetical lists of difficult or foreign words and their meanings gathered from the explanations (or glosses) inserted in the spaces of a manuscript—similar to the explanations modern students write above difficult words in literary or foreign texts. Glossaries were frequently devised in ancient classical times as well as during the Middle Ages when they were geared for young monastic students and focused on Scriptural texts. The earliest glossary for English to come down to us is the *Corpus Glossary* (eighth or ninth century).[6]

Vocabularies

From the tenth through the eighteenth century, highly popular books of word lists called *vocabularies* were produced. Whereas each glossary listed only the difficult words of a specific text, vocabularies were designed to teach the Latin language and therefore comprised both common and difficult words. Each list in a vocabulary was centered about a certain category, with each Latin word in the category followed by an Anglo-Saxon equivalent. The lists were not alphabetical, and they covered such diverse topics as agricultural implements, birds, religious terms, foods, weapons, colors, and so forth, with the specific topics and numbers of groups differing from vocabulary to vocabulary. One of the most popular of all vocabularies was James Greenwood's *London Vocabulary* (1700).

Foreign Language Teaching Manuals

A sixteenth century variation of the vocabularies was the foreign language teaching manual. Instead of individually listed words and their translations, however, manu-

---

[5]Mitford M. Mathews gives an excellent description of the standard types of information to be found in a "good" modern English dictionary. He also identifies the point in time when each type was first introduced. ("An Introduction to the Dictionary" in *Words, Words, and Words about Dictionaries*, Jack C. Gray (Ed.), Chandler, San Francisco, 1963, pp. 35–51.)

[6]Modern glossaries are not derived from glosses, of course, but they resemble the original glossaries in that both are lists of the obscure or technical words in a specific written work.

als contained whole Latin sentences, with their English translations written directly above or below them. The sentences were based on topics similar to the topics of the vocabularies. One of the earliest as well as the most popular of the teaching manuals was John Stanbridge's *Vocabularia*, first published in 1496.

Such manuals were produced abroad as well as in England. The great Moravian educator, Johann Amos Comenius, tried his hand at them and wrote a German–Latin manual, *Orbis Sensualium Pictus* (1657), which was almost immediately translated into an English–Latin manual by Charles Hoole.[7] Since Comenius's works were immensely influential with other educators, the innovations he introduced have had lasting effects on subsequent study tools. Thus, his listing of sentences in the order of their increasing difficulty became the cornerstone of all graded instruction. Also, aided by the invention of the copper plate for engraving,[8] Comenius was able to include 150 pictorial illustrations in his *Orbis*. This use of illustrations was adopted by James Greenwood in his *London Vocabulary*, and illustrations have since appeared in every kind of instructional and reference material.

Incidentally, Comenius's preface to this work has been cited—wholly erroneously according to Mathews—as evidence that Comenius was the first advocate of a whole word approach to the teaching of reading. The error arose when a nineteenth century writer on the history of reading instruction, Rudolph Rex Reeder, took some sentences out of context and arrived at a conclusion he found pleasing.[9]

Interlingual Dictionaries

The most important interlingual dictionaries for the development of English language dictionaries were the English–Latin and the Latin–English works intended for youngsters going into the religious life. They first arose in the middle of the fifteenth century, with the English–Latin *Promptorium Parvulum, sive Clericorum* (ca. 1440, author unknown) and the Latin–English *Medulla Grammatice* (ca. 1460).

Subsequent to these, there was a continuous output both in England and on the Continent of various Latin and modern language interlingual dictionaries. In the sixteenth century, the modern language compilations were stimulated by the worldwide colonization and contact with exotic languages noted earlier.

The English Schoole-Maister

Among the many compilations that contributed to the evolution of the English dictionary, one stands out as the final link between earlier works and true dictionaries. This is Edmund Coote's *The English Schoole-Maister* (1596), the teacher's manual mentioned earlier for its role in the development of English spelling. Coote's book

---

[7]Different authors give different translations of the title, all equally awkward. This translation, *The World in Pictures*, is given by Matthew Spinka in *John Amos Comenius: That Incomparable Moravian*, University of Chicago Press, 1943. Charles Hoole's translation is *The World of Things Obvious to the Senses drawn in Pictures. (The Orbis Pictus of John Amos Comenius*, C.W. Bardeen, Syracuse, NY, 1887. Reissued by Singing Tree Press, Detroit, 1968.)

[8]Dunkel, 1963, p. 209.

[9]Mathews, 1966, pp. 141–143.

lists about 1,400 difficult English words, set down in three different typefaces to indicate whether a word was borrowed from French, borrowed from Latin, or was a native word. Although the word lists are merely part of a much larger work and not its main body, they are the first known attempt at this kind of intralingual listing and were heavily drawn upon by the authors of the first dictionaries—both the entries and definitions, as well as the basic concept. *The English Schoole-Maister* is therefore considered the direct predecessor of the first English dictionary.

A Table Alphabeticall—The First True English Dictionary

Robert Cawdrey's *A Table Alphabeticall* (1604) is thought of as the first true English dictionary because it is "the first volume in English devoted entirely to a listing of difficult English words explained by other English words rather than by those from another language, such as Latin."[10] An alphabetical listing of some 2,500 words and their meanings, together with a rough indication of word derivations (words of French or Greek origin are marked), Cawdrey's dictionary was popular enough in its day to have had four editions through 1617.

One aspect of Cawdrey's book—the audience for whom it was intended—is of special interest. His title page states:

"A Table Alphabeticall, conteyning and teaching the true writing and vnderstanding of hard vsuall English wordes, borrowed from the Hebrew, Greeke, Latine, or French.&c.

"With the interpretation thereof by plaine English words, gathered for the benefit & helpe of Ladies, Gentlewomen, or other vnskilfull persons."[11]

Cawdrey's singling out of women in this way might seem startling to anyone not acquainted with the prevailing attitudes toward female illiteracy. Scragg, discussing women's limited education during this period, notes that women's spelling was at times derided—as was all poor spelling. Scragg points out that Cawdrey's immediate predecessor, Coote, also believed that his book, *The English Schoole-Maister,* would be more useful to women, although Coote refers to "both men & women" in his preface.[12]

Other authors of early wordbooks who describe their target audience refer to "all such as desire to understand what they read"[13] or to "Ladies and Gentle-women, young Schollers, Clarkes, Merchants, as also Strangers of any Nation"[14] or to "the Curious . . . the Ignorant and . . . young Students, Artificers, Tradesmen, and Foreigners who are desirous thorowly to understand what they Speak, Read, or Write."[15]

---

[10]Peters, 1968, p. 283.

[11]Robert Cawdrey, *A Table Alphabeticall,* Edmund Weaner, London, 1604. Facsimile edition with introduction by Robert A. Peters, Scholars' Facsimiles & Reprints, Gainesville, FL, 1966, Title Page.

[12]D.G. Scragg, *A History of English Spelling,* Manchester University Press. Published in the U.S.A. by Harper & Row, Barnes and Noble Import Division, New York, 1974, p. 89.

[13]Thomas Blount, *Glossographia,* Thomas Newcomb, London, 1656, Title Page. Reproduced in Starnes and Noyes, 1946.

[14]Henry Cockeram, *The English Dictionarie,* H.C. Gent, London, 1623, Title Page. Starnes and Noyes, 1946, p. 26.

[15]Nathan Bailey, *An Universal Etymological English Dictionary,* London, 1721, Title Page. Reproduced in Starnes and Noyes, 1946.

Other Early Dictionaries

The dictionaries that followed Cawdrey's increased the number of their entries and added features that were then incorporated into subsequent dictionaries. In compiling their works, all the early lexicographers made extensive use of *A Table Alphabeticall* as well as of other earlier works, as Cawdrey himself had done.

One work, published not long after Cawdrey's, should be mentioned because of its extraordinary impact on future dictionaries. This is John Minsheu's *Ductor in Linguas or a Guide into the Tongues* (1617), an interlingual rather than English language dictionary, in which each word is followed by its etymology and by its translation in 10 different languages. It was the first English etymological dictionary and was used as a source for all later dictionaries. Minsheu was an imaginative as well as astute scholar, and a number of his etymologies that were dismissed as absurd by earlier researchers have turned out to be accurate.[16]

---

[16]Ernest Weekley, "On Dictionaries," *The Atlantic Monthly*, June 1924. Reprinted in *Dictionaries and That Dictionary*, James H. Sledd and Wilma P. Ebbitt (Eds.), Scott, Foresman and Company, Glenview, IL, 1962, pp. 12–13.

18

The English Dictionary from the Eighteenth Century On

Dictionaries evolved throughout the seventeenth century and were expanded by the addition both of new categories of terms and of obscure words with increasingly elaborate definitions. The eighteenth century, however, brought new lexicographical approaches.

UNIVERSAL DICTIONARIES

One new approach was the attempt to list and define compactly all the words in the English language rather than just the hard words. The first to undertake this task was John Kersey, the author of several dictionaries culminating in the *Dictionarium Anglo-Britannicum* (1708).

A more scholarly and much fuller work than Kersey's appeared in 1730: Nathan Bailey's *Dictionarium Britannicum* (*A More Compleat Universal Etymological English Dictionary*). Bailey was the author of several earlier compilations, for which he adopted freely from his own works as well as the works of others, particularly Kersey's. The *Dictionarium Britannicum* was not as widely used as Bailey's extremely popular earlier work, *An Universal Etymological English Dictionary* (1721), but it is superior in construction, and its two editions (1730 and 1736) appear to have formed the working base for Samuel Johnson's dictionary.

SAMUEL JOHNSON'S GREAT DICTIONARY

Although other dictionaries—those of Bailey in particular—continued to be published and used, from 1755 on all existing dictionaries were overshadowed by the one published in that year: Samuel Johnson's A *Dictionary of the English Language*.[1] This milestone compilation became the model for all future dictionaries, especially those published during the following century. Upon its publication, the history of English dictionaries entered a new phase. Further refining, broadening, and abridging took place, but the basic dictionary format was established by Johnson.

The first (1755) edition of Johnson's dictionary was a two-volume work, almost 2,300 pages long, containing separate sections on the history and the grammar of the English language and a thoughtfully selected listing of words and their definitions, all introduced by a preface in which he described his design and his beliefs about the language. The words he listed were defined according to their uses, and quotations from reputable authorities were given to illustrate the definitions.

In recent years, the rapturous phrases that had earlier characterized appraisals of Johnson's dictionary have been substantially modified. The contemporary view is that Johnson was not an originator but mainly a compiler of all that had gone before. Johnson had started his dictionary as a commission by a group of booksellers who felt the times were right for such a work—to do for English lexicography what had already been attempted for the French and Italian by the dictionaries of the French and Italian Academies. The *Dictionary* was based not only on the chain of dictionaries described above but on a number of other English and foreign dictionaries and books on language. Sledd and Kolb also point to the enormous efforts by his publishers to promote the work, and they attribute much of the *Dictionary*'s success to those efforts.[2]

There is general agreement, however, on the importance of Johnson's work to the lexicographers who followed and, especially, on the originality and excellence of his definitions. Clifford states that Johnson's definitions "have been the basis for the work of all modern lexicographers."[3] Even as they carefully try to avoid an overexuberent evaluation of Johnson, Sledd and Kolb do not quarrel with Wheatley's statement (in 1885): "The definitions are full, clear, and above all praise for their happy illustration of the meaning of words. These can never be superseded, and the instances in which Johnson's successors have been able to improve upon his work in this respect are singularly few."[4]

In the end, however, the most important effect of Johnson's *Dictionary* was probably its role in the firm establishment of dictionaries as the ultimate authority on all they contain. This authority has come to include not only the legitimacy, meaning, and derivation of each word—on which Johnson lavished his special attention; for most persons, dictionaries have also become the final arbiters of correct pronunciation and spelling. Johnson himself, aside from indicating syllabic stress, did not include pronunciation in his dictionary. Pronouncing dictionaries like Walker's (see the next section) contributed this now standard feature. Johnson did,

---

[1]Samuel Johnson, *A Dictionary of the English Language*, 1755. Facsimile Edition, Arno Press, New York, 1980. This first huge folio edition was "drastically condensed" for a second edition in 1756. The second edition sold at least 40,000 copies, more than 10 times the sales of the first edition. The fourth edition (1773), with many changes, is now considered to be the best. (James L. Clifford, *Dictionary Johnson*, McGraw Hill, New York, 1979, p. 145.)

[2]James H. Sledd and Gwin J. Kolb, *Dr. Johnson's Dictionary*, University of Chicago Press, 1955, pp. 204–205. Their scholarly appraisal was in commemoration of the 200th anniversary of the publication of the *Dictionary*.

[3]Clifford, 1979, p. 147.

[4]Sledd and Kolb, 1955, p. 41.

however, play a prominent part in establishing for private writing the spelling forms that printers had established for printed matter.[5] His spellings both recorded those printer's forms and helped fix them.

PRONOUNCING DICTIONARIES

Parallel to the compilation of dictionaries devoted to the meanings and etymologies of words, the eighteenth century saw the production of a number of pronouncing dictionaries. In these, some of the contemporary orthoepists tried to indicate the "correct" sounding of words, devising diacritical markings for that purpose. John Walker's *A Critical Pronouncing Dictionary and Expositor of the English Language* (1791) was the most highly regarded of all. In fact, Walker's influence in America was a source of great irritation to Noah Webster, earnestly trying to establish American styles of spelling and pronunciation.

The need for dictionaries that are solely concerned with pronunciation has been recognized in modern times, and two outstanding works are currently available, one for British and one for American speech. Daniel Jones's *An English Pronouncing Dictionary*[6] and Kenyon and Knott's *A Pronouncing Dictionary of American English*[7] are excellent listings of words and their current standard pronunciations in the two English-speaking countries.

NINETEENTH CENTURY DICTIONARIES
Individual Compilations

Johnson's dictionary and its revisions were dominant in England and North America from the time of its first publication to the end of the eighteenth century. Although no other lexicographer working on his own ever produced a dictionary that equaled Johnson's, several made significant contributions. Among them were two Americans, Noah Webster, with five dictionaries, including *An American Dictionary of the English Language* (1828),[8] and Joseph Worcester, the author of several dictionaries, of which the best was *A Dictionary of the English Language* (1860).

Group Compilations

In addition to these, many individual lexicographers have continued to produce various types of dictionaries up to the present day. From the middle of the nineteenth century, however, most of the comprehensive and prestigious dictionaries have not

---

[5]Scragg, 1974, p. 82.
[6]Daniel Jones, *An English Pronouncing Dictionary*, 13th ed. Revised by A.C. Gimson, London, 1967.
[7]John S. Kenyon and Thomas A. Knott, *A Pronouncing Dictionary of American English*, G. & C. Merriam, Springfield, MA, 1953.
[8]John Morgan, *Noah Webster*, Mason/Charter, New York, 1975, pp. 163–164. (See Chapter 20 below for much more about Noah Webster.)

been compiled by individuals. Instead, in the tradition of such compilations as those produced by the French Academy and the Italian Academia della Crusca, English language dictionaries were now commissioned by professional groups and publishers and parceled out to staffs of lexicographers under the editorship of one or more highly reputed scholars.

Oxford English Dictionary

One outstanding example is the *Oxford English Dictionary* (or *OED*). Initially called *A New English Dictionary on Historical Principles*, it was sponsored by the Philological Society after attempts to improve Johnson's dictionary showed that revision would not be adequate. Because of the many changes that had taken place in English and in lexicography since Johnson's time, an entirely new dictionary would have to be compiled.

In this new dictionary, every word used in the English language since the start of the twelfth century would be listed, together with the history of each: all its past and present forms, spellings, uses, and meanings. Furthermore, quotations to illustrate each of these would be presented.

In 1859, the Society issued a call for volunteers to gather material for the new work, and hundreds of contributors from all over the world responded. Several editors in turn took charge of the project; the one most associated with its initial publication is Sir James A.H. Murray. Under his editorship, the first installment was published in 1884, and the rest were issued volume by volume until the dictionary was completed in 1928, by then under a new team. Its bibliography and first supplement followed in 1933. During those years, most of the work was done and the expense carried by Oxford University, hence the ultimate adoption of the name, *Oxford English Dictionary*.

The work inspires great affection as well as admiration among linguists, having been described as "the noblest of all dictionaries,"[9] and "that great monument to English scholarship."[10] Baugh simply states that the *OED* is "the greatest dictionary of any language in the world."[11]

Between 1936 and 1944, an American extension of the *OED*, called the *Dictionary of American English* (*DAE*), was published under the editorship of Sir William A. Craigie (one of the later *OED* editors)[12] and James R. Hulbert.

Century Dictionary

Another important group dictionary, produced in the United States, is the *Century Dictionary*—a beautiful, informative work that includes a wide range of words. The first edition was published in 1889–1891 and the last in 1914, but much of the material in it is still useful. A condensed and updated version, the *New Century Dictionary*, was published in 1927 and has been reissued regularly ever since.

---

[9]Weekley, 1962, p. 20.
[10]Pyles, 1971, p. 21.
[11]Baugh, 1957, p. 399.
[12]Two other fine linguists who were principal editors of the *OED* after Murray were Henry Bradley and C.T. Onions.

Webster Dictionaries

A third major group compilation, also American, was based on Noah Webster's *An American Dictionary of the English Language* (1828) and its revised editions. When Webster died in 1843, the G. & C. Merriam Company bought the publishing rights to the dictionary and began to produce a series of ever-enlarged group revisions that culminated in the mighty *Webster's Third New International Dictionary* (1961).[13] Although other dictionaries with the name "Webster" began to appear after the copyright expired—Morgan notes that more than 50 entries with "Webster" appear in *Books in Print*[14]—these others must all include a statement that they are not produced by the publishers of the original Webster's dictionaries.[15]

Webster's Third International is considered the best modern American dictionary, although its adherence to the principle that dictionaries should reflect rather than set standards caused a great stir when the latest edition was published—showing that the prescriptive tradition of 250 years earlier still had great force 20 years ago. The inclusion of such forms as *finalize* and *ain't* led to accusations of bolshevism,[16] subversion, and decay. These were countered by the prevailing view of modern lexicographers and linguists, expressed by Barnhart in his introduction to the *American College Dictionary:* "It is not the function of the dictionarymaker to tell you how to speak, any more than it is the function of the mapmaker to move rivers or rearrange mountains or fill in lakes."[17]

• • • • •

From the foregoing summary of the evolution of English language dictionaries, it can be seen that these works, initially a response to the seventeenth- and eighteenth-century desire for authoritative prescriptions for the language, became firmly established in modern life, long after the desire that had originally inspired their production moved away from the center stage. Perhaps because prescriptions were at last available—in dictionaries, grammar books, and, most tellingly, in the hearts and lessons of the schoolmasters—the emphasis changed during the eighteenth century from the setting down of rules to that of refining and transmitting them.

Schoolmasters in particular laid great store by existing language rules, and the study of English became formalized much as the study of Latin had been. Their students—both those who became schoolmasters in turn and those who became part of the educated general public—revered and handed on the rules they had been

---

[13]*Webster's Third New International Dictionary of the English Language*, G. & C. Merriam, Springfield, MA, 1961.

[14]Yet Webster was not the first American lexicographer, but Samuel Johnson, Jr. (*A School Dictionary*—1798). See Gibson, 1936, 1937.

[15]Morgan, 1975, p. 203.

[16]Sledd and Ebbitt, 1962, p. 129. Such an accusation must have been especially damning so soon after the days of Senator Joseph McCarthy.

[17]James R. Hulbert, "The Authority of the Dictionary," in Sledd and Ebbitt, 1962, p. 43. It is this desk-size dictionary (Clarence L. Barnhart [Ed.], Random House, New York, 1947) that Bolinger credits with blazing the dictionary trail away from the prescriptive purpose, a trail followed soon after by the authors of *Webster's Third International* (Bolinger, 1975, p. 585).

taught. Ironically, at that same time, latter-day lexicographers and other language scholars were beginning to turn away from prescriptions, looking instead toward daily usage and the lessons of historical change for their linguistic enterprises. Nevertheless, an increasingly school-trained lay populace held on to the forms that already existed and that were recommended by "authoritative" sources. The free and guiltless individualism of earlier times was no longer possible, at least not in England.

In eighteenth and early nineteenth century America, however, language forms were substantially more mobile. New words and other new language features were borrowed from the languages spoken by other residents here. Both the greater freedom and the new borrowings had their effect on Modern English. For that reason, as well as for its relevance to readers of this book, we now turn our attention to the fortunes of the English language in this country.

19

Transplanting the English Language to America

EIGHTEENTH CENTURY ENGLISH

By the end of the eighteenth century, the English language had settled into a form similar to its present one. Although there have been some changes in spelling forms and in pronunciation, the style and vocabulary of written English have remained markedly constant. The eighteenth century writings of Jonathan Swift and Henry Fielding present few obstacles to the literate reader of today. The establishment of a prescriptive tradition in the eighteenth century, coupled with the structured circumstances in which written communication has been learned (from the schoolmasters intent on preserving prescriptions) and used (in circumstances controlled by the graduates of the schools) during the last two centuries have served to discourage divergent written forms.

Spoken language, however, being much more spontaneous, is much more difficult to confine. The difference between the pronunciation of the eighteenth century and of current English is thus considerably greater. This difference includes such modifications as a shift in syllabic stress and a change in the pronunciation of an individual phoneme within a word.

In addition, for both written and spoken language, a number of words and expressions entered the language, some as borrowings from foreign languages and others as slang or colloquialisms that became absorbed into the standard lexicon.

During these two centuries also, the history of the English language embarked on a new phase, one that saw the emergence of new dialects in different parts of the world as a result of previous intensive colonization. (See pp. 109–111.)

THE RISE OF AMERICAN ENGLISH[1]

British participation in the efforts of European countries to establish footholds in far-off regions resulted in enclaves of English-speaking colonies all over the world. In each colonized place, the English language was subject to a host of influences that fostered words with pronunciation patterns different from the standard ones as well as from those found in other English colonies.

The English spoken in the North American colonies was, on the whole, closer to standard British than was that of Australia, South Africa, and most other English colonies. The relatively few differences of the early days were later augmented, however, by those resulting from circumstances unique to United States history and to the evolution of the United States as an independent republic.

INFLUENCES ON AMERICAN ENGLISH

Some influences on the English language were present throughout American history, while others were felt only at certain times. One important influence that operated from the start and has continued to this day has been the numerous contacts in this country between speakers of English and speakers of foreign languages.

Three types of foreign language contact took place here: 1) with Native American languages, 2) with languages spoken by European colonists in neighboring or newly acquired territories, and 3) with languages brought over by successive waves of immigrant groups. In most cases, the contacts resulted in vocabulary borrowing rather than in changes of pronunciation patterns or of grammatical style. School leveling brought about by the spread of free public schools mentioned below (pp. 180–181) was greatly responsible for the adherence to traditional pronunciations and style even when individual words were freely adopted.

The foreign language borrowings first filtered into the English of those in the immediate neighborhoods of foreign speakers. Some borrowings remained there for a time and were then dropped; some continued to be used in that part of the country; and some were ultimately adopted by all speakers of American and even of British English. Thus, from the Dutch settlers of New Amsterdam and the Hudson Valley region the word *erve* (a small inheritance) was used in the New York area for a number of years but then dropped. On the other hand, the word *stoop* (front steps or porch)—also of Dutch origin—is still found in common use in the New York area while the similarly derived words *waffle* and *Yankee* are used everywhere.

The numbers of speakers of a foreign language were not always related to the language's impact on American English; there are very few Italian, Swedish, or Polish borrowings, for example, even though there were large numbers of immigrants from these countries. On the other hand, there were significantly more borrowings from the much smaller Dutch group. The period in which the major contact oc-

---

[1]The term *American English* is used here for the language of the United States. Although Baugh describes Canadian English as "a variety of American English" (1957, p. 388), and thus permits "American English" to cover the vast portion of English spoken in this hemisphere, there is controversy on this point. I choose to use the term, with apologies to the relatively small numbers of those who speak the dialects of Bermuda, Jamaica, and other English-speaking places in the Americas.

curred and the nature of the group's contact with the English-speaking culture were far more important than its size. The earlier the contact, in most cases, and the greater the degree to which aspects of the culture had an impact on American life, the richer was the contribution of the foreign language.

Native American Languages

At the time of the first settlements in the early 1600s, there were about 1,300,000 Native Americans speaking about 350 languages from about 25 different language families spread out over what is now the United States. Starting at least as early as 1608, evidenced by Captain John Smith's mention in that year of a *rahaugcum* or *raugroughcum* (eventually, *raccoon*),[2] as English-speaking colonists settled in new locations they adopted words used by the Native American groups nearby. These were usually words for new animals and plants or for Native American foods, customs, objects, and relationships. Such familiar English words as *chipmunk, hickory, moccasin, pecan, totem,* and *woodchuck* are among the derived words that have become fully accepted.[3] Because the Native American languages contained many sounds that do not occur in English, words were often adopted with pronunciations that only approximated the original.

The most intensive borrowing and use of Native American words took place in the seventeenth century, and the greatest number of loan words by far came from the Algonquin language family, spoken by the tribes along the Atlantic coast, who were the first to meet the English colonists. The words *moose, opossum, persimmon, powwow, wigwam,* and the aforementioned *raccoon* are among a number of Algonquin words borrowed before 1628.

Languages of Other European Colonists

The Spanish along the Mexican border and in the Southwest, the French from the St. Lawrence River down along the Great Lakes and the Mississippi to New Orleans, and the Dutch in New Netherlands all made significant contributions to American English. They had greater influence on the language than did most of the immigrants who arrived expressly to settle in the English-speaking regions. This was because such immigrants wished to be absorbed into American society and to learn English—seeing it as the language of a culture superior to the one they had left—while the neighbors of the English-speaking groups continued to maintain their own languages.

American Borrowings from French

French words began to enter English back in the seventeenth century through contacts with the explorers, traders, and missionaries of the frontier along the Canadian

---

[2]Albert H. Marckwardt, *American English*, Oxford University Press, New York, 1958, p. 28.

[3]Raven I. McDavid, Jr., *The American Language, by H.L. Mencken,* (The Fourth Edition and the Two Supplements, abridged, with annotations and new material), Knopf, New York, 1963, p. 111.

border and down the central Mississippi Valley. Later sources for French borrowings were the more settled communities in the Louisiana territory—like New Orleans—and, to a more limited extent, the Acadian French community of southeastern Canada (now New Brunswick and Nova Scotia). This is the group of "Evangeline" fame that was deported from Acadia after they refused to submit to British rule. The Acadians settled in New England and other parts of this country, including the New Orleans/Louisiana area. The term *Cajun*—used for the French-speaking community of Louisiana—is derived from *Acadian*. The word *chowder* (from French *chaudiere* or pot) is believed to have entered English from this group.[4]

Some of the French loan words were actually derived from Native American speech, having entered the French language on this continent before they were transmitted to English-speaking settlers in the course of frontier life. The words *gopher* and *toboggan* are examples of Native American–derived frontier words that entered from French, while the words *prairie* and *rapids* are examples of loan words initially French in origin.

American Borrowings from Spanish

The Spanish language contributed to American English with the greatest consistency for the longest period of time. Its influence began with the "hacienda" culture centered about the independently owned estates (or *haciendas*) established by the Spanish colonists when the sixteenth century conquest of Mexico resulted in their acquiring territories as far north as present-day Texas and southwestern United States. In contrast to the impermanent French settlements of that era—which were primarily exploratory and commercial—the Spanish settlements deepened in culture and set down firm roots throughout the years that led to the Mexican War of 1848. Many Spanish words entered English in those centuries as well as in the years of American statehood that followed. Borrowing peaked during the early frontier contacts of the seventeenth century and in the nineteenth century, when the Mexican War resulted in annexations of territories with large Spanish-speaking populations.

In addition, new words from the Spanish of Florida, South America, and the islands up and down the western Atlantic have been added continuously and are still being added today as a consequence of active, ongoing commerce and immigration.

In the same way that Native American–derived French words were borrowed, Native American–derived Spanish words also came into American English (*coyote*, for example). In addition, African-derived Spanish words such as *rhumba* and such mixtures as the word *filibuster*—originally Dutch but absorbed into Spanish via French—entered American English as a result of the wide-ranging sweep of Spanish culture throughout this hemisphere.

The sum of American Spanish borrowings is very large, especially if those confined to specific regions here are added to the many that have been adopted by both American and British English. Listings of such words have reached as many as 800 for a combination of regional loan words and loan words in the English language as a whole.[5]

---

[4]Steven T. Byington, "Mr. Byington's Brief Case II," *American Speech*, Vol. 19, April 1944, p. 122.
[5]Sorvig, cited by Marckwardt, 1958, p. 42.

American Borrowings from the Dutch

Most of the Dutch borrowings in Standard American English were contributed by Dutch settlers in what is now New Jersey and the Hudson River Valley. The words *boss, cookie, dope, sleigh,* and *snoop* are all examples of early Dutch borrowings, pre-1800. These were augmented by such Dutch-derived regionalisms as the word *stoop* (mentioned above) that lingered on in the New York area.

Languages of the Immigrant Groups

From the very start, English-speaking America attracted a steady stream of new arrivals—a stream that became a flood at those times when troubles abroad impelled large numbers of people from one country or another to come here to better their lot. Each of the immigrant groups brought either a foreign language or, in the case of English-speaking immigrants, a distinctive English dialect. Because of their great numbers, it was inevitable that traces of their foreign languages and of their different English dialects should enter American English. The number of traces that did in fact enter is nevertheless surprisingly small in comparison to the contributions of the languages spoken by the Native Americans and the French, Spanish, and Dutch colonists. The difference in relative influence is probably due to the fact, noted above, that the immigrants usually wished to assimilate and to speak the language of the country, while the Native Americans and the colonizing groups had little desire to relinquish their own cultures.

　　Constituting a special case were those whose original language was African. In most instances they had little choice of language because they spoke diverse African languages when they arrived and were dispersed too widely to permit any of their languages to be maintained. English was therefore the common language, strongly influenced in pronunciation and style by the Southern dialects. Not surprisingly, therefore, very few African borrowings have entered American English; *tote, banjo, yam, jazz,* and *gumbo* are among those that have been identified.

AMERICAN ENGLISH IN COLONIAL TIMES

Dialects of the First Settlers

The English settlements in America were established in the early 1600s by different groups and in different regions. Most notable were the Puritans in what became New England and the settlers in Virginia. The social classes and geographic origins of these two groups, as well as the dates of their arrival, led to the language patterns that have distinguished American from British speech to this day.

　　The Virginian settlers tended to be of the upper classes, while the original settlers of New England, as well as those who joined them for some years afterward, were largely of the middle and lower classes. The New Englanders were also substantially homogeneous in their geographic origins—most came from the southeastern part of England, in and near London.

By fortunate circumstance, the lower and middle class southeastern English dialect of the New England settlers was similar to the upper class "London" dialect of the Virginians. Ultimately, this similarity helped establish the speech patterns for the whole new country, when the American standard was set by the speech of New England.[6]

Archaic Features of American English Speech

Perhaps the most interesting feature of American speech can be traced to the time of the early American settlements. The first colonists still spoke sixteenth-century Elizabethan English when they arrived. In their speech, therefore, a number of important changes, including the Great Vowel Shift (see pp. 107–108 above), had not yet fully crystallized. Some characteristics of the earlier speech were retained in America even as the speech of England evolved into the significantly altered language of the eighteenth and nineteenth centuries.

This explains a number of differences between modern British and modern American language forms—vocabulary, pronunciation, usage—and accounts for what Marckwardt calls "an archaic element pervading all of American English."[7] (Marckwardt hastens to add that no contemporary American dialect has preserved the older language unchanged, however. In saying this, Marckwardt is alluding to amateurish perceptions that isolated groups like some of the Kentucky or Ozark mountaineers speak Elizabethan English because of certain forms they have retained.)

Thus, the vowel sounds in *bite*, *hide*, and *tile* (all the same phoneme) as well as the vowel sounds in *cow*, *out*, and *owl* (all the same phoneme) have a range of pronunciations in modern American speech that includes some of the Elizabethan pronunciations dropped long ago from Received Standard speech.[8] Remnants of pronunciations that existed before the Great Vowel Shift can be found in other American long vowel and diphthong pronunciations as well.

Another early form that has been retained in America is the pronunciation of *a* before voiceless fricatives (*f*, *s*, and *th* as in *thin*) and clusters with initial nasals. The words *calf*, *pass*, *bath*, *example*, and *dance* are examples of these. It was noted above (pp. 101–102) that short vowel pronunciations have changed very little throughout the centuries, and in the London dialect of Elizabethan English, the *a* vowel in these words was pronounced as it is in most of America—that is, as the *a* in *ax*. Some time after the American colonies had been established, perhaps in the mid-eighteenth century and certainly about the year 1800, the upper-class London pronunciation of the *a* in such words began to change into the familiar broad *a* (as in *father*) of Received Standard Pronunciation. Nevertheless, in most of America, the earlier *a* as in *ax* pronunciation remained.

In words like *secretary*, *necessary*, and *military*, Elizabethan pronunciation clearly retained the next to last syllable with a secondary stress and so does Amer-

---

[6]Krapp, 1925, Vol. 1, pp. 20–21.

[7]Marckwardt, 1958, pp. 60–61.

[8]Hans Kurath, *A Phonology and Prosody of Modern English*, University of Michigan Press, Ann Arbor, 1964, p. 26.

ican English. In British English, however, that syllable was dropped in the late eighteenth–early nineteenth century and such words are now pronounced in Great Britain as if they were spelled *secret'ry, necess'ry, milit'ry*, and so on.

Another American characteristic that Marckwardt attributes to the Elizabethan language of the early settlers is an exuberant overstatement and "admiration of the big word." He states that "the American of today still loves the mouth-filling phrase or word,"[9] and calls this an Elizabethan tendency that survived in America despite the rise in England during the late seventeenth and the eighteenth century of an opposing tendency toward understatement.

Krapp also calls attention to this characteristic, seeing an "ingenuity and inventiveness" in American speech that British speech of the eighteenth and nineteenth centuries held in check. Unlike Marckwardt, however, Krapp believes that this quality—which he also calls Elizabethan—was not inherited from Elizabethan England but is a homegrown American characteristic.[10]

Additional examples of Elizabethan vestiges in American language forms may be found in Marckwardt's *American English* (pp. 62–77).

Effects of Contact Between the Colonists and England

Certain of the American colonies remained in close contact with England during the colonial years while others did not. Where this contact was substantial, the American speech adopted changes that took place in British speech. In Elizabethan times, for example, the *r* following a vowel (as in *barn, bird, over*, and so on)[11] had a hard, consonantal pronunciation that was brought over by the early settlers. This pronunciation was lost in standard British speech some time after 1700[12] but was kept in much of America.

The pattern of regions that retained or lost the *r* after a vowel reflects the pattern of contact with England in colonial times. Thus, American leaders in the southern and New England regions stayed in touch with the upper classes of England and their speech lost the pronunciation of the *r* after the vowel as it faded from London speech. In Pennsylvania, however, where contact with England upper classes was much more limited, the *vowel-r* retained and still retains its consonantal quality. Only in the South, in much of New England, and in New York City[13] has the consonantal *vowel-r* been lost.

Another example of how the degree of contact between the colonies and England resulted in regional differences in American speech is the aforementioned

---

[9]Marckwardt, 1958, p. 102.
[10]Krapp, 1925, Vol. I, pp. 51–52.
[11]Except before another *r*—as in *mirror*—or before a vowel—as in *miracle*.
[12]Dobson, 1968, p. 914.
[13]McDavid raises the strong possibility that New York City's loss of the consonantal *vowel-r* may be traced to the years 1776–1783, when most of the city's population fled and was replaced by the British garrison of the North American Expeditionary Force. Thousands of British soldiers, officers, and military dependents may have left their linguistic mark on the American Loyalists who joined them and remained in the city after the British departed. (Raven I. McDavid, Jr., "The Speech of New York: The Historical Background," Paper presented at the Annual Conference of the National Council of the Teachers of English, New York City, 1977.)

pronunciation of the *a* in words before *f, s, th,* and clusters with initial nasals. Although most of America retained the Elizabethan pronunciation of short *a* (*calf, bath,* and about 150 other such words), Virginian and New England speech changed, as London speech did, to a broad *a* pronunciation as in *father.* This pronunciation is still found in eastern New England but was gradually lost in Virginia.

The retention of the broad *a* in New England may be attributed to two historical trends. In the Boston area, the broad *a* was reinforced after the Revolutionary War and throughout the nineteenth century by a phenomenon peculiar to that city. That is, the upper classes of Boston "made a cult of culture" that centered about the glorification of all things English. This attitude touched speech patterns, which were in time relayed to all groups in the Boston area. The broad *a* in that special category of words was thus preserved in Boston and is still used by some for stage and "acquired pedantic or 'fashionable' use."[14] It has also been preserved in Maine among all classes because of contact with London back in colonial days.

British Attitudes Toward American English

For the first century or so of its existence, colonial American speech was not very different from British speech. In the eighteenth century, however, as divergences between American and British English became noticeable, comments regarding specific Americanisms and American speech in general began to appear, with British reactions to American speech mostly favorable. Read notes that, before 1800, the British "conceded that the general level of purity in pronunciation was . . . even higher than in Great Britain."[15] Read attributes this sentiment to the fact that "America was still regarded as a land of promise, and the attitude toward speech reflected that outlook."[16]

Furthermore, the English who visited America were struck by the fact that American speech was much freer of regional dialects than was British speech: All Americans spoke conspicuously alike. This characteristic has continued to hold true so that one of the significant differences between British and American speech is the existence in Britain of many, widely varying regional and social dialects while American speech is greatly uniform.

In contrast to the respect accorded to American pronunciation, however, the introduction of new words from the sources described above met with disapproval. In his discussion of British approval of the English language in America, Read further points out that "only in the matter of vocabulary did they, on the basis of their supposition that all change in language is reprehensible, find grounds for censure."[17] One such critic was Samuel Johnson, who openly hated everything American and deplored new American words as well.

---

[14]Gray and Wise, 1959, p. 301.

[15]Allen Walker Read, "British Recognition of American Speech in the Eighteenth Century," *Dialect Notes,* Vol. 6, Pt. 6, 1933, p. 334.

[16]Read, 1933.

[17] Read, 1933.

American Attitudes Toward Colonial American English

Americans, too, were caught up in the eighteenth century desire for authoritative "correctness" and for preserving existing language forms. Benjamin Franklin, for example, was one who believed that "introducing new words, where we are already possessed of old ones sufficiently expressive, I confess must be generally wrong, as it tends to change the language."[18]

This belief, as well as a desire to emulate British English, prevailed before and immediately after the Revolutionary War. With the gaining of freedom from England, however, and the establishment of an autonomous nation, many American attitudes underwent profound change. Among them were attitudes toward language; these turned from deprecation and apology to self-assertiveness and justification of American forms. Ultimately, efforts began to be made to identify American forms and set them within prescriptive contexts.

---

[18]Quoted in Baugh, 1957, p. 448.

20

Noah Webster

The changed view of American English in the post–Revolutionary War years was greatly influenced by an enormous patriotic fervor that had started before the War and so increased afterward that it permeated every aspect of American life. This patriotism was inspired and nurtured by an astonishing number of eloquent leaders who undertook to establish the basic institutions of the new republic. Of these leaders, one man stands out for his impact on the American language: Noah Webster, the remarkable force behind an impressive number of "firsts" in an era filled with beginnings. Webster engraved his mark on every aspect of the language: on its forms, the way it was taught, and the publishing and selling of the books in which it was set down.[1]

While Webster was himself one of the forces that shaped American English, some of the other forces that acted on the language in his time acted on Webster's life as well. Because of that intertwining of environment, personality, and language, the story of Webster's life tells much about the history and fortunes of American English.

WEBSTER'S EARLY LIFE

Noah Webster (1758–1843) was born in West Hartford, Connecticut, just before the outbreak of the Revolutionary War. After a childhood in which his studious bent was recognized very early, he went on to Yale for an education that—while its curriculum was the conventional classical one—prepared him for an activist, political life perhaps more than it promoted his intellectual growth.

Yale at that time (1774–1778) was at the peak of a nationalistic, revolutionary excitement. One of Webster's inspirations while he studied there was the tutor Timothy Dwight (later president of Yale). The essence of Dwight's sentiments is expressed in the following excerpt from his valedictory address to the Yale seniors in 1776, soon after the Declaration of Independence had been made known to them:

---

[1]While there is divergence of opinion on the precise extent to which Webster was directly responsible for specific language-related practices, particularly spoken language forms, the evidence of his lifelong interest and involvement is overwhelming.

"You should by no means consider yourselves as members of a small neighborhood, town or colony only, but as being concerned in laying the foundations of American greatness. Your wishes, your designs, your labors, are not to be confined by the narrow bounds of the present age, but are to comprehend succeeding generations, and be pointed to immortality."[2]

If such words are spine-tingling even 200 years later, imagine their effect on a high-spirited 18-year-old Webster, surrounded by other impassioned young patriots (Nathan Hale, a Yale alumnus, was hanged by the British that same year). Webster became fixed on the ideal of nationalism, a notably generous ideal in an age marked by intense local loyalties. That ideal was never to leave him, even when his opinions changed about the best ways to advance it.

His experiences as a schoolmaster were another dramatic influence that determined the substance of Webster's future concerns. After leaving Yale, Webster wanted to become a lawyer but, probably because of financial need, taught school for 2 years (1778–1780).[3] This was in an era when schools and teachers were greatly looked down upon in America, an opinion that reflected and was reinforced by the fact that many teachers were of low, even detestable character. Warfel points out that, before the Revolutionary War, convicts transported as punishment for their crimes were hired as private tutors.[4] Webster's dismay at the educational practices of the day—the practical and economical difficulties as well as the guiding values— is set down in several essays he later wrote. He criticizes the deteriorated schoolhouses (worse than they had been when he was a child), "the impossibility of obtaining books," and the prevailing practice of corporal punishment. Webster expresses concern for the emotional and physical well-being of children, emphasizing that "the pupil should have nothing to discourage him."[5]

Webster returned to his study of the law in 1780 and was admitted to the bar a year later. Because conditions at that time were poor for lawyers, however, he decided almost immediately to return to teaching—this time to start his own academy. For reasons that are still obscure but that may be related to a disappointed romance, he closed the academy after 3 months. Although his enterprise did not last long, his intense preoccupation with it helped clarify Webster's thoughts about education. His ideas on the subject were further crystallized when, after spending the rest of the year in study, writing, and job-hunting, he moved to Goshen, New York, to teach school once more. Webster's beliefs about government and politics also developed during these years and were expressed in essays he began to write for newspapers.

Grammatical Institute of the English Language

A year after Webster settled in Goshen, his ideas on education bore their first fruit. In 1783 he published the book that ultimately sold more copies in America than any

---

[2]Harry R. Warfel, *Noah Webster, Schoolmaster to America*, Macmillan, New York, 1936, p. 29.

[3]E. Jennifer Monaghan, *Noah Webster's Speller*, unpublished doctoral dissertation, Yeshiva University, New York, 1980.

[4]Warfel, 1936, p. 52. An intriguing bit of information in light of the long-standing stereotype of teachers as being proper and conventional.

[5]Morgan, 1975, p. 32.

other book except the Bible.[6] This was the first book of his *A Grammatical Institute of the English Language*,[7] a three-part work consisting of a speller, a grammar, and a reader. Although all three books became popular, the effect of the speller was spectacular: More than 100 million copies have been sold to date.

Webster wrote the book early in his life and had it reissued frequently in the years to come, often with changes in text and, at times, even in name. In 1787, for example, it was revised and reissued as *The American Spelling Book* and in 1829 as the *Elementary Spelling Book*. Such was its popularity that Commager notes, "No other secular book had ever spread so wide, penetrated so deep, lasted so long."[8] So long, in fact, that Clifton Johnson, writing in 1904, stated that "there are schools where it is studied even at present."[9]

Problems of Publishing in America

The spelling book was also the first successful book to be published in the newly established United States—books bought here generally originated in England. For a number of reasons, the early American printers confined their work to periodicals, reprints of English books, and certain other, circumscribed ventures. For one thing, while England's small size made transportation and therefore marketing easy, it was hard for printers here to deliver books over America's vast distances. These same distances often made it difficult for authors to check on how accurately their work was being reproduced, and many of them were therefore reluctant to call upon American printers.

Other serious problems were due to the absence of copyright laws: No one could stop rampant pirating by printers who reproduced and then sold books originally published by other printers.[10] This practice discouraged the publication of new books here, since it greatly lessened the profits a publisher could make after investing the time and money needed to edit, print, and distribute a manuscript.

WEBSTER'S PUBLISHING TACTICS

In his day, Webster surmounted the problems of producing and marketing his speller by acting as his own publisher. He dealt with the pirating by lobbying for

---

[6]McDavid, 1963, p. 483.

[7]The term *Institute* here means a summary of the basic principles of a subject. John Calvin, the founder of Calvinism, used the term in the same way in his *The Institutes of the Christian Religion* (1583).

Webster adopted the title at the suggestion of Dr. Ezra Stiles, the president of Yale, dropping his own original choice, *The American Instructor*. That Webster regretted the *Grammatical Institute* title may be seen from the fact that later editions of the spelling book were called *The American Spelling Book* and *The Elementary Spelling Book*.

[8]Henry Steele Commager, "Schoolmaster to America," Introductory Essay in *Noah Webster's American Spelling Book* (1831 ed.), Classics in Education No. 17, Teachers College Press, New York, 1962, p. 5.

[9]Clifton Johnson, *Old-Time Schools and School-books*, Macmillan, New York, 1904. Reprinted by Dover, New York, 1963, p. 184.

[10]So merciless was this pirating that no British author of that time ever received one penny from the American printings of his book. (E. Jennifer Monaghan, personal communication.)

copyright laws with great perseverance—approaching, state by state, the legislatures of the 13 original states. As a result of his efforts, along with those of others, the federal Constitution (written in 1787 to be ratified in 1788 and effective in 1789) contained recognition of authors' rights.[11] The federal copyright laws then enacted essentially remained in effect until the new copyright law was recently passed.[12] There is no question that Noah Webster deserves a great deal of the credit for the early passage of the first author/publisher protection laws in this country.[13]

Webster also made sure to supervise the production of his book personally. He moved to Hartford, Connecticut, where it was being printed. Then, he addressed himself to the question of how to market an American-published book successfully in face of the great distances between potential purchasers. He came up with an impressive array of ingenious techniques to advertise and to sell his book. Some of these techniques remained unique to Webster; others were subsequently adopted by other publishers and have continued to be used.[14]

Thus, Webster organized a philological group with the name but not the scholarly functions of The Philological Society of England (see p. 136 above). Almost the sole action of America's philological society was to recommend Webster's speller to the schools of the United States. He was also wisely generous in his promotion efforts. Webster presented quantities of his books to reputable educational institutions and then made sure that those gifts were well publicized. With his Connecticut royalties, he underwrote a scholarship for a worthy Yale student (stipulating, however, that the student must not be a duelist or a seducer). In fact, Webster scarcely hesitated to publicize anything about his books or their author. He continually initiated interest in himself by openly or anonymously writing provocative articles in periodicals. At the same time, he capitalized on the writings of others by responding to criticism in a way that stimulated heated, long-term published disputes about his work.

Webster unabashedly solicited and often obtained testimonials from well-known persons. The number of endorsements he was able to gather added up to hundreds, although the glowing praise he sought from Washington, Franklin, and Jefferson did not materialize. Jefferson found his brashness, together with his politics, so offensive that in a letter to James Madison (1801) he called Webster "a mere pedagogue, of very limited understanding and very strong prejudices and party passions."[15]

Webster's Sales Tours

There is one promotional technique most often associated with Webster: Starting with a hugely rewarding, 13-month sales tour of the 13 states (1785–1786), he made a great number of sales tours throughout America for the rest of his life.

---

[11]Article I, Section 8 (*Powers of Congress*), Paragraph 8 gives the Congress power "to promote the progress of science and useful arts by securing for limited times to authors and inventors the exclusive rights to their respective writings and discoveries."

[12]Public Law 94-553: General Revision of Copyright Law was passed by Congress on October 19, 1976, and became effective on January 1, 1978.

[13]See Bruce W. Bugbee (*The Genesis of American Patent and Copyright Law*, Public Affairs Press, Washington, D.C., 1967) for perspective on Webster's role.

[14]Morgan, 1975, pp. 70–74.

[15]McDavid, 1963, p. 14. Jefferson's disdain of "pedagogues" is consistent with the low esteem in which schoolteachers were held for a long time.

Webster used these trips to contact nationally prominent persons about his books as well as to secure publishing copyrights. As he went from village to village, often on horseback, he gave lectures and met with local leaders—teachers, clergymen, lawyers, school committees, and the like.

The face-to-face contact between author and public on which Webster capitalized so adroitly may be seen as an early form of the current practice of having authors appear on television talk shows to promote their writings (and of producers, directors, performers, and the like to promote their drama, dance, or music productions).

Another selling technique tied in with Webster's sales tours was placing his books at such unconventional sales outlets as the general store, the post office (which was often headed by the local tavern keeper), and with local printers. He would also give local printers copies of his speller and tell them to follow the spelling forms it contained. In light of the power of printers to determine spelling forms (see pp. 120–122 above), this practice was to have substantial effects on the spread of Webster's spelling patterns. Furthermore, his lifelong travels about the country helped familiarize Webster with American language patterns. His perceptions of those patterns as he continued to write and revise his books were vitally important in view of the part he was to play in the future of the English language in this country.

Patriotic Emphasis in Webster's Textbooks

To complete the three-part *Grammatical Institute*, Webster published his grammar book in 1784 and his reader[16] in 1785. In addition, after the first publication of the three textbooks, Webster worked on several little introductory texts to be used before each part of the *Institute*.[17] Although all his books were used throughout the country, none was as overwhelmingly popular in its category as the spelling book was among spelling books.

By 1790, Webster had published six elementary textbooks, with some revisions already issued. That store of books acted as examples for other American authors who, both then and shortly afterwards, were producing a huge number of similar schoolbooks. It was through this influence on others, over and above the direct in-

---

[16]The "reader" of the eighteenth and much of the nineteenth century was very different from the modern text that is part of a carefully sequenced series. From the sixteenth through the nineteenth centuries a "reader" was a self-contained book of selections meant for young persons, which were chosen without the slightest concern for the meanings, spelling patterns, or frequencies of the words within them, and just as little concern for the length, structure, or complexity of sentence—the characteristics by which modern reading texts are carefully developed. It was the content of the selection rather than its readability in the modern sense or its usefulness as an illustration of language patterns that was important; its role in fulfilling the social-cultural aims of the times was all that was considered (Fries, 1963, pp. 6–7).

[17]One of these little books was *The Little Reader's Assistant* (1790), a work that Rollins characterizes as "an early abolitionist tract" though it appeared to be "just another reader for schoolchildren." Rollins ties its antislavery component to Webster's antislavery activities at that period. Two stories in particular contain lurid descriptions of atrocities done to African slaves by whites—to which Webster adds his own feelings of outrage and calls for justice. (Richard M. Rollins, *The Long Journey of Noah Webster*, University of Pennsylvania Press, Philadelphia, 1980, pp. 66–67.) See also p. 159 n. 14 below.

fluence of his works themselves, that Webster's impact on the American language and on American education made itself felt.

One outstanding feature of Webster's new books was quickly adopted by the authors of other textbooks published during the first years of the American republic. This was the great preoccupation with nationalism and Americanism that first appeared in the 1787 revision of Webster's reader. Webster worked on this revision while he was in Philadelphia for the Constitutional Convention. In that environment, his ever-smoldering nationalism flared up powerfully, and he doubled the size of the reader by inserting new patriotic selections, thus introducing to American children's books such innovations as American geography, the speeches and writings of American patriots, and his own strongly felt nationalistic beliefs. He changed the title to *An American Selection of Lessons in Reading and Speaking* and put this motto on its title page: "Begin with the infant in the cradle; let the first word he lisps be Washington."[18] Together with the other five school texts, this book became Webster's vehicle for imbuing young Americans with patriotic fervor.

Webster's Further Career

Although Webster continued to revise and oversee the production of his school textbooks, in 1787 he shifted from his early vocations as lawyer and schoolmaster and turned to writing and editing. From 1787 to 1788, and again from 1793 to 1798, he was the publisher and editor of first, the *American Magazine,* and then two New York newspapers, using them to circulate his ideas and thereby intensifying his influence throughout the country. When he retired from publishing, Webster had produced enough original copy "to fill 20 volumes,"[19] in addition to his translations of hundreds of French newspaper columns done to provide his readers with news of Europe.

Webster did not leave his newspapers in 1798 in order to remain idle but to dedicate himself to an enterprise he had contemplated for a number of years—the compilation of a series of English language dictionaries, starting with the *Compendious Dictionary* (1806) and culminating in *An American Dictionary of the English Language* of 1828[20] (see p. 137 above). After that, Webster issued several more texts for students and teachers, wrote a landmark *History of the United States* (1832), and published an expurgated translation of the Bible (1833). Even as he worked on these writing projects, Webster found time to make his regular sales tours of the country, to be elected to the Massachusetts state legislature, to help found Amherst College (1820–1821), and to continue to work on revisions of his earlier works.

The last of his works Webster saw published was *A Collection of Papers on Political, Literary and Moral Subjects,* issued in 1843. Webster died in the spring of that year at the age of 85 just as he finished correcting a new printing of his speller.

---

[18]Warfel, 1936, p. 90. Webster took this quotation from Mirabeau, a French noble who defied Louis XVI and became a popular leader during the first 2 years of the French Revolution.

[19]Morgan, 1975, p. 133.

[20]There were two editions after 1828, published in 1829 and 1841.

21

Early American Spelling

Webster holds the prime position in the establishment of distinctly American spelling traditions. Nevertheless, other persons have played significant roles throughout the years and have contributed an assortment of views and accomplishments. Some of those will be discussed in the following chapters, as we focus not only on the written language itself but move on to connecting our written language to the methods used to teach it. This procedure will lead ultimately to the alternative definition of *phonics* given at the start of the book (pp. 2–3), namely, phonics as a method of teaching beginning reading.

Let us start by looking at American spelling and spelling/reading instruction in the colonies and then go on to the changes that took place after the Revolutionary War.

SPELLING IN COLONIAL TIMES

In the early settlements and the colonies, spelling and the teaching of spelling and reading were the same as they were in England. In both places the children learned to spell and read from hornbooks, followed by primers.

Hornbooks[1]

A hornbook was not a book in the modern sense but was, originally, a small, often wooden, often paddle-shaped tablet. It was also called, at various times, an *Abece-*

---

[1] An oft-cited source is Andrew W. Tuer, *History of the Hornbook*, Leadenhall Press, London, 1897. Reissued by Benjamin Blom, Bronx, NY, 1968.

dario, an *ABC*, an *Abee-cee book*, a *horn*, a *criss-cross row*, or, in later years, a *battledore*[2] (after the similarly shaped paddle used in badminton). Written or carved on it were the letters of the alphabet, a syllabarium (organized lists of such syllables as *ab, eb, ib, ob, ub*—see p. 25 above) and a brief passage, including the Lord's Prayer. Children learned to name the letters, to call off the syllables, and to memorize the text before going on to read from a regular book.

In time, instead of the inscription being set down directly on the tablet, a thin, translucent sheet of horn was nailed to it, hence the name *hornbook*. A sheet of paper or parchment would be fastened or slipped under the horn, which thus acted as a protection against moist little fingers or, perhaps, the pressures of a *fescue*. The latter was a kind of pointer used along with the hornbook to indicate what was being read. In addition to this characteristic form, there were some hornbooks made of metal or ivory, and variations arose in the text.

The first hornbooks seem to have come from England, exactly when is not known, although references to them appear as early as the fourteenth century. They were used in the American colonies right from the beginning and were found, at least in some classrooms, until the nineteenth century.

New England Primer

In addition to the hornbook, children in England learned to spell and read from primers. These were real books with alphabet tables, syllabaria, and religious text like those of the hornbooks, although with longer lists, pictures, and many more religious selections. (The name *primer* can be traced back—at least as far as the thirteenth century—to the Latin *primarium*, a book of essential religious selections intended for adults.)[3]

The first such book intended for American children was the *New England Primer*. Initially printed in England in 1683 and then in Boston from 1690 on, the *New England Primer* was the only textbook used for the next 50 years. Even when other textbooks were introduced and became popular (such as Webster's in the late 1700s), the *New England Primer* continued to be printed and used, especially in certain of the church schools. Johnson states that, "For a hundred years this book beyond any other was the school-book of American dissenters."[4] One copy I have examined was printed by the Massachusetts Sabbath School Society as late as 1842, and, in 1849, George Livermore, the first collector of *New England Primers*, noted that in the preceding dozen years, 100,000 copies of the nineteenth century editions alone of the *Primer* had been circulated. Livermore's statement is mentioned in an old facsimile edition of the earliest known copy (1727), reprinted in paperback by Teachers College Press.[5]

Among the features that characterize the *New England Primer* are writings and catechisms about Puritan teachings and beliefs. One standard inclusion, for ex-

---

[2]W.J. Frank Davies, *Teaching Reading in Early England*, Pitman, London, 1973 (First published in the U.S.A. by Harper & Row, New York, 1974), pp. 95–99.

[3]Davies, 1973, p. 101.

[4]Johnson, 1963, p. 72.

[5]Paul Leicester Ford (Ed.), *The New England Primer*, Dodd, Mead, NY, 1897. Reprinted by Teachers College Press, New York, 1962, p. 19.

ample, is the tragic story of Mr. John Rogers, a minister of the gospel in London, "the first martyr in Queen Mary's reign." In what is actually a much-garbled version of what happened to an entirely different martyr, the *Primer* states that in the year 1554, Rogers was burned at the stake in full view of his wife and their 10 or 11 children.[6] A lengthy poem of stern religious advice from Rogers to his children is included in all editions of the *New England Primer*, while a supplemental, also religious, response entitled "Verses for little children" was acquired in the years between the 1727 and the 1842 editions.

The New England Primer differs from the standard British primer of its time in another respect. In British primers, a small cross was traditionally placed at the beginning of each alphabet listing. That practice, which inspired the name *Christ's-Cross-Row* or *Cris Cross Row* for the first line of the alphabet, was considered "popery" by the Puritans, who dropped it completely.

The spelling patterns of the *New England Primer* reflect the British spelling of the times. British spelling patterns were just about settled by 1650 (see p. 123 above), and it is therefore not surprising that the spelling in the 1727 edition is almost identical to our own, 250 years later. Among the few deviations to be found in its pages is the use of the contracted form in several verbs (*sav'd, offer'd*) and the spellings *farewel, whipt (whipped), italick* and *Catholick, entred (entered), kalender, prophaning,* and *courageous.*[7]

Examination of the six alphabet listings in the 1727 edition reveals that the roles of the letters *i/j* and *u/v* were far from settled. Instead of both letters in each pair being listed, as they would be today, either the *i* or the *j* is excluded from five of the six alphabets and either the *u* or the *v* is excluded from four of the six alphabets. Moreover, in the two alphabets where both *u* and *v* appear, the sequence is *u, v,* in one case and *v, u,* in the other. (See pp. 39–40 above on the history of these four letters.)

Other Early School Texts

In addition to the hornbook and the *New England Primer*, various school textbooks for further study of spelling and reading were available in Britain and in America from at least the middle of the seventeenth century.[8] In both places, spelling, reading, and even grammar were traditionally included in the same book. However, the British interest in spelling forms that was popular in sixteenth and early seventeenth century England (see pp. 122–124 above) was not evident in America until almost the start of the nineteenth century. Before then, the books used here all conformed to whatever spelling patterns were current in England.

In mid-eighteenth century, the most widely accepted school text in America was Thomas Dilworth's *New Guide to the English Tongue*, published in London in 1740 and reprinted in Philadelphia by Benjamin Franklin in 1747. Dilworth's work is

---

[6]Ford, 1897, pp. 32–37.

[7]A page from an edition of 1762 reveals that in that year, *courageous* was spelled with an *-eous* ending rather than an *-ious* (Ford, 1897, Frontispiece).

[8]Monaghan points out that Stephen Daye published a spelling book in Cambridge, Massachusetts, in about 1643 (1980, p. 46).

a combined speller, grammar, and reader. Deeply religious in content, it also includes references to British royalty and lists British place names. Nevertheless, by 1765 it was being used in New England schools and was the early text by which Webster himself was educated. In fact, from 1750 until Webster published his speller in 1783, Dilworth's speller "held almost indisputed command in the teaching of orthography in American schools."[9]

Dilworth's book was also known as the *Aby-sel-pha*, a name that relates to spelling methodology as least as old as Elizabethan times. Mencken notes that Aby-sel-pha is "a corruption of *abisselfa*, itself a corruption of *a-by-itself-a*."[10] He connects this to the way children were trained to spell, referring to an article by Allen Walker Read in which Read quotes the following marvelously specific instructions to teachers that appear in F. Clement's *The Petie Schole* (London, 1587). These instructions were set down in 1576: "Teache the childe, in spelling his syllabes, to leaue the consonant, that commeth before a vowell, to the syllabe following, exãple: in this word, *manifold*, Let him spell, for the first syllabe *m* and *a* onely, for he may not take *n* vnto them, because, *i* the vowel followeth: to the second syllabe he must take but *n* and *i*, for *f* hath *o*, the vowell next after him. To the third syllabe he must take the foure letters that remaine, *f, o, l*, and *d*. In this order than let him spell it, saying: *m, a, ma: n, i, ni: f, o, l, d, fold, manifold*. And like wise of all other words. An other example, to spell this word *imagine*, he must take for the first syllable, but only the vowel, *i*, saying *i*, by it selfe, because *m*, hath *a*, the vowell after it. For the second syllabe he hath *m*, and *a*: for *g*, he may not take to them, because *i*, the vowel followeth: therefore to the third syllabe he must take the three letters, which remaine, *g, i*, and *n*. Then he can spell it thus: *i*, by it selfe, *m, a, ma, ima: g, i, n, gin, imagin*."[11]

Read calls this method of spelling "cumulative syllabification" and cites references indicating that American school children at the end of the eighteenth century were still learning in this way. The nickname given to Dilworth's book indicates that the spelling method used with it was also this cumulative syllabification.

This method also predates the complex rules involving open and closed syllables that were decreed more recently—that is, the rule that the consonant following a short vowel is retained by the short vowel, thus "closing" the syllable (e.g., *tablet*), while the consonant following a long vowel is released to the next syllable so that the first syllable is "open" (e.g., *ma-son*). Webster later criticized Dilworth's method of syllabication, taking Dilworth to task for such divisions as *clu-ster, ha-bit, no-stril*, and *bi-shop*. Webster changed them to *clus-ter, hab-it, nos-tril*, and *bish-op* in his own speller.[12]

Another British school text used in colonial America was a book by Daniel Fenning called *The Universal Spelling Book* (1756). Webster drew upon as well as attacked both Dilworth's and Fenning's spellers, using the same or similar passages, fables, and word lists—reorganizing them and adding his own material, however. One aspect of the earlier works, especially Dilworth's, was modified somewhat by

---

[9]Warfel, 1936, p. 61. Also, Monaghan (1980, p. 77) notes Dilworth's heavy reliance upon Coote's *The English Schoole-Maister*.

[10]H.L. Mencken, *The American Language*, Knopf, New York, 1919. Fourth revision, 1936, *Supplement One*, 1945; *Supplement Two*, 1948; *Supplement Two*, p. 271.

[11]Allen Walker Read, "The Spelling Bee: A Linguistic Institution of the American Folk," *Publications of the Modern Language Association* (PMLA), Vol. 56, No. 2, June 1941, pp. 498–499.

[12]Warfel, 1936, p. 64. Webster's divisions in such instances are the ones we use today.

Webster. Although he kept the heavily religious values, Webster did not use the name of the Deity. He believed that such use on "every trifling occasion" would diminish reverence "for the Supreme Being."[13]

One book, published somewhat later and not mentioned by Webster, was apparently the very first American spelling book. This is Anthony Benezet's *The Pennsylvania Spelling Book* (1779).[14]

SPELLING AFTER THE REVOLUTIONARY WAR

As it was noted above (p. 147), only after the separation from England did independent attention begin to be paid to language forms in America. Such attention also included spelling patterns. It was not in the spelling books, however, that divergences arose. Noah Webster, whose spelling books were much more popular than any others, chose to keep the traditional forms found in British spelling books, although his personal views varied.

Webster's Views on Spelling

In 1783, when Webster published his first spelling book, his views on spelling were so conservative that he even mocked those who advocated such changes as *favor* for *favour*, a change that Webster himself ended up instituting permanently in America.[15] These views are reflected in the conservative spelling patterns he kept in the many editions of his spelling books.

Three years later, however, in a striking reversal of position, Webster came out in favor of total spelling reform (see pp. 163–164 below). Then, from this other extreme, he moved back slowly to a stand not much less conservative than he had started from. By the time he finished his first dictionary in 1806, Webster had moved from advocating spelling reform to stating simply that "The orthography of our language might be rendered sufficiently regular, without a single new character, by means of a few trifling alterations of the present characters, and retrenching a few superfluous letters, the most of which are corruptions of the original words."[16]

---

[13]Monaghan, 1980, p. 109; also, see pp. 121–123.

[14]Richard E. Hodges, "In Adam's Fall: A Brief History of Spelling Instruction in the United States," in *Reading & Writing Instruction in the United States: Historical Trends*, H. Alan Robinson (Ed.), ERIC Clearing House on Reading and Communication Skills, National Institute of Education and the International Reading Association, Newark, DE, 1977, p. 2. A first edition of the book, called *A First Book for Children*, was published in 1778 (Monaghan, 1980, pp. 67–70).

Webster, however, met Benezet, a Quaker schoolteacher and agitator against slavery, who aroused Webster to active antislavery as early as 1789. Webster felt strongly enough to assign part of the proceeds of his *Dissertations on the English Language* (1789) to the Pennsylvania antislavery movement and, in 1791, to help found an abolitionist group in Hartford, Connecticut (Rollins, 1980, pp. 66–67).

[15]John W. Clark, "American Spelling," Ch. 9 in Spelling, by Vallins, 1965, p. 186. (Also, see below, pp. 174–175).

[16]The statement is from p. vi of Webster's *Compendious Dictionary* (1806). Written in a note to the dictionary's preface, it follows a statement that reveals an unattractive side of Webster's character, a statement in which he baldly disavows his well-documented support for Franklin's Reformed Alphabet (see pp. 163–164 below). Such uncalled-for ingratitude toward Franklin (by then deceased) may give insight into why Webster aroused so much animosity in many of his contemporaries.

Even this position proved to be too extreme for most of Webster's educated contemporaries, who were starting to get caught up in the tide of nineteenth century authoritarianism. Bowing to their will, Webster became still more conservative—not so much because he believed his reforms to be unsound but because he encountered so much resistance to change. Thus, in 1809, after a clamorous, negative response to the spelling changes he had included in his dictionary 3 years earlier, Webster wrote in the postscript of a letter to his brother-in-law, Thomas Dawes, "My proposed corrections are few, and my orthography differs from that of the English, not more than English authors differ from each other. The truth is a reformation of orthography might be made with few changes, and upon a plan so simple as not to require an hour's attention to be perfectly master of it; and it might be introduced in a tenth part of the time required to render general the practice of reckoning money by dollars and cents. But I shall not attempt it. If men choose to be perplexed with difficulties in language, which ordinary men are never able to surmount, I will not contend with them, by endeavoring to remove such difficulties against their will."[17]

Despite this statement, it was difficult for contentious Webster not to contend, and though he gradually eliminated many of his innovations in subsequent editions of his dictionaries, he persisted in retaining some of his favorites. In the end, Webster was far more successful than any previous or subsequent reformer in having the forms he held most dear become part of American spelling.

Reasons for Webster's Influence on American Spelling

Webster's effectiveness, despite the opposition to his ideas about spelling forms, was due in large part to the period of time in which he did his work. Thus, one of the main problems faced by Mulcaster and his fellow orthoepists in pre-authoritarian sixteenth century England (see pp. 122–124 above) was how to deal with the fluid state of the written language—multiple spellings were still fairly common. A similar fluidity, although to a lesser degree, was to be found in much of American spelling during the late eighteenth and early nineteenth century. Consequently, since forms were not yet fully settled, Webster was able to make changes in his dictionaries. To add to the luck of Webster's timing, American authoritarianism was full-blown by the mid-nineteenth century, shortly after his last dictionary revision, and those changes he persisted in championing became fixed and permanent in America.

By contrast, Samuel Johnson compiled his dictionary in England when British spelling was already fixed. Therefore, even with his lustrous reputation, Johnson

---

[17]Noah Webster, Letter to Thomas Dawes (Postscript), *Monthly Anthology and Boston Review*, Vol. 7, p. 208ff. Reprinted in M.M. Mathews (Ed.), *The Beginnings of American English*, University of Chicago Press, 1931, pp. 51–52. The last sentence here reflects a view Webster expressed in the earlier part of the same postscript, namely, that retaining the nonphonemic elements in English spelling was the desire of an elitist group. "Ordinary men," who are unable to spend the necessary time in school, are shut out from the easy access to written language that is the privilege of the educated classes. This concept, which is in accord with Webster's populist creed, is reminiscent of Diringer's and Childe's linking the invention of the first alphabet to the openness of a democratic society (see pp. 30–31 above). Also, Rudolf Flesch linked his recommended phonics approach to the democratic ideal of equal opportunity (see pp. 175–176 below).

was unable to make independent determinations in favor of the forms he might have preferred. He could only record the spellings in contemporary use (see pp. 134–135 above).

Another reason for the effectiveness of Webster's efforts on behalf of spelling was his astute alignment with the schoolmaster tradition. He consciously made full use of teaching guides like Coote's and spelling books like Dilworth's. (Webster's involvement in dictionaries was also in line with this tradition—Mulcaster was one of the first to suggest such compilations.) Over and above his superb promotional techniques, the fact that Webster's spellers were deliberately in accord with ingrained contemporary teaching practices made all of his ideas—even innovative ones—much easier to accept than if he had been constantly advocating radical departures. In return, the teachers helped make Webster's name a household word in the most literal sense, and as the number of educated American households grew, Webster's reputation grew as well. As a result, with the rise of mid-nineteenth century American authoritarianism, Webster became the consummate spelling authority in this country.

The Five Reactions to English Spelling

Not only in Webster did the nonphonemic patterns of written English inspire reactions different from the nonquestioning acceptance usually found here before the Revolutionary War. At the end of the eighteenth century, varying opinions about these patterns emerged in the way that such reactions were then emerging in England and had previously emerged in the sixteenth century. The earlier reactions in England had fallen into three categories, ranging from a strong desire to make basic changes in the alphabet to an almost total acceptance of existing spellings (see p. 123). Because the forces at work in the later years differed from the earlier forces, reactions tended to fall into five categories that only partially resemble the three categories of the earlier English period.

One difference between the two periods was that while the fixing of the language in the seventeenth century in England had practically solved that period's problem of an assortment of spellings for the same word, eighteenth century American spelling, as noted above on p. 160, was somewhat less fixed than the British spelling of the same century. The American spelling was fluid enough to allow new forms, although nowhere nearly as open to individual whim as spelling had been in sixteenth century England.

In addition, as their name orthoepists denotes, those in the earlier period were mainly interested in speech and pronunciation and looked at spelling from the point of view of letter–sound correspondence. From the late eighteenth century on, however—to our own time, in fact—the scrutinizers of English spelling (both in America and in Great Britain) came with a variety of orientations and ended up with a wide range of perceptions of written English. Such viewers of English spelling fall into the following five categories:

1. Those who, looking for strict sound–letter correspondences, believe that the "defective" English alphabet should be changed by altering or adding to the existing characters or by contriving an entirely new alphabet. Here I include all new, augmented, and diacritically marked alphabets.

2.   Those who emphasize the existing spelling rules while noting the inconsistencies in certain designated forms. All in this group believe that the existing alphabet should be retained; a considerable number of them, however, wish to bring their pet inconsistencies in line to achieve greater spelling pattern uniformity.

3.   Those who react with resignation—perceiving many inconsistencies, but who, instead of attempting to change them, advocate working around them by treating written English as if it were a logographic rather than an alphabetic system. (See Chapters 2, 3, and 4 for discussion of the types of writing systems.)

4.   Those who perceive many inconsistencies but many consistencies as well. Those in this group address themselves principally to the problem of teaching children to read. They recommend that consistent patterns be taught first and inconsistently spelled words be introduced subsequently.

5.   Finally, those who perceive many of the nonphonemic spelling patterns as strengths rather than weaknesses of the system because they retain meaning-loaded historic patterns. In this view, written English is valued for its pictographic features.

These five views and some of their more forthright advocates in the United States (and, where appropriate, in Great Britain) are discussed in detail in the next six chapters. Since the five views have had great impact on methods used to teach children to read and spell, their effects on teaching practices are also examined.

22

Alphabet Reform

From the time of their initial appearance in the sixteenth century, a great number and wide assortment of augmented, altered, and completely new "regular" alphabets have been devised and tried out in England (see pp. 122–123 above). Similar attempts at alphabet change have emerged in this country as well. None has even approached the possibility of supplanting our present spelling, yet the power of the desire to make written English precisely match spoken English is evident from the fact that the invention of alternative systems has persisted for so very long in both countries.

BENJAMIN FRANKLIN AND NOAH WEBSTER

In America, the first such invention was devised by Benjamin Franklin, who set down his ideas for an augmented alphabet in a correspondence with a young friend, Mary Stevenson (1768).[1] Franklin proposed regularizing the existing spelling forms, adding six new letters to the English alphabet, and dropping the letters *c*, *j*, *q*, *w*, *x*, and *y* on the grounds they were superfluous.

Franklin did little more with this alphabet, although he later gave his approval when Noah Webster proclaimed himself Franklin's disciple and in 1786 devised another alphabetic system, based on Franklin's suggestions. It was here that Webster shifted dramatically from the conservative position on spelling reform he had held when he published his speller only 3 years before. Although Webster was aware of the failure of similar modified alphabets in Great Britain, he said that American minds were now "in a ferment, and consequently disposed to receive improve-

---

[1]Benjamin Franklin, "A Reformed Mode of Spelling. A Scheme for a new Alphabet and reformed mode of Spelling; with Remarks and Examples concerning the same; and an Enquiry into its Uses, a Correspondence between Miss S_____n and Dr. Franklin, written in the Characters of the Alphabet," in *Political, Miscellaneous, and Philosophical Pieces ... by Benjamin Franklin*, Benjamin Vaughn, London, 1779, p. 472.

ments."[2] Therefore, believed Webster, most Americans would be able to relinquish British language forms. He decided to take advantage of this perceived receptivity by having his modified alphabet made into law by an act of Congress. Webster then tried to enlist Franklin's help in this plan, suggesting that possible opposition to the idea might be counteracted if Franklin would obtain support from prominent political figures—Washington, perhaps, to start with.

Krapp sees Webster's efforts and initial optimism about the success of legislating language as "characteristic of the pathetic faith of men in the early days of the American republic in the power of government to cure all the evils of life by edict and decree."[3] Perhaps because he was older, had seen more, and had perceptions less rosy, Franklin did not respond with equal enthusiasm. Eventually, the two men gave up the idea. (See pp. 159–160 above for Webster's subsequent views on spelling.)

NINETEENTH CENTURY ALTERNATIVE ALPHABETS

Franklin and Webster seem to have been the earliest American advocates of an alternative alphabet; they were also the earliest to stop campaigning for one. The number of others who pushed for such reform soon increased, particularly from the start of the nineteenth century. Krapp lists more than 10 authors who proposed reformed spelling or devised modified alphabets solely between 1793 and 1860 and states that, following those years, such efforts were "legion."

One of the earliest names on Krapp's list of American alphabet reformers is Dr. William Thornton, creator of the Universal Alphabet (1793).[4] Thornton, whose experience in teaching deaf persons had led him to reject the English alphabet because it was nonphonemic, suggested a phonics method to go along with his alphabet's sound–spelling regularity. That seems to have been the first report in the United States of a truly *phonics* approach[5] but little use seems to have been made of Thornton's suggestion until the publication of Edwin Leigh's method 70 years later (see pp. 165–166 below).[6]

Among the American alphabets listed by Krupp because they appeared before 1860 are James Ewing's Columbian Alphabet (1798), Amasa Sproat's Monalpha (1807), and B.J. Antrim's Pantography (1843)—as well as others with more prosaic

---

[2]Harry Warfel (Ed.), *Letters of Noah Webster*, Library Publishers, New York, 1953, p. 50.

[3]Krapp, 1925, Vol. 1, p. 332. Also, see pp. 172–173 below for what must surely have been the last attempt to legislate language change by "edict and decree."

[4]Scragg, 1974, p. 105.

[5]That is, teaching the sounds rather than the names associated with the letters of the alphabet. The distinction of being the first in modern times to introduce a phonics approach to reading belongs to a German teacher, Valentin Ickelsamer (?1501–?1542). His influence was tremendous, not only in Germany but throughout Europe and especially in England. His techniques are still used today by advocates of phonics methods, even by those who are unaware of the original source. (W.J.F. Davies, 1974, p. 129. Also, Mathews, 1966, pp. 31–34.)

[6]Edmund Burke Huey, *The Psychology and Pedagogy of Reading*, Macmillan, New York, 1908. Reprinted by MIT Press, Cambridge, MA, 1968, pp. 259–260, 266. (See also Pitman and St. John, 1969, p. 79.) With respect to early phonics methods, Huey (alone, of the sources I consulted) refers to the "phonic method" of the Jansenists in the Port-Royal schools—presumably in France during the late seventeenth and early eighteenth centuries (1968, pp. 258, 266.) Huey gives no description of that method, however.

titles. None of them were successful or are known to have been particularly influential, but their existence is a sign of the ongoing restiveness about spelling in America.

ISAAC PITMAN AND PHONOTYPY

The proliferation of reformed spellings in America paralleled concurrent efforts in Great Britain, where, after a number of years in which Johnson's retention of spelling patterns held the center stage, a movement toward reform started up again at the end of the eighteenth century.[7] This new interest continued in Great Britain through the following century just as the American reform efforts did, and one notable British attempt at alphabet change was tried here as well. That was the augmented alphabet invented by Sir Isaac Pitman with the collaboration of an eminent philologist and alphabet reformer, Alexander John Ellis. Pitman, who had earlier developed Phonography, the familiar shorthand used by stenographers, was also the grandfather of Sir James Pitman. (The latter was following a family tradition when he created the i.t.a about 100 years later. It is discussed on pp. 168–169 below.)

From 1844 to 1852 Sir Isaac and Ellis perfected their augmented alphabet—called *Phonotypy*—which they intended to be used with printing just as Phonography had been used with handwriting. That is, instead of replacing conventional printing (or *heterotypy*), Phonotypy would simply serve as a bridge to literacy. This educational goal differed from the goals of many previous alphabet reformers, who had generally sought to institute their new systems as permanent replacements for the old one. Phonotypy was therefore introduced as a beginning teaching tool in a number of schools in Great Britain, with Phonetic Schools set up for the express purpose of using it.

Phonotypy was also tried out in the United States. In the years between 1852 and 1860 it was used with 800 school children in Waltham, Massachusetts. Although good results were reported and use of the new alphabet spread to 500 schools in this country, it did not last here.[8] The story of Phonotypy is reminiscent of the later fortunes of the i.t.a.: Both systems originated in England, were tried out there and in the United States with reported success but, in the end, neither was adopted on a substantial, permanent basis.

EDWIN LEIGH AND PRONOUNCING ORTHOGRAPHY

The most successful of the alternative alphabet systems in this country was Dr. Edwin Leigh's Pronouncing Orthography (1864), but this one, too, failed to survive. It was a highly complex system in which Leigh preserved the conventional spellings but tried to give precise clues to the pronunciations. He set down over 70 forms—

---

[7]Scragg, 1974, pp. 105–106. Scragg points to the late eighteenth century philosophy of Rousseau as a prime source for the renewed spelling reform movement. Rousseau's principle of appealing to children's reason was linked by spelling reformers to the desirability of making the spelling system more consistent and hence more "reasonable."

[8]Mathews, 1966, pp. 169–170.

all the standard letters with slight alterations to signal their different pronunciations. Thus, there were five variations in the form of the letter *a* for the five pronunciations it represents, according to Leigh, in the words *aim, any, air, arm,* and *ask.* Silent letters were retained but printed in thinner lines than sounded letters. Leigh also developed a series of readers in which the first two books were printed in Pronouncing Orthography and the rest in conventional spelling. Several other series— including the famous *McGuffey Readers*—were transcribed into it as well. Of special importance is the fact that, with his system, Leigh introduced a true phonics approach to reading and spelling. The sounds, not the names of the letters in a word, were pronounced and then blended—apparently the first such approach to be advocated in this country since Thornton's suggestion.

For a short time, Pronouncing Orthography was highly successful and, during the 20 years between 1866 and 1886, it was adopted, at least in some schools, in St. Louis, Boston, Washington, New York, and other large cities. It is to this widely spread exposure of Leigh's system here that Huey attributes the growth of the phonics method in America. Huey also gives reasons for the fading of Pronouncing Orthography itself even though the phonics approach associated with it was picked up. He assigns the major blame to the fine details on each letter in Leigh's system.[9] The subtle markings made the system hard to learn and, for those who did manage to learn it, difficult to concentrate on meaning while reading it. The details also gave trouble to printers, a factor not often mentioned in discussions of why alternative alphabets did not succeed. In view of the power of printers—Caxton, as we have seen, or even the printers who were helpful to Webster in promulgating his spelling forms—their reluctance or opposition may well have operated against alphabet reform in other instances as well as in the case of Leigh's system.[10]

THE PHILOLOGISTS AND ALPHABET REFORM

Following Leigh and his contemporary alphabet reformers, others continued to come forward with new ideas for altering the symbols of written English, reaching a peak in this country during the last part of the nineteenth century. At that time, interest in spelling reform grew on the part of such scholars as the philologists belonging to the university-based *American Philological Association,*[11] an interest reflecting a cyclical swing in scholarly interest in basic language education.[12] A key action of this group was the Convention for the Amendment of English Orthography (Philadelphia, August 1876), a conference that resulted in the formation of a new body: the American Spelling Reform Association.[13] This group set right to work and, by 1879, had completed a 32–letter Spelling Reform Alphabet. Since the philologists at that time were much concerned with reform as a means of making written

---

[9]Huey, 1968, p. 261.

[10]See p. 176 n. 17 below for additional support for this suggestion.

[11]Founded by William Dwight Whitney.

[12]Bloomfield's concern with beginning reading during the middle decades of this century (see pp. 196–197) followed by the current linguistic and psycholinguistic vogue, are the most recent manifestations of this cyclical interest.

[13]Two years later, the British Spelling Reform Association was founded in England.

language easier to learn, instructions for using the Spelling Reform Alphabet as a beginning reading tool were also formulated. However, that "scientific" alphabet, as well as numerous other elaborately presented alphabets that were inspired by the founding of the American Spelling Reform Association, fell on inhospitable soil. In this country at least, interest in such introductory alphabets declined very soon thereafter.

Mathews attributes the quick decline to resistance from several quarters. For many educational practitioners, the philosophy of the times had moved toward the "whole" approach of John Dewey, G. Stanley Hall, and Colonel Francis Parker (see pp. 187–189 below), and they were unreceptive to the focus on details that was the basis of the philologists' alphabet reform. Of those still interested in changing the written language, most now favored the compromise position of simplified spelling, which uses the conventional alphabetic characters (see pp. 171–172 below). Some were afraid that even though a new alphabet was intended to be used as an introductory tool, it might grow to displace the current alphabet.[14]

In any case, it was not until the 1940s—when the great linguist Leonard Bloomfield turned his attention to the subject—that beginning reading once again captured the serious concern of language scholars in this country. More than a decade passed after that before the recent torrent of linguistics and psycholinguistics swept over the field of reading. Their emphasis in this recent period has not been on ways to change the alphabet, however, but on ways to use linguistic insights in dealing with existing language forms. (See pp. 195–200 below.)

GEORGE BERNARD SHAW'S ALPHABET

In Great Britain, on the other hand, interest in a new alphabet remained steady through much of the twentieth century, with a number of prominent scholars, as well as persons outstanding in other fields, enlisted in the cause. Among the latter, George Bernard Shaw (1856–1950), stands out as "the most trenchant publicist for a complete rejection of the roman alphabet."[15]

Shaw was in the ranks of those who did not want to use the existing forms in any way. He favored starting from scratch, with entirely new characters. In addition to extolling the pronunciation advantages of direct sound–spelling relationships, Shaw pointed out that more concise spellings, free of extraneous silent and doubled letters, would save space and therefore lower paper and printing costs. He thus addressed himself to the practical aspects of instituting a new writing system, aspects that were often neglected by other innovators but that have exerted great, though frequently quiet, power on the forms of written language.

Shaw did not devise any new alphabet himself, but he left a sum of money in his will as a prize for the inventor of the best new alphabet of 40 characters with perfect sound–spelling correspondences, of which 16 were to be vowel characters. In a contest to fulfill this provision, an alphabet by Kingsley Read was chosen from among the 4 best of 467 entries. Read's alphabet was modified by the other three

---

[14]Mathews, 1966, p. 174.
[15]Pitman and St. John, 1969, p. 102.

best entries and the final product used in following Shaw's further instructions. That is, Shaw's play *Androcles and the Lion* was printed with the new and the traditional alphabets on facing pages, and copies were sent to public libraries in Great Britain, the British Commonwealth, and the United States.[16]

SIR JAMES PITMAN AND THE I.T.A.

Experimentation with various introductory alphabets had proceeded uninterruptedly though quietly in England during the first four decades of this century. There was a burgeoning of interest in new alphabets after World War II because of the widely publicized discovery that a large number of the young men called to serve in the armed forces were very poor readers. The dismay generated by that discovery was carried over in Great Britain to the years immediately following the war and was capitalized on by various proponents of spelling change. The most successful of the efforts made by such persons is that associated with Sir James Pitman (Isaac Pitman's grandson).

Convinced by none other than George Bernard Shaw of the value of a new alphabet over a mere simplification of spelling forms,[17] Sir James spoke before the House of Commons early in 1953 and tied the "deplorable" results of the reading instruction of the day to the conventional English spelling. He likened spelling and the task of learning to read it to the task of Chinese children in learning to read the logograms of written Chinese. (His view of the cause of poor reading ability was paralleled in the United States 2 years later when Rudolf Flesch, also addressing himself to a lay audience, attributed poor reading of American children to "our Chinese word-learning system."[18] See pp. 178 and 184 below for other, earlier references to a "Chinese" writing system.)

Sir James was instrumental in the passage by the House of Commons of a bill calling for research into "The assistance to children likely to result from the use (in the earlier stages of teaching reading) of matter printed in a spelling which uses the letters of the alphabet consistently and from a transfer, in due course, to the reading of matter in the existing orthography."[19]

The "spelling" that was developed by Pitman and his helpers to carry out this investigation was the charismatic initial teaching alphabet or i.t.a.—probably the most famous modern reformed alphabet.

The i.t.a. (first called the *Augmented Roman Alphabet*) was completed after years of work and introduced in Great Britain in 1960 and 2 years later in America.

---

[16]George Bernard Shaw, *Androcles and the Lion*, The Shaw Alphabet Edition, Penguin Books, Harmondsworth, 1962. Among the finalists in Shaw's contest was UNIFON—a capital letter reform alphabet devised by a Chicagoan, John R. Malone. UNIFON (from "*uni*formly *pho*nemic") was used with both adult nonreaders and young beginning readers, with reported success. (See Aukerman, 1971, pp. 334–350. Also, John R. Malone, "The UNIFON System," *Wilson Library Bulletin*, 40, September 1965, pp. 64–65 and p. 48 n. 18 above.

[17]Pitman and St. John, 1969, p. 112.

[18]Rudolf Flesch, *Why Johnny Can't Read*, Harper, New York, 1955, p. 7 and elsewhere.

[19]Quoted in Mathews, 1966, p. 176.

Experiments with it continued in both countries through much of the 1960s.[20] So much funding was made available for it that i.t.a. became "the most widely researched approach in beginning reading in the history of our language."[21] John Downing, then of the Institute of Education of the University of London, was outstandingly steadfast and diligent on behalf of the i.t.a. experimental studies in Great Britain as well as in America. In the United States, Albert J. Mazurkiewicz and Harold J. Tanyzer are among those associated with i.t.a. publications and experiments, notably, the *Early-to-Read* i/t/a series,[22] and with experiments using the series—starting with the public schools of Bethlehem, Pennsylvania, under the auspices of the Ford Foundation.

Both the British and the American experimental studies were scrutinized in an independent evaluation of i.t.a. sponsored by the Schools Council (the official curriculum body of England and Wales). Starting in 1966 and carried out by F.W. Warburton and Vera Southgate, the evaluation was based on a meticulous examination of all published i.t.a. research as well as additional interview and questionnaire data gathered specifically for the Schools Council evaluation. Warburton and Southgate found that: "The evidence suggests that, for most children in most schools, the use of i.t.a. as an *initial* teaching alphabet would considerably raise the children's standard of reading and their rate of scholastic progress, although it seems likely that this advantage will be lost after the transition."[23]

Nevertheless, despite this and subsequent reports in its favor, and after being heralded and greatly subsidized on both sides of the Atlantic, the i.t.a., like earlier alternative alphabets, quickly lost its glow—perhaps because, just when it might possibly have taken hold, the educational climate changed.

CURRENT DECLINE OF
INTEREST IN ALTERNATIVE ALPHABETS

First of all, a wealth of new phonics and (so-called) linguistic beginning reading programs cancelled out the "Chinese character" argument for a new alphabet, since most of these new programs featured the immediate introduction of words whose sound and spelling matched, and thus emphasized the regularity of English spelling. Moreover, the political and educational climate of the 1960s and 1970s led many educators to focus on the content of children's readers rather than on the spelling pat-

---

[20]For descriptions of the 1960s i.t.a. experiments, see F.W. Warburton and Vera Southgate, i.t.a.: *An Independent Evaluation*, Murray and Chambers, London, 1969. Also, see John Downing, *Evaluating the Initial Teaching Alphabet*, Cassell, London, 1967; Downing, 1973, pp. 221–227; and Pitman and St. John, 1969.

[21]Aukerman, 1971, p. 335.

[22]Albert J. Mazurkiewicz and Harold J. Tanyzer, *Early-to-Read i/t/a Program*, i/t/a Publications, New York, 1966.

[23]Warburton and Southgate, 1969, p. 276. By "transition" they mean the shift to conventional spelling (or t.o.—traditional orthography—in *i.t.a.* parlance). One of the questions often raised about alternative alphabets and other systems that use nonstandard clues as part of initial reading (e.g., diacritical markings or color-coding) is whether the need to make a transition will have a deleterious effect on achievement.

terns that the words contained. There was also newly aroused interest in such factors as individualization and programming of instruction, which divided and diverted the attention of the educational community just as it had been diverted at the
end of the nineteenth century when the enthusiasm about new alphabets petered
out at that time.

Today, although interest in alphabet change may be said to be at a low point—
certainly for introductory reading—a degree of such interest still does exist. For example, one famous early reading program, DISTAR, uses alphabetic modification
within an approach most noted for its rigidly structured, hard-hitting lessons.[24]
Looking back and seeing how tenaciously the idea has remained alive, though often
dormant, there is little doubt that ingenious individuals who find our present system
unbearably abrasive will continue to arise and will have at it again.

---

[24]*DISTAR* (from Direct Instruction Systems for Teaching Arithmetic and Reading), Science Research Associates, Chicago, 1969, 1975.

23

Simplified Spelling

The second reaction to the complex English spelling patterns also goes back many years. This is the compromise position taken by Richard Mulcaster, who was the first to set down cohesively the views of those in his day who were opposed to any change in the alphabet. In his famous *Elementarie* of 1582 (see p. 123 above) Mulcaster recommended changing certain specific spelling patterns—often to conform to existing analogous patterns—rather than making the more drastic changes suggested by the alphabet reformers of his time. Mulcaster's influence was far-reaching. Not only were his altered spelling forms picked up directly by the authors of spelling books, but also rooted in Mulcaster (via Edmund Coote) was the traditional schoolteacher method of teaching spelling and reading. That method ultimately affected all who passed through the educational systems of Great Britain and North America. In the United States, the person most associated with the second reaction is Noah Webster.

WEBSTER'S POSITIONS ON SPELLING REFORM

As was noted above (pp. 159–160), Webster started out in a strongly conservative position, shifted abruptly to the cause of alphabet modification, and, when his activities on behalf of his alternative alphabet met with little support, changed his goal to that of simplifying the existing spelling forms. By 1790, he had published his *Collection of Essays and Fugitive Writings*, in which he used simplified spellings that involved the omission of silent letters in addition to many changes in the direction of uniform spellings of specific speech sounds (e.g., *ee* for all *long e* pronunciations and *z* for *s*, as in *iz* for *is* and *reezon* for *reason*). Webster's retreat in the face of the ridicule with which those writings were met was the beginning of the gradual, lifelong modification of his position on simplified spelling.

During his lifetime, Webster's influence as the ultimate authority on American spelling had its start, and his authority continued to grow after his death. It reached such heights that even though the language scholars of the middle and late nineteenth century—who were newly aroused to study English spelling—did not consider Webster to have had scientific credentials, they felt it necessary to examine the spelling changes in his dictionary.

THE AMERICAN PHILOLOGICAL ASSOCIATION

It was, in fact, Webster's non-British spellings that led the American Philological Association to study the entire question of spelling reform.[1] One direction the group took spurred the invention of the 32-letter alphabet. Simultaneously, the Association explored the more moderate possibility of altering spelling forms, as Webster had done. As a result, by 1886, they endorsed a number of spelling changes, changes that involved 3,500 words. Many of those changes had been previously recommended by Webster, and some of them were already widely used in America. The Association also recommended some new, generally clumsy changes, but little came of them.

THE NATIONAL EDUCATION ASSOCIATION

Not much more of note was done about changing spelling forms until 12 years later. In 1898, the National Education Association made a try at it, although with a decidedly more modest list of only 12 suggestions: *tho, altho, thru, thruout, thoro, thoroly, thorofare, program, prolog, catalog, pedagog,* and *decalog.*[2] Although only *program* and possibly *catalog* have been fully assimilated into American spelling, a number of the other 10 forms may still be found in informal notes and the rather outdated literary writing of early twentieth century spelling reform enthusiasts.

SPELLING REFORM IN THE TWENTIETH CENTURY

Attempts to institute the second approach to English spelling continued after the start of this century and have never ceased.

President Theodore Roosevelt and the Simplified Spelling Board

The year 1906 marked the founding of the Simplified Spelling Board, a group ornamented with such sponsors as Mark Twain, William James, Nicholas Murray Butler (president of Columbia University), and some of the most eminent linguists of the time. Furthermore, the group was subsidized by Andrew Carnegie with an uninflated $283,000.

---

[1]McDavid, 1963, p. 489. (Also, see pp. 166–167 above.)
[2]McDavid, 1963, p. 490.

The Board's first year was filled with dramatic events. In March, it published a list of 300 spellings, some familiar and some innovative.[3] Included were such forms as *honor* for *honour, center* for *centre, plow* for *plough,* and others long urged by American spelling reformers, as well as the practice of adding a *t* for the dental suffix of the past forms of verbs (the old Germanic form—see p. 65 above) instead of final *-ed* and its variations (*kist* for *kissed* and *mixt* for *mixed*). The changes consisted mainly of omitting unsounded letters rather than substituting one letter for another to achieve sound–spelling uniformity.[4]

The head of the Simplified Spelling Board was Brander Matthews, a well-known man of letters and professor of dramatic literature at Columbia University, who also happened to be a friend of President Theodore Roosevelt. Roosevelt had himself had problems with spelling at one time and seems to have been sympathetic to simplified spelling for that reason. With the encouragement of Matthews, Roosevelt lent his prestige and what he believed to be his power to the cause of spelling reform. In August 1906 he sent an official order to the United States Government Printing Office, serving notice that from then on the rules of simplified spelling were to be followed in all government printing. Roosevelt also had his own secretary use the simplified forms for all presidential correspondence.

On the volatile question of spelling, however, the power of even so strong a president as Roosevelt was not enough to overcome the resistance of either the government printers—who balked at his order (not surprisingly in light of the historical conservatism of printers)—or the alarm of the traditionally educated Congress. The national press was of little help—newspapers gleefully held up to ridicule examples of the new forms. Finally, when Roosevelt actually wrote his annual message to Congress in simplified spelling, the consternation was great enough for Congress to suggest to the president that he rescind his order on government printing. Clever as he was and sensing the depth of feeling, Roosevelt immediately withdrew the decree, writing to Matthews in December of 1906 that "it was evidently worse than useless to go into an undignified contest when I was beaten."[5]

Despite this lost battle, Roosevelt retained his sympathetic views on simplified spelling. He became a member of the Simplified Spelling Board and used some of the new forms in his private writing. Any time his own writings were quoted in the press, however, all simplified spellings were changed to traditional forms.

Recent Simplified Spelling Systems

The Simplified Spelling Board lost much of its momentum after the death of Andrew Carnegie in 1919. Two years later, the National Education Association withdrew its earlier endorsement of spelling reform. Nevertheless, the Simplified Spelling Board and its descendant, the Simpler Spelling Association, continued to function, joined

---

[3]A list of these 300 words may be found in George Ranow's article "Simplified Spelling in Government Publications," *American Speech,* Vol. 29, February 1954, pp. 36–41.

[4]Clyde H. Dornbusch, "American Spelling Simplified by Presidential Edict," *American Speech,* October 1961, pp. 236–238.

[5]Dornbusch, 1961, p. 238. (Quoted from a letter to Brander Matthews, December 16, 1906, *The Letters of Theodore Roosevelt,* Vol. 5, Letter no. 4171.)

by the Spelling Reform Association (see pp. 166–167 above) and the Simplified Spelling League. These American groups stayed in touch with the British Simplified Spelling Society, and all moved from the conservative nineteenth century changes to work toward a new reformed system using the current alphabet. Their efforts culminated in New Spelling (1955) and Godfrey Dewey's World English Spelling (1968),[6] which were influenced by an earlier system: R.E. Zachrisson's Anglic (1932). Zachrisson, a Swedish linguist, believed that spelling reform would make it easier for foreigners to learn English and thus further his primary goal of using English "as an international auxiliary language."[7]

Another Swedish linguist, Axel Wijk, devised Regularized English some 25 years later. It was a relatively conservative system that left 90%–95% of the original spelling intact.[8] Wijk's system was praised by linguists but it, like the other recent reformed systems, never attained general acceptance.

DIFFERENCES BETWEEN BRITISH AND AMERICAN SPELLING SINCE WEBSTER

In the end, only a handful of specifically American spellings have become accepted but, demonstrating Webster's impact, the largest number of words that have distinctly American spellings are those Webster espoused. Particularly associated with him are the patterns of -*or*/-*our* as in *favor/favour*, -*er*/-*re* as in *center/centre*, and -*se*/-*ce* as in *offense/offence*.

Some other major clear-cut differences between American and British spelling are: *check/cheque, jail/gaol, program/programme, plow/plough, ax/axe, tire/tyre, inquire/enquire, connection/connexion, curb/kerb, wagon/waggon* and the elimination in America of the ligatures "æ" and "œ" in words like the British-spelled *archæology* and *amœba*, in which the ligature represents a Greek or Latin diphthong. In American spelling, either the two vowels comprising the ligature are separated (as in *archaeology* and *amoeba*) or the *a* or *o* is dropped altogether (as in the also-accepted spellings *archeology* and *ameba*).

One other difference between Modern British and American spelling is not patterned with total consistency but is real nonetheless. This is the question of doubling the *final l* in derived or inflected forms in the way that other final consonants are doubled or not. Usually, the single final consonant in an accented short-voweled final syllable is doubled when a suffix beginning with a vowel is added, as in *permitted* (but not in *inhabited*). (See pp. 65–66 above for the old Germanic basis of this rule.) American spelling extends this rule to words in which the final consonant is *l* while British spelling makes exceptions for such words. Thus, in England the *l* may be doubled in a word like *traveller*, even though the last syllable is unaccented,

---

[6]Godfrey Dewey, *World English Spelling*, Simpler Spelling Association, New York, 1964.

[7]R.E. Zachrisson, "Four Hundred Years of English Spelling Reform," *Studia Neophilologica*, Vol. 4, Nos. 1–2, 1931, p. 49. See also R.E. Zachrisson, *Anglic, an International Language*, Almqvist and Wiksell, Stockholm, 1932.

[8]Axel Wijk, *Regularized English; an Investigation into the English Spelling Reform Problem with a New Detailed Plan for a Possible Solution*, Stockholm Studies in English, Vol. 7, Almqvist and Wiksell, Stockholm, 1959, p. 114.

or the *l* may be made single in a word like *enrolment*, even though the suffix begins with a consonant.[9]

SPELLING REFORM TODAY

Despite the efforts at spelling reform described above, American spelling became as fixed after Webster as British spelling had been during Johnson's time. Since then, alterations in England and America have been few and very slow to be accepted, even though efforts to make changes have abounded and continue to be presented to this day.

An added reason for the recent quiet on the question of spelling change is the lack of support from a large group of potential allies—those who perceive the English alphabet as a viable phonemic code but see far fewer flaws in it than do the spelling reformers. Representing that point of view is Rudolf Flesch who, in his cataclysmic book *Why Johnny Can't Read* (1955), maintains that written English can be taught with a phonics method because it is predominantly phonemic (he calls it "phonetic")[10] and can therefore be taught with a phonics method. Although he says nothing about a need for spelling reform, Flesch's own view most nearly corresponds to the second of the five categories discussed here: he is traditional in his approach to reading instruction and his perception of English spelling is that "our English system of writing is *of course* phonetic, but has a few more exceptions to the rules than other languages."[11]

When Flesch's book first exploded into the arena of those concerned with teaching children to read and spell, his quarrel was only with the prevailing whole word approach, against which he counters a purely phonics approach. Flesch put up a staunch defense of the alphabetic nature of written English and then pointed to the regularities of that written language as a reason for using a phonics method like his own. Flesch did not offer any criticisms of the "exceptions," nor did he recommend any changes in the existing written forms.

Nevertheless, while Flesch is much more content than Webster ever was about leaving spelling patterns as he found them, Flesch firmly identifies himself with Webster's approach, stating that "The Blue-Backed Speller was a fourteen-cent medicine that cured you of illiteracy."[12] Like Webster, too (although not, as Webster,

---

[9]John W. Clark, 1965. Clark gives a full description of the differences between American and British English in this chapter.

[10]Flesch was using the same terminology he found in other authors he was quoting (e.g., Paul Witty and Roma Gans). For this, Flesch was scolded several years later—in 1962—by Charles Fries, who picked up on what he identified as a widespread misuse of the terms *phonetic* and *phonetics* and devoted Chapter 5 of his book to detailing the differences between *phonics*, *phonetics*, and *phonemics*. In that chapter, Fries tries to make clear that phonetics "is an internationally respected science dealing with the descriptive analysis of speech sounds" (1963, p. 139). It does not mean "those practices in the teaching of reading that have aimed at matching the individual letters of the alphabet with specific sounds of English pronunciation" (Fries, 1963, pp. 143–144). That, rather, is Fries's definition of *phonics* (see p. 3 above). Neither does the term *phonetics* mean the individual sound system of any one language—that is a definition of *phonemics* (see pp. 27–28 above). In all fairness, Fries does point out that this interchange of meanings began many years ago—appearing as early as 1570 in the writings of John Hart, (see p. 123 above)—and was widespread in the nineteenth century. For additional discussion of these terms, see Jeanne S. Chall, *Learning to Read: The Great Debate*, McGraw-Hill, New York, 1967, p. 14.

[11]Flesch, 1955, p. 13.

[12]Flesch, 1955, p. 46.

linked to a desire to alter spelling forms), Flesch sounds a patriotic note, saying, "There is a connection between phonics and democracy—a fundamental connection. Equal opportunity for all is one of the inalienable rights, and the word method interferes with that right."[13] Going further in this vein, Flesch states, "I say, therefore, that the word method is gradually destroying democracy in this country; it returns to the upper middle class the privileges that public education was supposed to distribute evenly among the people."[14]

That extreme sentiment is rarely heard today, although there are certainly many active proponents of phonics programs. Today's adherents of Flesch's view of our spelling system find adequate room to put that view into practice within the contemporary trend toward eclectic beginning reading programs.[15] Perhaps for this reason they, like Flesch, are not identified with spelling reform. Instead, the heirs to the late nineteenth and early twentieth century desire to make specific English spelling forms more phonemic are to be found in organizations like the British-based Simplified Spelling Society and the Phonemic Spelling Council in this country.[16] Both organizations have numbered some outstanding linguists and scholars among their members, and both continue to be active in a limited sphere. The leadership within the Simplified Spelling Society of John Downing, and of Emmett Betts within the Phonemic Spelling Council, resulted in efforts to strengthen ties between those organizations and reading educators.

Thus, in 1975, the Simplified Spelling Society held a weeklong conference, for the first time since its establishment in 1908, that included many aspects of reading and reading acquisition. In addition, in recent years, the Society has cosponsored meetings at the International Reading Association's annual convention. The Phonemic Spelling Council has, among its activities, also cosponsored meetings at these annual conventions, starting in 1970. The attendance at the Phonemic Spelling Council meeting at the 1980 convention showed a definite increase: Whereas a few short years earlier there had been only a handful in the audience, this time a large room was filled. The possibility still exists that through either one of these or through another channel some of the earlier intense interest in orthographic change may flare up again.[17]

---

[13]Flesch, 1955, p. 130. Also see p. 160 n. 17 above.

[14]Flesch, 1955, p. 132.

[15]Helen Popp, "Current Practices in the Teaching of Beginning Reading," in *Toward a Literate Society: The Report of the Committee on Reading of the National Academy of Education*, John B. Carroll and Jeanne S. Chall (Eds.), McGraw-Hill, New York, 1975, p. 138. Flesch criticized current beginning reading instruction once more. He addressed himself, again to parents, in "Why Johnny *still* Can't Read," (*Family Circle*, November 1, 1979, pp. 26, 43–46), and provoked strong reactions—both supportive and antagonistic—from parents, teachers, and reading educators. This preceded the publication of his new book *Why Johnny* Still *Can't Read*, Harper & Row, New York, 1981.

[16]The Phonemic Spelling Council was formerly the Simpler Spelling Association, which, in turn, had been the Simplified Spelling Board discussed above (pp. 172–173).

[17]On July 12, 1977, it was reported in the *New York Times* that Edward Rondthaler, a retired printer and the inventor of Soundspel—a simplified spelling system that uses our entire alphabet—was prepared to devote his life to promoting his new system. The role of printers in spelling change that has been noted earlier was underscored by Rondthaler when he said, "I'm only suggesting a method here that uses our 26 letters. That's the only one our printers will accept—I know that—and it's the only one that has a chance with the public. I want to use my entree to the printing industry not to oppose it—too strongly. I'm sure they'll oppose it." (*The New York Times*, July 12, 1977.)

24

Rejection of the Alphabetic Code I

Horace Mann

The third reaction to the nonphonemic spelling patterns of written English has been to perceive such patterns as so numerous that the only way to deal with them is to respond to each word as if it were a logogram. This view is bound up with the whole word approach to teaching reading[1]—a logical method to use in teaching written words that are indeed not phonemic. As background to understanding this third view, it should be noted that though modern arguments for a whole word approach to reading have emphasized the imprecise sound–letter relationships of English, the approach itself originated for altogether different reasons.

FRIEDRICH GEDIKE (1754–1803)

The first person to advocate a whole word approach to beginning reading instruction in an alphabetic language was not a teacher of written English, but a dedicated, highly influential German teacher named Friedrich Gedike. Gedike, inspired by his era's "back to nature" philosophies of education like that of Jean Jacques Rousseau, became interested in methods of teaching beginning reading. He reasoned that starting with small units and building with them was a method that only God should use. Humans must do the opposite—that is, go from wholes to their individual parts. Thus, while God started with units to build a flower, a person wishing to learn about the flower must start with the whole flower and dissect it down to its units. In the same way, to learn to read, one must start with the total finished product—the

---

[1]The whole word approach, often referred to as *analytic* or *look-say*, consists of first presenting a block of written language, rather than single letters, and then breaking the block into its components. When such an approach is used in response to the nonphonemic spelling of individual words, the block of language is usually an individual word. Analytic approaches have also been those in which the initial "block" was a book, a story, a sentence, or a phrase.

book—and then go to the units within it. Gedike felt, however, that a whole book would be too large a unit with which to begin, so he developed a method in which the initial units were whole words.

In 1779, Gedike set down his theories in his book *Aristoteles and Basedow* and, 12 years later, published a primer incorporating a word method, *Kinderbuch . . .* (the lengthy German title is translated as "Children's Book for the First Practice in Reading without the ABC's and Spelling").[2] In the preface to the primer, Gedike states, "It is neither necessary nor useful *to begin* learning to read with a knowledge of the individual letters, but it is not only far more pleasant but also far more useful for the child if it learns to read *entire words* at once, because in this way it will be occupied immediately with whole ideas, but on the contrary the ABC's and spelling supply the child with only fragments of ideas."[3]

Thus, the impetus for Gedike's devising the whole word approach (which he called *analytic*) came from his concern with making learning to read pleasurable and with deriving meaning from reading, rather than from any desire to bypass a nonphonemic writing system. (His lack of concern with the writing system is not surprising, since written German has few spelling anomalies.) The teachers of his day were critical of his method, however, seeing it as an experimental rather than a practical approach. He was accused of treating written German as if it were Chinese (that is, *logographic*—though that term was adopted much later), with the same derogatory overtones with which the accusation was made in later centuries (see pp. 168 and 184).

Although Gedike accurately denied that he ignored the alphabetic nature of the German writing system and maintained that his method would actually facilitate children's ability to determine unknown words independently, his method was not adopted for general use in the schools of his day. A number of educators in Germany and in other European countries came to know of it, however. Among them was Jean Joseph Jacotot, a French educator who taught in Belgium.

JEAN JOSEPH JACOTOT (1790–1840)

Jacotot went further with Gedike's basic concept, greatly emphasizing the idea of "whole" by presenting the beginning reader with an entire book, read aloud. Jacotot chose *Les aventures de Telemaque* by Fenelon (1669), an exciting yet profound 400-page book describing the adventures of Telemachus in search of his father Odysseus—a book written initially to instruct the son of Louis XIV. After the pupils were familiar with the book, it was broken down into sentences, into words, and finally into letters. Because of the rich content of the book, Jacotot was able to keep the children interested as well as to relay much information about a variety of subjects in addition to language.[4]

Jacotot's method gained popularity in Germany, but the cumbersome technique of using an entire book as the "whole" was soon modified. Because in Jaco-

[2]Mathews, 1966, p. 39.
[3]Mathews, 1966, p. 39.
[4]Jean Joseph Jacotot, *Enseignement universe! . . . Langue maternelle*, 3rd ed., Louvain, 1827 (described in Mathews, 1966, pp. 43–45).

tot's approach the words served to introduce the letters of the alphabet almost immediately, those who picked up his method moved into a direction Jacotot did not mean to take. The method became one in which the "whole" was simply a single word, not to be learned for its own sake. Rather, the letters in it were analyzed, sounded (not named), written, and then put back together into the word.[5] Thus, children were quickly moved into synthesizing the letters they learned rather than being helped to focus on the meaning of what was read. As the method was used in the schools of Germany, the introduction of words turned into a transitory diversion, followed by the same copious practice with letters that had existed before Jacotot and Gedike. In the end, Jacotot's "whole" method grew to be a system of using words to introduce phonics elements rather than the meaning-emphasis method first conceived by Gedike.[6] It was such a method that Horace and Mary Mann saw on their trip to Prussia in 1843.

HORACE MANN (1796–1859)

Horace Mann was described by Mathews as "by far the most eloquent advocate the orthodox look-and-say method of teaching children to read has ever had."[7] The story of how Mann arrived at his beliefs about the teaching of reading and how he advanced those beliefs merits telling—not only because of his preeminent place in the history of American education but also because his arguments proved so valuable to later proponents of the whole word approach.

Mann's Early Career

Horace Mann was born and raised on a Massachusetts farm. After a childhood and adolescence of almost constant toil, he broke the pattern set by his American ancestors by leaving the family farm to take a degree at Brown University and to study law in Litchfield, Connecticut. Mann's intelligence and eloquence were recognized from the start of his years at Brown. One classmate later recalled him to be "the best law student and the best-read scholar in the school."[8]

---

[5]Paulo Freire, the Brazilian educator, has used a similar system with adults in modern times, although he centers on syllables rather than on individual phonics elements.

Starting with one meaningfully presented written word, *tijolo* (brick), Freire derives three syllables, *ti, jo, lo*. With careful sequencing, he teaches related written syllables, *ta-te-ti-to-tu, jaje ji jo ju,* and *la-le-li-lo-lu*. The students then synthesize these syllables into such words as *loja* (store), *tela* (screen), *juto* (jute), and so on—first orally and then in writing. (Paulo Freire, *Education for Critical Consciousness*, Seabury Press, New York, 1973, pp. 53–55.)

Freire states that, by starting from and building carefully on this introduction, "Generally, in a period of six weeks to two months, we could leave a group of twenty-five persons reading newspapers, writing notes and simple letters, and discussing problems of local and national interest." (Freire, 1973, p. 53, n.16.)

[6]Mathews, 1966, pp. 46–49. This method eventually came to be known by such names as *Analytic-Synthetic Method* and *Normal-Words Method*.

[7]Mathews, 1966, p. 75.

[8]Jonathan Messerli, *Horace Mann*, Knopf, New York, 1972, p. 71.

Mann met with further success when he set up a law practice in Dedham, Massachusetts—achieving both financial comfort and social prominence within 5 years. Mann, like Webster, was patriotic to the point of chauvinism and decided to leave private practice and enter public life. In 1828, he was elected to the Massachusetts state legislature, where he remained for almost 10 years—advancing in time to the presidency of that body.

Mann's service in the state legislature was interrupted for several years while he struggled with a personal tragedy. His first wife, Charlotte, became ill shortly after their marriage in 1830 and slowly faded until she died 2 years later. Mann went into a prolonged period of mourning and depression that lasted until he developed a close friendship with Mary Peabody (the sister of Nathaniel Hawthorne's wife, Sophia), a friendship that led to their marriage in 1843. Despite the burden of his emotions after his first wife's death, Mann was able after a time to return to the state legislature and to continue to work for the humanitarian ideals he championed throughout his life.

Mann and the Massachusetts Board of Education

In 1837, in his position as president of the senate, Mann participated in a successful campaign to establish a board of education of the state of Massachusetts. This was an advisory body to help improve the quality of public education in the state, and Mann was offered and accepted the post of secretary of the new board—in effect, its administrative head. Messerli identifies that offer as "Mann's summons to shape the destiny of American education."[9]

Mann's interest in education, like Webster's, was grounded in his patriotism. Rather than looking on publicly supported and publicly controlled education as a form of charity to the poor—as even some of its supporters held it to be—Mann believed that education was the key to the democratic ideal of the wisdom of the majority, that the better educated the populace, the greater would be its collective wisdom. This principle of Jeffersonian democracy was much in vogue, and Mann expanded it to include moral as well as intellectual wisdom. (His was an age when school texts added the moralistic content of readers like McGuffey's to the patriotic content found earlier in Webster's books.) Thus, public education seemed to be another way to achieve the improvements in American life that Mann had been trying to bring about through politics.[10]

An indication of the general quality of public education in Massachusetts (at that time the hub of the cultural Northeast) is the fact that, in the year of Mann's election (1837), Henry David Thoreau and Herman Melville each tried to teach school—Thoreau in Concord and Melville outside of Pittsfield—but both gave up after a short time because they found the conditions intolerable.[11]

---

[9]Messerli, 1972, p. 247.

[10]Lawrence A. Cremin (Ed.), *The Republic and the School: Horace Mann on the Education of Free Men,* Teachers College Press, New York, 1952, p. 7.

[11]Messerli, 1972, p. 254. In that year, too, pupils revolted against the cruelties and beatings that had been inflicted upon them and drove 300 teachers from their schools (Mathews, 1966, p. 76).

After reading whatever he could on the subject of education, Mann decided to see Massachusetts public schools first-hand by making a tour of the state—an undertaking reminiscent of Noah Webster's tours to publicize his books. In addition to learning about actual conditions in the schools, Mann hoped to arouse interest in public education and thereby develop a base of sympathetic citizens to support his educational goals.

Alone and on horseback, as well as by boat to Martha's Vineyard and Nantucket, Mann traveled throughout the state. In addition to visiting schools at each stop, he would contact private individuals and organize town meetings, encouraging the formation of local educational associations. Mann found the tour so rewarding that in following years he made similar tours to visit each county in the state.

Mann's Educational Reforms

Upon his return from the tour, Mann prepared the first of what were to be 12 memorable annual reports. This initial report, delivered on January 1, 1838, listed some of the major needs of the school system and was the cornerstone of the significant reforms that Mann was later able to institute. Main areas of concern described in the report were the dreadful physical facilities and the "intense want of competent teachers in the common schools"[12]—which he blamed on the lack of public concern.

These and other educational issues were addressed energetically by Mann while he was secretary. Because of his careful, tireless leadership, Mann was directly responsible for profound alterations in the Massachusetts public schools as well as for much that took place in American education during the generations that followed. Outstanding were the teacher-training (or normal) schools he founded, models for the many teachers colleges that were established in the nineteenth century. In addition, he set up an elaborate structure to ensure thorough supervision of the public schools in each county and, concerned with pupils' physical well-being, he provided models for the design of school buildings with adequate light, ventilation, and comfort.

Mann's Trip to Europe

The high spot of Mann's years as secretary of the board of education was probably his visit to Europe in 1843. This was his honeymoon trip with his second wife, Mary Peabody, and the newly married couple spent much of their 6-month tour visiting European schools, prisons, and asylums, hoping to gather ideas for similar institutions back home.

Although the trip as a whole left the Manns with a distaste for the extremes of riches and poverty of European society, they were enthusiastic about some of the educational systems they observed. Upon their return, Mann prepared his landmark Seventh Annual Report, in which he described much that had impressed him during his European visit. He was especially taken with the educational practices in Prussia—the competence of the teachers, the orderliness and motivation of the children

---

[12]Messerli, 1972, p. 290.

(achieved without the corporal punishment that permeated American schools), and the efficiency with which the Prussian schools were organized and administered.

Mann's Beliefs About Reading and Spelling

Mann also lauded the Prussians for their approach to beginning reading, a reaction that was not surprising in view of his earlier statements about reading as well as the teaching practices previously advocated by Mary Mann. From his initial readings on the subject of education, Mann had grown increasingly persuaded that the word method of Gedike and Jacotot, as well as of a number of American educators who had followed in the tradition started by the two Europeans, was superior to the Websterian alphabet/spelling method still much in use. As early as his Second Annual Report (1838) Mann had pointed out the advantages of teaching words before letters, although he was not yet as deeply convinced on the matter as he was soon to become. He was more concerned at that time with the need to arouse the desire to learn—one of his key beliefs about education—and the method of teaching reading was secondarily tied to that need.

Nevertheless, even then he laid great stress on the importance of reading for meaning: "But one thing should be insisted upon, *from* the beginning, and especially *at* the beginning. No word should be taught, whose meaning is not understood."[13] Further, "Reading is divisible into two parts. It consists of the *mechanical*, and the *mental*. . . . With the mental part . . . reading becomes the noblest instrument of wisdom; without it, it is the most despicable part of folly and worthlessness."[14]

Three years later, Mann took an even stronger position in favor of a whole word method in a lecture entitled "On the Best Mode of Preparing and Using Spelling-Books" (1841). Perhaps his increased experience with what actually took place in hundreds of classrooms was responsible, or perhaps it was his deepening relationship with Mary Peabody, who, about that time, published a primer based on a whole word method using words and sentences—a book much admired by Mann. At any rate, in this lecture he caustically denounced alphabetic lists, referring to the letters in them as "skeleton-shaped, bloodless, ghostly apparitions, and hence it is no wonder that the children look and feel so death-like, when compelled to face them. The letters are more minute too, than any objects which ever attract the attention of children. Children require some medium between the vast and the microscopic. They want some diversity, also, but the forms of the twenty-six letters have as little variety as twenty-six grains of sand."[15]

The rest of Mann's discussion of the alphabetic approach to reading and spelling also paints pictures designed to convey his revulsion: "it is upon this emptiness, blankness, silence and death that we compel children to fasten their eyes"; "the odor and fungousness of spelling-book paper"; "a soporific effluvium seems to emanate from the page, steeping all their faculties in lethargy."[16]

---

[13]Cremin, 1952, p. 41.
[14]Cremin, 1952, pp. 42–43. This concept of "mechanical" and "mental" parts of reading is reminiscent of Chomsky's concept of surface and deep structures of language. (See p. 204 below.)
[15]Mathews, 1966, pp. 77–78.
[16]Mathews, 1966, p. 78.

His description of the whole word method is somewhat more cheerful and, according to Mathews, reveals Mann's familiarity with the work of other whole word advocates, particularly Gedike and Jacotot. Thus, Mann says that lessons in which words are taught first "will be like an excursion to the fields of elysium, compared with the old method of plunging children, day by day, for months together, in the cold waters of oblivion, and compelling them to say falsely, that they love the chill and torpor of the immersion."[17] He talks, too, of how one presents a whole animal to a child rather than individual parts—echoing Gedike's example of starting with a whole flower rather than with its individual units—and speaks of Samuel Worcester, Thomas H. Gallaudet, and Josiah Bumstead, who were among the earliest in the country to have introduced whole word instruction.

Thus, Mann was fully prepared to be pleased with the Prussian whole word method when he was abroad, and the Seventh Annual Report reflects the delight aroused by the experience. In a section of the Report called "Methods of Teaching Young Children on Their First Entering School," he goes into great detail about the problems caused by introducing letters and syllables without words and stresses the boredom and lack of mental stimulation involved in memorizing the letters. "A parrot or an idiot could do the same thing."[18] (A little more than 100 years later Rudolph Flesch was to write with equal conviction, "The truth is, of course, that any normal six-year-old child *loves* to learn letters and sounds. He is fascinated by them. They are the greatest thing he's come up against in his life.")[19]

Mann's glowing description of the superiority of the word method is followed by a recommendation that whole "regular" words should be introduced first. Letter sounds should be brought to pupils' attention as small combinations are gradually introduced, "so that the sound of a regular word of four letters is divided into four parts; and a recombination of sounds of letters makes the sound of the word."[20] Mann uses the term *phonics* here, giving it the meaning it has retained, namely, "the sounds of the letters."[21] Moreover, he expresses the desire to spread the technique of using entire words and then phonics in place of the alphabetic-spelling method long in use. Mann also recommends his wife's primer as the best example of the whole word approach.

THE BOSTON SCHOOLMASTER CONTROVERSY

Mann's reports to the board of education were well publicized, and the Seventh Report brought praise from prominent educators and government officials both in America and Europe. However, one pocket of dormant rage at Mann's ideas—the Association of Masters of the Boston Public Schools—responded with a memorable

---

[17]Mathews, 1966, p. 81.

[18]Nila Banton Smith, *American Reading Instruction*, International Reading Association, Newark, DE, 1965, p. 78.

[19]Flesch, 1955, p. 74. Flesch, incidentally, does not seem to be aware of Mann's true position with respect to phonics. On p. 128 of his book Flesch states, "Horace Mann . . . observed the teaching of phonics in Prussia and recommended it enthusiastically for use in American schools."

[20]Messerli, 1972, p. 406.

[21]Messerli, 1972, p. 406. Messerli implies that Mann was the first to use the term *phonics* in this way, and I have not found evidence to dispute him.

eruption. The Boston schoolmasters were an entrenched and powerful group who considered themselves to be the elite of Massachusetts schoolteachers. They had chosen to exempt Boston schools and Boston teachers from the criticism in Mann's earlier reports, although Mann himself had never exempted them. This Seventh Report hit too close to home, however, and they reacted with fury.

Six months after the Report was issued, a committee of the Association published a 144-page pamphlet called *Remarks on the Seventh Annual Report of the Hon. Horace Mann, Secretary of the Massachusetts Board of Education.* In it, they bitterly rejected every educational idea that Mann put forth and were particularly sharp on the question of reading and spelling. They accurately pointed out that Mann was confused about the reading method he had seen in Prussia and went on to disparage what they believed to be the whole word method. They noted such evils that resulted from it as a neglect of spelling and an inability to transfer recognition of a word to the same word in another context or with different type. They also attacked Mrs. Mann's whole-word primer.

Mann's reaction to the Remarks was not long in coming—2 months later he wrote a 176-page *Reply to the "Remarks of the thirty-one Boston Schoolmasters on the Seventh Annual Report of the Massachusetts Board of Education."* In it, he bitingly accused the schoolmasters of sacrificing children's welfare to preserve their own selfish interests. He accused them of distorting the operation and the results of the word method and ended by listing the achievements of the Massachusetts Board of Education during his tenure as its secretary.

Mann's "Reply" provoked an even lengthier "Rejoinder . . ." from the schoolmasters, to which Mann responded with an "Answer to the Rejoinder. . . ," carrying the controversy to the middle of 1845. Mann's "Answer . . ." brought the formal correspondence to a close, although the friction between Mann and the Boston schoolmasters continued informally for about a year longer. The publicity given to the issues raised, however, was notably effective in bringing about many of the changes that Mann sought. On the question of corporal punishment alone, Mann noted gleefully in April of 1846 that, "One of the already ripened and gathered fruits of the controversy is, that it is admitted on all hands, that, since the controversy began, corporal punishment has diminished in the masters' schools at least eighty per cent!"[22]

Continuing Disputes About the Whole Word Method

Impassioned debate about whole word versus phonics as the better method for beginning reading was not confined to Mann's struggle with the Boston schoolmasters. Mann's arguments in favor of using whole words were attacked in professional journals and in papers presented to professional groups—generally by educators who still favored the older alphabetic approaches. One such critic pointed out that the letters will have to be mastered at some time in any case, that in the word method the children are not taught to master new words independently, that spelling ability is hampered, and that "The new method reduces English to the status of Chinese" (the old accusation—see pp. 168 and 178 above) "and deprives the

---

[22]Mary Mann, *Life of Horace Mann*, Lee & Shepard, Boston, 1888, p. 246.

child of all the advantage which English possesses by virtue of its being a language written in letters."[23]

The question of whether written English has large numbers of irregular patterns was addressed both by Mann and his critics, who made the same points that were to appear repeatedly in the arguments of proponents of each point of view throughout the years that followed. Thus, one eloquent supporter of first introducing children to the letters of the alphabet maintained that, "Any careful classification of the words of our language must demonstrate the fact that the anomalies are few";[24] to which Mann replied, summing up the opposite perception, "In regard to this, we think our correspondent to be in great error. The exceptions exceed the rule, immensely."[25]

---

[23]Mathews, 1966, p. 90. These objections were summarized by Samuel S. Greene in a speech before the *American Institute of Instruction* (1844).

[24]Mathews, 1966, p. 92. The author of this statement himself chose a letter—*Q*—as a pseudonym.

[25]Mathews, 1966, pp. 92–93.

Rejection of the Alphabetic Code II

Through the Nineteenth Century to Today

In the years that followed, Mann's view of English phonics increasingly prevailed. This was due in large part to the support of three powerful figures in American education. The influence of these three educators resulted in the adoption throughout America of the method of instruction associated with Mann's view, namely, the whole word approach. And despite many swings of the pendulum in different directions and to varying degrees, that view is probably the one most widely held in American schools today.[1] The three educators were Colonel Francis Parker, John Dewey, and G. Stanley Hall.

PARKER, DEWEY, AND HALL

Colonel Francis Wayland Parker (1837–1902) was the superintendent of the Quincy, Massachusetts, public schools from 1875 to 1883 and the principal of the Cook County Normal School in Chicago from 1883 to 1899. In both the Quincy and the Chicago schools he became famous for educational innovations that eventually developed into the progressive education movement. The Quincy System, as Parker's program came to be known, was characterized by a richly broadened curriculum and by minute attention paid to arousing, sustaining, and moving along with each child's interest.

Parker's position was extreme with respect to reading. Nevertheless, he and the teachers in his schools played an enormous part in the spread of the whole word

---

[1]Nevertheless, today's eclecticism makes room for strong, structured phonics instruction so that for beginning reading classes in contemporary American schools that are organized around a meaning-emphasized program, more often than not some phonics instruction is either introduced early within that program or presented alongside it by means of a supplementary program.

approach across the country. His system called for a words-to-reading approach, followed by a great stress on reading for meaning. Parker went considerably further than prior advocates of a whole word approach, particularly with respect to what had been a cornerstone of the alphabetic-spelling approach: the introduction of letter names. According to Mathews, "The names of the letters were withheld for at least the first two years to prevent the child from becoming confused about the names and sounds of the letters."[2]

Parker's influence on the teaching of reading as well as on other aspects of education was further extended when he left his post at the Chicago Normal School. At that time, he was instrumental in the establishment of the Francis Parker School, which embodied his principles of education, and he became the first director of the University of Chicago's School of Education. There, he spent the last few years of his life laying the groundwork for the institution that was to become one of the outstanding centers of American teacher education. It was at the University that Parker came into close contact with John Dewey.

Dewey (1859–1952) had come to the University of Chicago in 1894 to head the Philosophy, Psychology, and Pedagogy departments. Two years later he founded the Laboratory School there to try out his ideas about progressive education. As it happened, Dewey had been previously exposed to Parker's educational philosophies by Dewey's teacher at The Johns Hopkins University, G. Stanley Hall.

Hall (1846–1924) was a psychologist who pioneered in the field of child study. He had been trained in Germany, where he encountered the theories and some of the research methods with which he later became identified in this country. Hall, like William James, was one of the psychologists associated with the progressive education movement that arose here in the latter part of the nineteenth century. Both Hall and James stressed the importance of devising a curriculum based on a knowledge of child development. Hall felt that the school must be designed around the child's needs rather than be set up to mold a child's education according to preconceived adult goals.[3]

Hall was also interested in the teaching of reading, particularly reading instruction in Germany and other parts of Europe. He did not himself develop any one coherent theory about learning to read, although he was a confirmed supporter of Colonel Parker for many years and paid an annual visit to Cook County to see Parker's system in operation. Hall set down his ideas on reading in various published works.

Hall's writings about his study of reading began with *How to Teach Reading and What to Read in Schools* (1874) and culminated in a lengthy chapter of his major work, *Educational Problems* (1911). In that chapter, he discussed techniques used in the analytic and synthetic methods of teaching beginning reading (terms

---

[2]Mathews, 1966, p. 105. Although I did not find concrete evidence of a direct connection, this may well have been the start of the practice of withholding letter names that was characteristic of twentieth century whole word programs. It was not until the mid-1950s, with Donald Durrell and others at Boston University, that the teaching of letter names began to regain a measure of respectability among some whole word advocates. (See Chall, 1967, pp. 153–156.) In contemporary "linguistic" programs like the Bloomfield-Barnhart and the Fries/Merrill programs, however, which stem from entirely different historical referents, letter names are introduced and stressed from the very start. Also, see Richard L. Venezky, "The Curious Role of Letter Names in Reading Instruction," *Visible Language*, Vol. 9, No. 1, Winter 1975, pp. 7–23.

[3]Diane Ravitch, *The Great School Wars*, Basic Books, New York, 1974, p. 111.

Hall apparently coined)[4] and then went on to minimize the importance of learning to read at an early age. Hall argued, on the one hand, that it was possible to be illiterate and yet be happy, well educated, and even to achieve great eminence. On the other hand, he stated that learning to read was not difficult and could be postponed until a child's interest was high. (It is easy to see the connection between these views of Hall's and the ultimate intertwining of the reading readiness concept and the whole word approach.)

Through their professional respect for each other and the interchange of their ideas, the three men—Parker, Hall, and Dewey—came to have similar beliefs about reading and its place in the curriculum. Those beliefs, involving a whole word approach within a child-centered, incidental-learning curriculum rather than a pre-structured curriculum, were incorporated into the progressive education movement as it advanced from the late nineteenth century into the first decades of the twentieth century.

EDMUND BURKE HUEY

One other turn-of-the-century enthusiast of whole word reading for meaning should be mentioned: Edmund Burke Huey, professor of psychology and education at the Western University of Pennsylvania and author of *The Psychology and Pedagogy of Reading* (1908).[5] Huey was much influenced by Hall and a number of other researchers in psychology who were then engaged in investigations of reading processes. In his book, Huey presents a full description of his era's "reading for meaning" philosophy as well as of the setting in which he perceived the philosophy to have emerged. This work has seen a renaissance within the past 20 years—starting with an attack by Flesch, who practically accuses Huey of insanity in the latter's enthusiasm for the word method.[6] Frank Smith, a more recent champion of Huey's ideas, refers to Huey's book as "brilliant" and "a milestone," noting that it was republished in 1968 "not as a monument but as a book whose time has come."[7]

TWENTIETH CENTURY DEVELOPMENT OF WHOLE WORD READING INSTRUCTION

Upon Parker's death in 1902, Dewey was appointed to succeed him as director of the University of Chicago's School of Education.[8] In 1904, Dewey left this post for an appointment as professor of philosophy at Columbia University in New York City, where he remained for the rest of his life.

---

[4]Mathews, 1966, p. 133.
[5]Reissued in 1968 by Macmillan, New York.
[6]Flesch, 1955, pp. 52–53.
[7]Frank Smith, *Understanding Reading*, Holt, Rinehart and Winston, New York, 1971, p. 10.
[8]Robert L. McCaul, "Dewey and the University of Chicago," *School and Society*, March 25, 1961, p. 152.

Both in Chicago and in New York, Dewey exerted great influence on the educational philosophy of his colleagues and students, and thus on the training of teachers and administrators throughout the country. His advocacy of the whole word reading approach in the progressive education curriculum, while not precisely spelled out by Dewey (who was mainly concerned with the child-centered aspect of schooling), was picked up and widely promulgated. Although its spread met resistance from those who had been trained in and were faithful to the phonics approach, the whole word reading aspect of the progressive education movement gradually reached every corner of the country. By 1920, while there was still a good deal of phonics instruction in the schools, the "in" theoretical approach was the whole word approach. From about 1920 on, leaders in the field of reading began to attack the extensive phonics practice that still existed and that was even advocated in the commercial published reading programs.[9]

Gray and Gates

The two foremost leaders in reading education between 1920 and 1960 were persons who had felt Dewey's influence keenly. One was William S. Gray (1885–1960), dean of the University of Chicago's School of Education from 1918 to 1931 and then director of teacher education there. The other was Arthur I. Gates (1890–1976), director of the Institute of Educational Research at Columbia University from 1921 to 1930 and subsequently head of several key educational and research programs there.[10] In these important posts of higher education as well as through their authoritative contributions to key professional groups, both men were responsible for the attitudes toward reading instruction of teachers, administrators, researchers, and trainers of teachers throughout the United States as well as of many foreign educators who came to study at American colleges of education.

William Gray's beliefs about reading instruction came to be wholly centered on whole word reading, for either traditional or progressive education, and by minutely spelling out its methodology, he eventually formalized the twentieth century whole word doctrine in its most widely used form. Through the reading series he authored for the Scott, Foresman publishing company—*Curriculum Foundations*[11]—he made into household words the names of the series' main characters, Dick and Jane, and the approach to reading instruction they represent. Both in the teacher's guidebooks to this series and in his *On Their Own in Reading*,[12] written in his later years, Gray (and the authors writing the guidebooks under his aegis) listed step-by-step instructions for each aspect of a whole word program. He focused solely on the teacher's careful planning and control of each step of instruction, with almost no provision for incidental or divergent learning by children—a

---

[9]Chall, 1967, p. 133.

[10]Arthur I. Gates, "An Autobiography," *Leaders in American Education,* Seventieth Yearbook of the National Society for the Study of Education, Part II, University of Chicago Press, 1971, pp. 189–216.

[11]William S. Gray et al., *Curriculum Foundation Series,* Scott, Foresman and Company, Glenview, IL, various editions from 1940. Earlier, Gray was co-author with William Elson of the 1930 edition of the Scott, Foresman reading program, whose original copyright was 1912 (Chall, 1967, pp. 96, n.75, 328, and 334).

[12]William S. Gray, *On Their Own in Reading,* Scott, Foresman and Company, Glenview, IL, 1948, 1960.

radical departure from the nineteenth century progressive education philosophy. Nevertheless, he retained the earlier movement's whole word reading tenet and its practice of postponing the introduction of formal reading as part of the reading-readiness concept.[13] Gray's approach, followed by practically all the authors of the most widely used, commercially published reading programs, remained almost un-challenged as the second quarter of the twentieth century advanced.

Arthur Gates is described by Chall as "the most productive and creative re-search scholar both in reading and in other areas of educational and psychological research" since the 1920s.[14] He was also the senior author of a number of editions of the Macmillan basal reading series and was committed to the analytic approach. While his research and experience led him to realize the value of phonics for help-ing students recognize and pronounce words, Gates still maintained that "the sug-gestion that it [phonics] should usually be given such early and emphatic attention as to become the major approach to learning to read is one we cannot accept."[15]

With such staunch support, the analytic approach that was translated into the standard basal reading programs of the second quarter of the twentieth century re-tained its adherents even after the other features of the progressive education movement had receded from the center stage of conventional educational theory and practice. In 1964 it was reported that "basal readers from a graded series are used by 98 percent of first grade teachers."[16] True, after Flesch presented his alter-native view in 1955, (to the public at large rather than solely to a professional or scholarly community) a number of challenges and examinations of the basal reader/whole word method began to appear. Nevertheless, it was more than 10 years after Flesch before the powerful hold of the prevailing view began to loosen. At that time, Chall's classic study of the "great debate" about beginning reading[17] and the U.S. Of-fice of Education's studies of first grade reading[18] gave impetus and much greater respectability to alternative approaches.

Current Advocates of a Logographic Approach to Reading

At the present time, the heirs of Gedike, Mann, Dewey, Parker, Huey, Gray, et al., tend to call upon some of the recent linguistic and psycholinguistic[19] thinking in

---

[13]Chall, 1967, p. 153.
[14]Chall, 1967, p. 153.
[15]Chall, 1967, p. 153.
[16]Allen H. Barton and David E. Wilder, "Research and Practice in the Teaching of Reading: A Progress Report," in *Innovation in Education*, M.B. Miles (Ed.), Teachers College Press, New York, 1964. Quoted in Chall, 1967, p. 188.
[17]Chall, 1967.
[18]See Guy L. Bond and Robert Dykstra, "The Cooperative Research Program in First-Grade Instruc-tion," *Reading Research Quarterly*, Summer 1967, pp. 5–142.
[19]*Psycholinguistics* is a term coined in the early 1950s by the Social Science Research Council's Committee on Linguistics and Psychology as it sought to lay the groundwork for collaboration between the separate disciplines of structural linguistics and behavioral psychology to help solve a number of basic problems about language. See Sol Saporta (Ed.), *Psycholinguistics*, Holt, Rinehart and Winston, New York, 1961, Preface. A considerable body of psycholinguistic literature has been produced since that time by those who have combined the two disciplines in their work. John B. Carroll gives an excel-lent portrait of the early meshing of the two disciplines in *The Study of Language*, Harvard University Press, Cambridge, MA, 1955.

support of their view. Frank Smith (see p. 189 above) and Kenneth Goodman are among the most widely read authors in this group. Although they also include specific variations from the arguments of many of the earlier whole word advocates, Smith and Goodman, in a joint article, present what can only be interpreted as an analytic approach: "The child learning to read, like the child learning to speak, seems to need the opportunity to examine a large sample of language, to generate hypotheses about the regularities underlying it, and to test and modify these hypotheses on the basis of feedback that is appropriate to the unspoken rules he happens to be testing."[20]

Central to this contemporary form of the third, logographic, view is the concept that the written forms and sound–letter correspondences of individual words are only one aspect of reading. There are other vital aspects, namely, the syntax (or grammatical structure) of the material read and the semantics (or specific meanings implied by the author and inferred by the reader). In teaching children to read, phonics are to be minimized and new readers are to be given much opportunity to do exploratory reading of useful and relevant material.

In another article, Goodman himself once more brings up the old allusion to the Chinese writing system,[21] this time in a salutatory rather than in the derogatory way that phonics advocates have traditionally referred to it. Goodman notes, "The Chinese writing system may indeed have its faults but it has the virtue of being understood by speakers of oral languages which are not mutually comprehensible. And, of course, the Chinese writing system—once it is mastered—does function quite well for its users."[22]

It is not surprising that Goodman is one of the authors of the Scott, Foresman beginning reading program, *Reading Systems.*[23] In addition to great emphasis on reading for meaning, he advocates the stress on reading readiness associated with whole word programs. (In clear contrast, Flesch defines *reading readiness* as "the readiness of the *teacher* to let the child start reading.")[24]

On the question of sound–letter correspondences in English, Goodman and his associates consider them "unreliable" and note that many of the generalizations in old phonics programs are also unreliable—as well as being unscientific. Frank Smith goes even further, dismissing even the possibility of ever establishing such correspondences: "To suggest that accurate sounds can be reconstructed from the alphabetic representation is like suggesting that flour, eggs, and water can be reconstructed from cake."[25]

However, Goodman and his associates, as does Frank Smith, reject an exclusively whole word approach as firmly as they do a phonics approach, stating, "The assumed controversy between phonics and whole-word approaches to reading in reality turns out to be two sides to the same coin. Both treat words as ends in themselves. With phonics, words are assaulted letter by letter, whereas whole-word ap-

---

[20]Frank Smith (with Kenneth S. Goodman), "On the Psycholinguistic Method of Teaching Reading," in *Psycholinguistics and Reading*, Frank Smith (Ed.), Holt, Rinehart and Winston, New York, 1973, p. 180.

[21]See above, pp. 168, 178, and 184, for earlier allusions.

[22]Kenneth Goodman, "Psychological Universals in the Reading Process," in Frank Smith, 1973, p. 25.

[23]Scott, Foresman and Company, *Scott, Foresman Reading Systems*, Scott, Foresman and Company, Glenview, IL, 1971.

[24]Flesch, 1955, p. 70.

[25]Frank Smith, 1973, p. 128.

proaches take them in bite-size pieces. But reading in both cases is assumed to be naming words."[26]

Following from this, they do not advocate breaking the reading process into skills of word analysis or of comprehension—thereby differing significantly from Gray, who set down careful, step-by-step instructions for teaching specific skills. While they agree that there are patterns in language (of which phonemic patterns are only one aspect), they emphasize that a reader calls upon strategies other than language patterns. They point especially to the reader's own background of concepts and meaning and advocate that teachers focus less on word analysis skills (including phonics) and make greater use of reading for meaning.

Because of this variation, Goodman and Smith are removed from the direct descendants of Gray and his followers. Their views are most consonant (though not identical) with the views of Huey[27] and with the language experience philosophy on reading that originally evolved from the progressive education movement.[28] This philosophy was based on the idea that "Reading is developing meaning from patterns of symbols which one recognizes and endows with meaning. *Reading arouses or calls up meanings*. It does not provide them."[29]

---

[26]E. Brooks Smith, Kenneth S. Goodman, and Robert Meredith, *Language and Thinking in School*, Holt, Rinehart and Winston, New York, 1976, p. 271.

[27]This similarity is also noted by Popp, 1975, p. 105, n. 6.

[28]For details of this language experience approach, see Lillian A. Lamoreaux and Dorris M. Lee, *Learning to Read Through Experience*, Appleton, Century, New York, 1943. Revised by Dorris M. Lee and R.V. Allen, Appleton-Century-Crofts, New York, 1963.

[29]Lamoureaux and Lee, 1963, p. 2.

26

Emphasizing Regular Patterns First

Those who had the fourth and fifth reactions to written English came on the scene somewhat later than the first advocates of an analytic approach.

THE FOURTH REACTION:
EMPHASIZING REGULAR PATTERNS FIRST

Those in the fourth group were also much concerned with the problem of teaching young children to read written English—riddled, as most of them perceived it to be, with irregular patterns. The solution of the fourth group was to separate the regular from the irregular patterns and then to start reading instruction by presenting only regular patterns.[1] The linguists Leonard Bloomfield and Charles Fries were the most distinguished members of this group, although a low-keyed schoolmaster tradition in a similar vein went back to the early nineteenth century.

According to Mathews, the first person to set down the idea of initially introducing only regularly spelled words was Joseph Neef, an educator from Alsace who came to Philadelphia in 1806. Seven years later, Neef published a book on English reading instruction in which he awkwardly tried to translate his idea for sequencing regularly spelled words. Neef's work had little impact. Mathews flatly states: "His book appears to have failed utterly in arousing either interest or understanding."[2]

A few other efforts along the same lines appeared occasionally during the nineteenth century, but were never pursued with sufficient vigor to have any appreciable effect. In his Seventh Annual Report (see pp. 182–183 above), Horace Mann

---

[1]Here and elsewhere in these discussions, the terms *regular* and *irregular* are used as they were by the members of each group. In every case, such use should be considered wholly subjective—simply reflecting the perceptions of the members of the groups.

[2]Mathews, 1966, p. 153.

suggested that regular words be introduced first as part of the word method he advocates. That recommendation, however, was overshadowed by his emphasis on the importance of meaning.

Leonard Bloomfield

It was not until 1933 that a champion appeared for this fourth way of dealing with the existence of both phonemic and nonphonemic patterns in written English. In that year, Leonard Bloomfield, called "the father of modern American descriptive linguistics,"[3] published his major book, *Language*.[4] In it, Bloomfield recorded a comprehensive picture of the state of linguistic science at that time. In it may also be found a discussion of what Bloomfield saw as the implications of linguistic findings for various aspects of education—including reading.[5]

Like all those we have discussed up to now, Bloomfield was displeased with the nonphonemic forms of written English. He commented, "When one sees the admirably consistent orthographies of Spanish, Bohemian, or Finnish, one naturally wishes that a similar system might be adopted for English."[6] Moreover, contrary to Frank Smith's rejection of the possibility of devising an alphabet that would represent speech sounds accurately (see p. 192 above), Bloomfield maintained that "There would be no serious difficulty about devising a simple, effective orthography for all types of standard English."[7] Because of the insurmountable economic and political resistance such drastic action would meet, however, he saw no hope in trying to make a radical change. He also felt that a compromise solution of making selected, fragmentary changes would probably do more harm than good because of the overlapping and intricacies of many existing patterns.

Bloomfield also rejected the arguments of those who praise the values of nonphonemic patterns (pp. 201–205 below). He asserted that the advantages of some such patterns (for example, homonyms like *hear–here*) are balanced by the disadvantages of others (homographs like *read* and *tear*). He dismissed the arguments that certain historic spelling patterns add richness to the meanings of certain words by pointing out that the number of those who might benefit from the nonphonemic information of such patterns is limited to a small number of educated adults. A much larger and more important group are the many children who must learn to read the language.

Bloomfield's ideas about teaching children to read were based upon his perception that, in addition to its many unfortunate irregularities, English spelling contains many phonemically spelled words as well. He suggested that words with totally phonemic patterns be taught first, in sets similar to *word families*[8] (although he did not use that traditional schoolteacher term). Sets with an irregular pattern, such as

---

[3]Josef Vachek, *Written Language*, Mouton, The Hague, 1973, p. 11.
[4]Bloomfield, 1933.
[5]Bloomfield, 1933, pp. 499–503.
[6]Bloomfield, 1933, p. 501.
[7]Bloomfield, 1933, p. 502.
[8]That is, *bat, cat, hat,* and so forth.

fight, light, might and so forth, and various other nonphonemic words should be introduced systematically, with the precise sequences and times of introduction determined by experimentation based on rational linguistic understanding. Letters with deviant phonemic values might be distinguished by some mark or color.[9]

Bloomfield translated his ideas into practice by teaching his own son to read, setting down a series of lessons based on the process he recommends. Not long after (1937), he gave his notes describing these lessons to Clarence Barnhart, the lexicographer, who then used Bloomfield's approach to teach his own son to read. Encouraged by these successes, the two men decided to try out the method with larger numbers of children and sought professional and commercial help to do so. Unfortunately, the forces supporting the whole word approach were so entrenched that even these eminent men were unable to find substantial sponsorship. Only one small group of parochial school children in Chicago was exposed to Bloomfield's method—successfully, according to Barnhart.[10]

Twenty years later, after Flesch's great splash had induced a more receptive climate, Bloomfield's clearly expounded theory and specific exercises were published posthumously in the book *Let's Read* (1961). Clarence Barnhart later expanded the exercises into a commercially published series that has been used in various schools in the United States and in other English-speaking countries.[11]

Charles Fries

Charles Fries was another advocate of Bloomfield's view. He declared that, "English is very distinctly less well spelled than most of the languages using the Greco-Roman alphabet. But the view that English spelling is completely erratic or that it is so erratic that we must forego all the advantage of an alphabetic system is entirely without foundation."[12] Like Bloomfield, Fries was interested in beginning reading and was responsible for a reading series, the Merrill Linguistic Readers, which appeared soon after Barnhart published Bloomfield's approach.[13]

In order to demonstrate existing English language patterns, both spoken and written, Fries structured his materials even more purely than Bloomfield and from almost the very beginning, differentiated phonemic from nonphonemically spelled words. One striking feature both series have in common is the absence of pictures in the basic reading books—consistent with their views that pictures interfere with the new reader's concentration on the printed material. Fries's program was widely distributed and may still be found in schools throughout the country.

---

[9]These were far from new ideas—the use of marks was characteristic of many of the old alternative and modified alphabets, while color coding was used at least as early as the turn of the century.

[10]Bloomfield and Barnhart, 1961, pp. 12–15. Ironically, one of the few who tried out Bloomfield's method was Rudolf Flesch. Flesch read Bloomfield's article of 1942, used the method with his own daughter, and, Flesch states, "that's what started me on this whole business." (Flesch, 1955, p. 9.)

[11]Bloomfield and Barnhart, *Let's Read* series.

[12]Fries, 1963, p. 161.

[13]Fries, et al., 1967. Fries's ideas about reading are fully set down in his rich little book, *Linguistics and Reading* (1963).

Richard L. Venezky

Richard L. Venezky was a contemporary linguist who was engaged in evolving his views on how the structure of written English affects the reading process. His reactions are probably most akin to those of Leonard Bloomfield, although Venezky was much more cheerful in his appraisal of English spelling—perhaps because he found a fairly large number of patterns he considered regular.

Venezky's determination of which patterns are regular was based on more than letter–sound correspondences. He expanded the concept of regular phonemic patterns to include such patterns as soft and hard *c* and *g*. Because they appear in very specific positions within written words, he considered them to be phonemically regular.

Venezky further broadened his definition of *regularity* by maintaining that, "Whatever may have been the relationship between writing and sound when the first Old English writings were inscribed in Latin script and whatever may have been the reason for the subsequent development of this system, be they due to random choice or to an all-pervading National Orthographic Character, the simple fact is that the present orthography is not merely a letter-to-sound system riddled with imperfections, but, instead, a more complex and more regular relationship wherein phoneme and morpheme share leading roles."[14]

To understand Venezky's position on English orthography fully, as well as the positions of a number of other linguists, a complex but important modern linguistic concept needs to be explained—the concept of the morpheme.

Definition of Morpheme

A *morpheme*, like a grapheme and a phoneme (pp. 8–9 and 27–28 above) is a group of language units that in a given language are treated as if they were the same unit. Whereas phonemes are groups of related speech sounds (or *phones*), and graphemes are groups of related written forms (or *graphs*), morphemes are groups of related meanings or ideas (called *morphs*). Thus, each of the following English words ends with a morph that is pronounced differently, or spelled differently, or both. Each final morph, however, has the same meaning—that of plurality: *books* (final -*s* as in *this*), *bells* (final -*s* as in *was*), *peaches* (final -*es*), *oxen* (final -*en*), *fungi* (final -*i*), *criteria* (final -*a*), and *alumnae* (final -*ae*).

Each of these related endings is called an *allomorph* (parallel to allophone and allograph) of the same morpheme. (Note, however, that any of these endings may also occur as part or all of a different allomorph of a different morpheme. Thus, the *s* in *writes* is not an allomorph of the plurality morpheme but of another morpheme conveying the present singular of a verb. Similarly, the *en* in the word *hen* has nothing to do with plurality but is part of an allomorph of another morpheme that means a female domestic fowl.)

Morphemes may consist of entire words (called *stems* in this context) or of meaningful parts of words, namely, prefixes, suffixes, and bases. For example, the

---

[14]Richard L. Venezky, "English Orthography: Its Graphical Structure and Its Relation to Sound," *Reading Research Quarterly*, Spring 1967, p. 77.

prefix *in-* in the word *incomplete* is an allomorph of a morpheme meaning "not," and the base *-ceas-* in the word *unceasingly* is an allomorph of a morpheme meaning "stop." (Bases are frequently, although not always, capable of standing as an independent word, called a *free allomorph*; affixes, on the other hand, invariably appear with a base and are called *bound allomorphs*.) Any single word may contain one or more morphemes.

Just as suprasegmental graphemes and phonemes (see pp. 8 and 28 n. 2 above) occur simultaneously with the segmental graphemes and phonemes, suprasegmental morphemes occur as tones or pauses that convey identifiable meanings and emotions. Some suprasegmental morphemes are written as punctuation marks (e.g., *?* conveys the idea of questioning) or as spaces (conveying the idea of separation between units of language). It is not surprising that the number of morphemes of English, as of every language, is exceedingly large—far larger and much more difficult to list than are the graphemes and phonemes.

Venezky and Morphophonemic Relationships

When Venezky stated that morphemes as well as phonemes share leading roles in our present orthography, he was referring to the fact that certain morphemes change their spoken, phonemic forms but keep their written spellings. Thus, in the words *know* and *knowledge*, the morpheme represented by the grapheme *know* is pronounced differently. Linguists have been able to identify certain patterns of such phonemic change. The study of the patterns of how and when morphemes change phonemically within words or sentences is called *morphophonemics*. The formal study of morphophonemics is relatively new, although informal awareness of the existence of morphemic spelling patterns goes back further in time (see pp. 202–203 below).

For linguists who, like Venezky, are concerned with spelling, the recent morphophonemic studies have added a striking dimension to the assessment of written English. They note that it can be helpful to readers when the same spelling is kept for the same morpheme, despite variations in pronunciation. Such spellings supply clues to the meanings of words, clues that would be lost if the words were spelled phonemically, as, for example, if *know* and *knowledge* were spelled *noe* and *nollij* in a hypothetical phonemic system.

Not all linguists consider such clues to be equally valuable, however. Bloomfield, for example, as noted above (p. 196), believed that much of the nonphonemic morphemic information was useful only to a limited number of adult readers. On the other hand, those in the fifth category, discussed in the next chapter, find the retention of graphemic forms despite changes in pronunciation to be one of the great advantages of our spelling system.

Venezky, as the quotation on p. 198 indicates, took a middle view. He believed that both the phonemic and the morphemic patterns of written English play important parts and that both exist with a much greater degree of consistency than superficial observation would lead one to believe.

Venezky himself went much beyond superficial examination, having done an exhaustive study of the English spelling patterns.[15] He supplemented his examina-

---

[15]Venezky, 1965, 1970.

tion of the spelling forms themselves with additional data derived from experiments with live readers, to help his goal of constructing "a model of the reader's knowledge of orthographic regularity."[16]

It is because of this goal that Venezky is included in the fourth category: he tried to determine the best ways to capitalize on existing phonemic and morphemic spellings to help the reading process. Like Bloomfield, Venezky rejected the idea of total alphabet reform, although he was not averse to certain very specific alterations (e.g., dropping the *b* in *debt, doubt,* and *subtle*).[17]

Venezky did not come out with any clearly delineated program or sequence for teaching reading. His speculations, however, included the necessity of ensuring awareness of the patterns of written English. Although he accepted the idea that some readers may acquire this awareness as a result of their exposure to reading, as Goodman and Smith advise, Venezky seemed much more inclined to take instructional steps to make sure that the awareness does indeed take place. Yet, although Venezky was more positive about the nonphonemic patterns than many of those with whom I have grouped him, he still seemed to see the patterns as difficulties to be mastered, rather than as the happy helps they are considered to be by those in the fifth group, described in Chapter 27.

---

[16]Richard L. Venezky, *The Role of Orthographic Regularity in Word Recognition*, Working Paper No. 181, Wisconsin Research and Development Center for Cognitive Learning, November 1976, p. 47.

[17]Venezky, 1970, p. 123.

27

Nonphonemic Spelling Patterns as an Advantage of Written English

In the fifth reaction to nonphonemic English spelling patterns, such patterns are seen as positive, useful assets rather than as problems to be eliminated, modified, ignored, or worked around. This fifth reaction may best be presented by quoting a statement by two of its most prominent contemporary advocates, Noam Chomsky and Morris Halle. They write, "It is . . . noteworthy . . . that English orthography, despite its often cited inconsistencies, comes remarkably close to being an optimal orthographic system for English."[1]

In this view, emphasis is placed on the fact that morphemic spellings (such as the example given above of *know–knowledge*) convey meanings and relationships that would be lost if the two words were spelled with complete letter–sound correspondence. Also, many homonyms are clearly differentiated in our written language even though they are identical when spoken aloud. In such cases, retaining the different spellings is very helpful. Consider this sentence, for example: *The coal seller placed a load of coal in the coal cellar.* Upon hearing it spoken, one would have to think a moment to straighten out its meaning. The reader, however, grasps it immediately, probably without even realizing that the sentence is unusual in any way.

Another aspect of English spelling is the existence of what Bolinger calls "visual morphemes,"[2] that is, spelling patterns that convey emotional or cultural meanings despite their lack of precise letter–sound correspondence. Vachek gives

---

[1]Noam Chomsky and Morris Halle, *The Sound Pattern of English*, Harper & Row, New York, 1968, p. 49.

[2]Dwight L. Bolinger, "Visual Morphemes," *Language*, Vol. 22, 1946, pp. 333–340.

the example of the initial *gh* spellings on *ghastly, ghost, ghetto,* and *ghoul,* "which undoubtedly underline the strongly negative emotional colouring."[3] Similarly, the final *or* allomorph of the morpheme that means "one who" (as in *actor)* has been termed "a visual morpheme of prestige."[4] (Contrast *author* and *sculptor* with *writer* and *painter.*)

INITIAL APPEARANCE OF THE FIFTH VIEW

According to Scragg,[5] the foundation of this fifth view was laid by Henry Bradley, one of the editors of the *Oxford English Dictionary* (see p. 136 above). Bradley was apparently the first to allude to the values of nonphonemic spellings. In his book, *The Making of English,* he points out that the different spellings of words that are pronounced in the same way (i.e., homonyms) are generally the result of historical occurrences. Although at that time Bradley was experiencing the prevailing discouragement with English spelling, he was yet moved to note that these differences in spelling have "the merit of saving written English from a good many of the ambiguities of the spoken tongue."[6]

In time, Bradley came to hold even stronger views about the relative value of letter–sound correspondences. In 1913, speaking before the International Historical Congress, he said, "Many of the advocates of spelling reform are in the habit of asserting, as if it were an axiom admitting of no dispute, that the sole function of writing is to represent sounds. It appears to me that this is one of those spurious truisms that are not intelligently believed by any one, but which continue to be repeated because nobody takes the trouble to consider what they really mean."[7]

Bradley followed this statement by describing characteristics of written English that differentiate it from spoken English, many of which are advantageous to the reader. He did not go so far in his praise of English spelling as Chomsky and Halle, however. Rather, Bradley differentiated (as did Bloomfield later on—see p. 196 above) between the needs of the young learner and those of an "educated adult," noting that while the advanced reader can benefit greatly from the existing homonyms and familiar syllabic configurations, the beginner has vast problems with unphonetic spellings.

William Craigie, another editor of the *Oxford English Dictionary* also developed an optimistic picture of nonphonemic spellings. He approached the matter by examining the history of the language and then, in his book on English spelling (1927), tried "to give a clear and concise account of the several elements which have combined to produce the great variety so noticeable in the spelling of English." He continued by pointing out that, "The results of this combination are frequently so contradictory, and so incapable of being reduced to any one rule, that they have naturally created an impression that English spelling is a hopeless chaos. The first step

---

[3]Vachek, 1973, pp. 55–56.

[4]Raven I. McDavid, Jr., "Adviser and Advisor: Orthographic and Semantic Differentiation," *Studies in Linguistics 1.7,* New Haven, CT, 1942 (quoted in Vachek, 1973, p. 56n.).

[5]Scragg, 1974, pp. 114–115.

[6]Henry Bradley, *The Making of English,* Macmillan, New York, 1904, p. 212.

[7]Scragg, 1974, p. 114.

towards correcting that impression is to obtain a clear idea of the reasons for the variety in the forms, and of the sources from which they are usually derived. It will then be seen that most of the peculiarities have a historical basis, and to that extent are legitimate, however much they may be in opposition to each other and to the pronunciation of the present day."[8]

Craigie categorized English spellings into three major types, according to the origin and the pattern of the spelling. Many patterns that he identified within those types may be seen, in historical context, to have more order than is apparent from noting their letter–sound relationships. Craigie's three major English spelling types are: 1) native and allied normal types (for the most part, those that go back to Old English, Old French, and other Germanic languages, such as the Scandinavian); 2) classical and Romantic types (that is, words that entered at various times from French, Latin, and Greek); and 3) what Craigie calls exotic types (words from languages all over the world, in which either the foreign spellings or specific representations of the foreign pronunciations are to be found; e.g., the *c* in *cello*, the *aa* in *bazaar*, the *kh* in *khaki*, the *ll* in *llama*, and so on).

As a consequence of his study of spelling, Craigie's championing of nonphonemic spellings grew. In subsequent works, he pointed out the advantages of nonphonemic spellings and the difficulties that would arise if historical spellings were to be "reformed" into strict letter–sound correspondence.[9]

RECENT APPROVAL OF ENGLISH SPELLING

Other advocates of this view continued to appear throughout the next 2 decades. In the main, they have been linguists like Joseph Vachek and others listed by him who, though initially concerned with theoretical research on the subject of written English, have found themselves to be voices "defending present-day English spelling against the accusations usually brought forward against it."[10]

There has been relatively little communication between the linguists in this group and teachers of reading, however. Of those named by Vachek, for example, most are foreign linguists, writing in a variety of foreign scholarly journals. Rarely, in fact, have those who actually taught reading ended up as adherents of this fifth view of written English. Instead, such linguists as Bloomfield and Fries—who were deeply immersed in the complexities of devising a beginning reading program— were apt to see nonphonemic patterns as hurdles rather than aids for beginning readers (see p. 196 above).

While Chomsky and Halle, noted earlier for their enthusiasm about English orthography (p. 201 above) belong in this fifth category, Vachek only grudgingly accedes to their presence. In a tone reminiscent of those caught up in the "great debate" about phonics versus whole words, Vachek rejects one of their basic concepts and states, "Clearly, as a piece of apology for present-day English spelling, the argu-

---

[8]William A. Craigie, *English Spelling*, F.S. Crofts, New York, 1927, p. 1.
[9]Scragg, 1974, pp. 115–116.
[10]Vachek, 1973, p. 67.

mentation adduced by Chomsky and Halle is hardly convincing, and if it is mentioned here this is only done for the sake of completeness."[11]

In any case, Chomsky, like the other linguists in this group, does not associate his work on the structuring of the English sound system with the teaching of reading. However, Chomsky's study led him to certain theoretical constructions that have been seen as relevant to reading instruction. His study of phonology, for example, led him to perceive the existence of many complex phonological and spelling patterns, somewhat differently approached from the historical patterns discerned by the others in this fifth group. His view (which encouraged him and Halle to make the statement quoted above regarding the excellence of the English writing system) is supportive of those who have unearthed a considerably larger number of patterns than were thought to exist.

Those who stress reading for meaning have used as supportive of their view Chomsky's conception of the simultaneous existence of both deep and surface structures in language. That is, the idea that each utterance contains an underlying or deep meaning that is expressed in one of various possible sequences and syntactical forms. The specific sequence and syntax used comprises the surface structure of that utterance. Since "separate" is never "equal," it is easy to see how separating spoken language into these two levels might elevate one—the "deep" or meaningful part—over the other, called "surface" and implying "superficial." Thus, in reading instruction, focusing on meaning might seem to be more desirable than stressing surface forms.[12]

That is not Chomsky's view, however. His position on beginning reading instruction is actually close to Bloomfield's, namely, phonemically regular words should be taught first (although Bloomfield had a different perception of the regularity of written English—see p. 196 above). Chomsky certainly does not advocate an early emphasis on reading for meaning. Moreover, he disavows efforts to link his work with children's learning to read. In an invitational essay written as the first paper in a book entitled *Basic Studies on Reading*,[13] he concludes that, although there seem to be useful relationships among children's speech, general speech, and language perception and usage, and although his study may have important implications for human psychology, "For the moment, our understanding of sound structure does not, so far as I can see, lead to any very surprising conclusions regarding the problems of literacy or teaching of reading. It may very well be that one of the best ways to teach reading is to enrich the child's vocabulary, so that he constructs for himself the deeper representations of sound that correspond so closely to the orthographic forms. At the earliest stages, one would obviously make use of materials that do not involve abstract processes and do not depart too far from the surface phonetics. Beyond such relative banalities, I do not see what concrete conclusions can be drawn, for the teaching of reading, from the study of sound structure."[14]

---

[11]Vachek, 1973, p. 68.

[12]See p. 182 above on Horace Mann's separation of reading into "mechanical" and "mental."

[13]Harry Levin and Joanna P. Williams (Eds.), *Basic Studies on Reading*, Basic Books, New York, 1970.

[14]Noam Chomsky, "Phonology and Reading," in Levin and Williams, 1970, p. 18.

Despite this disclaimer, Chomsky has had great influence on the psycholinguists and educators who are interested in reading and, through them, a number of his concepts about language have made their way into the current literature of the reading field.

• • • • •

The foregoing summary of the five reactions to English phonics brings the body of the book to a close. Only a brief epilogue remains.

Epilogue

The goal of this book was to share a universe of interrelated spheres of history and scholarship. How to make use of the book's contents is best left to the judgment of each reader. No effort at critique or summary will be made here. My only concern at this point is one that has been expressed by authors of other comprehensive works: Despite painstaking scrutiny and consultation, inaccuracies may lurk on these pages. Diringer, at the end of *The Alphabet*, addresses the problem most aptly: "The necessity of brevity and simplicity may have led to false impressions. Indeed, it may be presumptuous to attempt so brief a survey as this of such a vast field. Yet, it is to be hoped that, in some measure, the chief purposes may be served no matter what the faults may be."[1]

---

[1]Diringer, 1968, p. 443.

Bibliography

Adams, Eleanor N.: *Old English Scholarship in England From 1566–1800*, Yale University Press, New Haven, 1917. (Reprinted by Archon, 1970)

Aukerman, Robert C.: *Approaches to Beginning Reading*, John Wiley, New York, 1971.

Bailey, Nathan: *An Universal Etymological English Dictionary*, London, 1721.

Balmuth, Miriam: "Reading Comprehension: Reading or Comprehension?," in *Literacy at All Levels*, Vera Southgate (Ed.), Ward Locke, London, 1972.

Barnhart, Clarence L.: *American College Dictionary*, Random House, New York, 1947.

Bartlett, John: *Familiar Quotations*, 14th ed. Emily Morison Beck (Ed.), Little, Brown, Boston, 1968.

Barton, Allen H. and David E. Wilder: "Research and Practice in the Teaching of Reading: A Progress Report," in *Innovation in Education*, M.B. Miles (Ed.), Teachers College Press, New York, 1964.

Baugh, Alfred C.: *A History of the English Language*, Appleton-Century-Crofts, New York, 1957.

Bede: *A History of the English Church and People*, Leo Sherley-Price (Trans.), Penguin Books, Harmondsworth, England, 1955.

Bennett, Paul A. (Ed.): *Books and Printing*, World Publishing Company, Cleveland, 1951.

Betts, Emmett Albert: "The Improvement of Reading in Elementary Schools," *The Educational Record Supplement for January, 1948*, pp. 141–161.

Blair, Peter Hunter: *An Introduction to Anglo-Saxon England*, 2nd ed., Cambridge University Press, London, 1977.

Bloomfield, Leonard: *Language*, Holt, New York, 1933.

Bloomfield, Leonard: "Teaching Children to Read," essay in Leonard Bloomfield and Clarence L. Barnhart, *Let's Read: A Linguistic Approach*, Wayne State University Press, Detroit, 1961. (Parts of this essay appeared as an article entitled "Linguistics and Reading," in *The Elementary English Review*, Vol. 19, No. 4, April 1942, pp. 125–130, and Vol. 19, No. 5, May 1942, pp. 183–186.)

Bloomfield, Leonard and Clarence Barnhart: *Let's Read: A Linguistic Approach*, Wayne State University Press, Detroit, 1961.

Bloomfield, Leonard and Clarence Barnhart: *Let's Read* (series), Clarence L. Barnhart, Inc., Bronxville, New York, 1966.

Bloomfield, Morton W. and Leonard Newmark: *A Linguistic Introduction to the History of English*, Knopf, New York, 1963.

Blount, Thomas: *Glossographia*, Thomas Newcomb, London, 1656.

Bolinger, Dwight L.: "Visual Morphemes," *Language*, Vol. 22, 1946, pp. 333–340.

Bolinger, Dwight L.: *Aspects of Language*, Harcourt Brace Jovanovich, New York, 1975.

Bond, Guy L. and Robert Dykstra: "The Cooperative Research Program in First-Grade Reading Instruction," *Reading Research Quarterly*, Summer 1967, pp. 5–142.

Borden, Gloria J. and Katherine S. Harris: *Speech Science Primer*, Williams & Wilkins, Baltimore, 1980.

Bradley, Henry: *The Making of English*, Macmillan, New York, 1904.

Brook, G.L.: *A History of the English Language*, Norton, New York, 1958.

Brown, Roger: *Words and Things*, Macmillan, New York, 1958.

Bugbee, Bruce W.: *The Genesis of American Patent and Copyright Law*, Public Affairs Press, Washington, D.C., 1967.

Bullokar, William: *A Booke at Large, for the Amendment of Orthographie for English Speech*, Henry Denham, London, 1580.

Burns, Paul C.: *Improving Handwriting Instruction in Elementary Schools*, Burgess, Minneapolis, 1968.

Byington, Steven T.: "Mr. Byington's Brief Case II," *American Speech*, Vol. 19, April 1944, pp. 118–125.

Campbell, A.: *Old English Grammar*, Oxford University Press, London, 1959.

Carroll, John B.: *The Study of Language*, Harvard University Press, Cambridge, MA, 1955.

Carroll, John B. and Jeanne S. Chall (Eds.): *Toward a Literate Society: The Report of The Committee on Reading of the National Academy of Education*, McGraw-Hill, New York, 1975.

Cawdrey, Robert: *A Table Alphabeticall*, Edmund Weaner, London, 1604. (Facsimile edition with introduction by Robert A. Peters, Scholars' Facsimiles & Reprints, Gainsville, FL, 1966.)

Century Dictionary, supervised by William Dwight Whitney, Century, New York, 1889–1891. (Various editions and supplements subsequently published.)

Chall, Jeanne S.: *Learning to Read: The Great Debate*, McGraw-Hill, New York, 1967.

Childe, Gordon: *What Happened in History*, Penguin Books, Baltimore, 1954.

Chomsky, Carol: "Reading, Writing, and Phonology," *Harvard Educational Review*, Vol. 40, No. 2, May 1970, pp. 287–309.

Chomsky, Noam: "Phonology and Reading," in *Basic Studies on Reading*, Harry Levin and Joanna P. Williams (Eds.), Basic Books, New York, 1970.

Chomsky, Noam and Morris Halle: *The Sound Pattern of English*, Harper & Row, New York, 1968.

Claiborne, Robert: *The Birth of Writing*, Time-Life Books, New York, 1974.

Clanchy, M.T.: *From Memory to Written Record (England, 1066–1307)*, Harvard University Press, Cambridge, MA, 1979.

Clark, Sir George: *The Later Stuarts 1660–1714*, Oxford University Press, London, 1961.

Clark, John W.: "American Spelling," Ch. 9 in *Spelling*, by G.H. Vallins, 1954. Revised edition by D.G. Scragg, Andre Deutsch, London, 1965.

Clifford, James L.: *Dictionary Johnson*, McGraw-Hill, New York, 1979.

Clodd, Edward: *The Story of the Alphabet*, Facsimile reprint of the 1938 edition, Gale Research Company, Detroit, 1970. (First edition, 1900; revised, 1913.)

Cockeram, Henry: *The English Dictionarie*, H.C. Gent, London, 1623.

Comenius, John Amos: *Orbis Pictus Sensualium* (1657). Reissued by Singing Tree Press, Detroit, MI, 1968.

Commager, Henry Steele: "Schoolmaster to America," Introductory Essay in *Noah Webster's American Spelling Book* (1831 ed.), Classics in Education No. 17, Teachers College Press, New York, 1962.

Coote, Edmund: *The English Schoole-Maister*, First Edition. At London. Printed by the Widow Orwin, for Ralph Jackson and Robert Dextar, 1596.

Craigie, William A.: *English Spelling*, F.S. Crofts, New York, 1927.

Cremin, Lawrence A. (Ed.): *The Republic and the School: Horace Mann on the Education of Free Men*, Teachers College Press, New York, 1952.

Crystal, David: *Linguistics*, Penguin Books, Baltimore, 1971.

Davies, Godfrey: *The Early Stuarts 1603–1660*, Oxford University Press, London, 1959.

Davies, W.J. Frank: *Teaching Reading in Early England*, Pitman, London, 1973. First published in the USA by Harper & Row, New York, 1974.

Dewey, Godfrey: *World English Spelling*, Simpler Spelling Association, New York, 1964.

Dewey, Godfrey: *Relative frequency of English spelling*, Teachers College Press, New York, 1970.

Dewey, Godfrey: *English Spelling: Roadblock to Reading*, Teachers College Press, New York, 1971.

DISTAR (Direct Instruction Systems for Teaching Arithmetic and Reading), Science Research Associates, Chicago, 1969, 1975.

Diringer, David: *The Alphabet*, Third Edition completely revised with the collaboration of Reinhold Regensburger, Hutchinson, London, 1968.

Doblhofer, Ernst: *Voices in Stone*, Viking, New York, 1961.

Dobson, E.J.: *English Pronunciation 1500–1700*, Oxford University Press, London, 1968.

Dornbusch, Clyde H.: "American Spelling Simplified by Presidential Edict," *American Speech*, October 1961, pp. 236–238.

Downing, John: *Evaluating the Initial Teaching Alphabet*, Cassell, London, 1967.

Downing, John (Ed.): *Comparative Reading*, Macmillan, New York, 1973.

Downs, Robert B.: *Horace Mann*, Twayne, New York, 1974.

Dunkel, Harold B.: "Language Teaching in an Old Key," *Modern Language Journal*, May 1963, pp. 203–210.

Ege, Otto F.: "The Story of the Alphabet," in *Books and Printing*, Paul Bennett (Ed.), World Publishing Company, Cleveland, 1951.

Elson, Ruth Miller: *Guardians of Traditions*, University of Nebraska Press, Lincoln, 1964.

Emsley, Bert: "Progress in Pronouncing Dictionaries," *American Speech*, Vol. 15, February 1940, pp. 55–59.

Feitelson, Dina: "Structuring the Teaching of Reading According to Major Features of the Language and Its Script," *Elementary English*, December 1965, pp. 870–877.

Fischer, John H.: "Chancery and the Emergence of Standard Written English in the Fifteenth Century," *Speculum*, 1977, pp. 870–899.

Fisher, D.J.V.: *The Anglo-Saxon Age*, Longmans, London, 1973.

Flesch, Rudolf: *Why Johnny Can't Read*, Harper & Row, New York, 1955.

Flesch, Rudolf: "Why Johnny *still* Can't Read," *Family Circle*, November 1, 1979, pp. 26, 43–46.

Flesch, Rudolf: *Why Johnny Still Can't Read: A Look at the Scandal of Our Schools*, Harper & Row, New York, 1981.

Ford, Emily Ellsworth Fowler (Ed.): *Notes on the Life of Noah Webster*, Emily Ellsworth Ford Skeel (Ed.), 2 vols., privately printed, 1912. Reprinted by Burt Franklin, New York, 1971.

Ford, Paul Leicester (Ed.): *The New England Primer*, Dodd, Mead, New York, 1897. Reprinted by Teachers College Press, New York, 1962.

Francis, W. Nelson: *The Structure of American English*, Ronald Press, New York, 1958.

Franklin, Benjamin: "A Reformed Mode of Spelling. A Scheme for new Alphabet and reformed mode of Spelling; with Remarks and Examples concerning the same; and an Enquiry into its Uses, a Correspondence between Miss S_____n and Dr. Franklin, written in the Characters of the Alphabet," in *Political, Miscellaneous, and Philosophical Pieces...by Benjamin Franklin*, Benjamin Vaughn, London, 1779, p. 472.

Freire, Paulo: *Education for Critical Consciousness*, Seabury Press, New York, 1973.

Fries, Charles C.: *Linguistics and Reading*, Holt, Rinehart and Winston, New York, 1963.

Fries, Charles C., Rosemary G. Wilson, and Mildred K. Rudolph (Eds.): *Merrill Linguistic Readers*, Charles E. Merrill, Columbus, OH, 1967.

Gates, Arthur I.: "An Autobiography," in *Leaders in American Education*, Seventieth Yearbook of the National Society for the Study of Education, Part II, University of Chicago Press, 1971, pp. 189–216.

Gelb, I.J.: *A Study of Writing*, University of Chicago Press, 1963.

Geschwind, Norman: "Anatomical Mechanisms of Acquired Disorders of Reading," Invited Address, 78th Annual Convention of the American Psychological Association, Miami Beach, FL, 1970.

Gibson, Martha Jane: "America's First Lexicographer Samuel Johnson Jr., 1757–1836," Part I, *American Speech*, December 1936, pp. 283–292; Part II, January 1937, pp. 19–30.

Gleason, H.A.: *An Introduction to Descriptive Linguistics*, Holt, Rinehart and Winston, New York, 1961.

Gleitman, Linda R. and Paul Rozin: "Teaching Reading by Use of a Syllabary," *Reading Research Quarterly*, Summer 1973, pp. 447–483.

Gleitman, Linda R. and Paul Rozin: "The Structure and Acquisition of Reading I: Relations between Orthographies and the Structure of Language," in *Toward a Psychology of Reading*, Arthur S. Reber and Don L. Scarborough (Eds.), Erlbaum, Hillsdale, NJ, 1977, pp. 1–53.

Goodman, Kenneth S.: "The Linguistics of Reading," *The Elementary School Journal*, April 1964, pp. 355–361.

Goodman, Kenneth S.: "Psychological Universals in the Reading Process," in *Psycholinguistics and Reading*, Frank Smith (Ed.), Holt, Rinehart and Winston, New York, 1973.

Gordon, Arthur E.: "The Letter Names of the Latin Alphabet," *Visible Language*, Vol. 5, No. 3, Summer 1971, pp. 221–228.

Gordon, James D.: *The English Language*, Crowell, New York, 1972.

Gray, Giles W. and Claude M. Wise: *The Bases of Speech*, Harper & Row, New York, 1959.

Gray, Jack C. (Ed.): *Words, Words, and Words about Dictionaries*, Chandler, San Francisco, 1963.

Gray, William S. et al.: *Curriculum Foundation Series*, Scott, Foresman and Company, Glenview, IL, various editions from 1940.

Gray, William S.: *On Their Own in Reading*, Scott, Foresman and Company, Glenview, IL, 1948, 1960.

Groff, Patrick: "Teaching Reading by Syllables," *Reading Teacher*, March 1981, pp. 659–663.

Hall, Robert A. Jr.: Review of Rudolf Flesch's "Why Johnny Can't Read—and what you can do about it," *Language*, Vol. 32, No. 2, pp. 310–313.

Hall, Robert A. Jr.: *Sound and Spelling in English*, Chilton Books, Philadelphia, 1961.

Hanna, Jean S. and Paul R. Hanna: "Spelling as a School Subject: a brief history," *The National Elementary School Principal*, Vol. 38, No. 7, May 1959, pp. 8–23.

Hanna, Paul R. and Jean S. Hanna: "The Teaching of Spelling," *The National Elementary Principal*, Vol. 45, No. 2, November 1965, pp. 19–28.

Hanna, Paul R. et al.: *Phoneme-Grapheme Correspondences as Cues to Spelling Improvement*. U.S. Government Printing Office, Washington, DC, 1966.

Harrigan, John A.: "Initial Reading Instruction: Phonemes, Syllables or Ideographs?" *Journal of Learning Disabilities*, February 1976, pp. 74–80.

Hexter, Jack H.: *Reappraisals in History*, 2nd ed., University of Chicago Press, 1979.

Hill, Christopher: *The Century of Revolution 1603–1714*, Norton, New York, 1961.

Hodges, Richard E.: "In Adam's Fall: A Brief History of Spelling Instruction in the United States," in *Reading & Writing Instruction in the United States: Historical Trends*, H. Alan Robinson (Ed.), ERIC Clearing House on Reading and Communication Skills, National Institute of Education and the International Reading Association, Newark, DE, 1977.

Huey, Edmund Burke: *The Psychology and Pedagogy of Reading*, Macmillan, New York, 1908. Reprinted by MIT Press, Cambridge, MA, 1968.

Hulbert, James R.: "The Authority of the Dictionary," in *Dictionaries and* That *Dictionary*, James H. Sledd and Wilma R. Ebbitt (Eds.), Scott, Foresman and Company, Glenview, IL, 1962.

Irmscher, William F.: *The Holt Guide to English*, Holt, Rinehart and Winston, New York, 1972.

Ives, Josephine P., Laura Z. Bursuk, and Sumner A. Ives: *Word Identification Techniques*, Rand McNally, Chicago, 1979.

Jacotot, Jean Joseph: *Enseignement universel...Langue maternelle*, 3rd ed., Louvain, 1827.

Jensen, Hans: *Sign, Symbol and Script*, Putnam, New York, 1969.

Jespersen, Otto: *Language, Its Nature, Development and Origin*, George Allen & Unwin, London, 1922.

Jespersen, Otto: *Essentials of English Grammar*, University of Alabama Press, 1964.

Johnson, Clifton: *Old-Time Schools and School-books*, Macmillan, New York, 1904. Reprinted by Dover, New York, 1963.

Johnson, Samuel: *A Dictionary of the English Language*, 1755. Facsimile edition, Arno Press, New York, 1980.

Jones, Daniel: *An English Pronouncing Dictionary*, 13th ed. Revised by A.C. Gimson, London, 1967.

Kavanagh, James F. and Ignatius G. Mattingly (Eds.): *Language by Ear and by Eye*, MIT Press, Cambridge, MA, 1972.

Kenyon, John S. and Thomas A. Knott: *A Pronouncing Dictionary of American English*, G. & C. Merriam, Springfield, MA, 1953.

Kottmeyer, William: *Decoding and Reading*, McGraw-Hill, New York, 1974.

Kramer, Samuel Noah: *History Begins at Sumer*, Falcon's Wing Press, 1956, Doubleday/Anchor, New York, 1959.

Krapp, George Philip: *The English Language in America*, 2 vols., Frederick Ungar, New York, 1925.

Kurath, Hans: *A Phonology and Prosody of Modern English*, University of Michigan Press, Ann Arbor, 1964.

Lamoreaux, Lillian A. and Dorris M. Lee: *Learning to Read Through Experience*, Appleton, Century, New York, 1943. Revised ed. by Dorris M. Lee and R.V. Allen, 1963.

Lefevre, Carl A.: *Linguistics, English, and the English Language Arts*, Allyn & Bacon, Boston, 1970.

Lehmann, Winfred P.: *Historical Linguistics*, Holt, Rinehart and Winston, New York, 1973.

Leonard, Sterling A.: *The Doctrine of Correctness in English Usage, 1700–1800*, University of Wisconsin Studies in Language and Literature, No. 25, Madison, 1929.

Levin, Harry and Joanna P. Williams (Eds.): *Basic Studies on Reading*, Basic Books, New York, 1970.

Malmstrom, Jean and Annabel Ashley: *Dialects—U.S.A.*, National Council of Teachers of English, Champaign, IL, 1963.

Malone, John R.: "The UNIFON System," *Wilson Library Bulletin*, Vol. 40, September, 1965.

Mann, Mary: *Life of Horace Mann*, Lee & Shepard, Boston, 1888.

Marckwardt, Albert H.: *American English*, Oxford University Press, New York, 1958.

Marckwardt, Albert H. and James L. Rosier: *Old English*, Norton, New York, 1972.

Martin, Samuel E.: "Nonalphabetic Writing Systems: Some Observations," in *Language by Ear and by Eye*, James F. Kavanagh and Ignatius G. Mattingly (Eds.), MIT Press, Cambridge, MA, 1972, pp. 81–102.

Mathews, Mitford M. (Ed.): *The Beginnings of American English*, University of Chicago Press, 1931.

Mathews, Mitford M.: "An Introduction to the Dictionary," in *Words, Words, and Words about Dictionaries*, Jack C. Gray (Ed.), Chandler, San Francisco, 1963, pp. 35–51.

Mathews, Mitford M. (Ed.): *Teaching to Read Historically Considered*, University of Chicago Press, 1966.

Matthew, D.J.A.: *The Norman Conquest*, Schocken, New York, 1966.

Mazurkiewicz, Albert J. and Harold J. Tanyzer: *Early-to-Read i/t/a Program*, i/t/a Publications, New York, 1966.

McCaul, Robert L.: "Dewey and the University of Chicago," *School and Society*, March 25, 1961, pp. 152–157; April 8, 1961, pp. 179–183; April 22, 1961, pp. 202–206.

McDavid, Raven I. Jr.: "Adviser and Advisor: Orthographic and Semantic Differentiation," *Studies in Linguistics 1.7*, New Haven, CT, 1942.

McDavid, Raven I. Jr.: *The American Language, by H.L. Mencken* (The Fourth Edition and the Two Supplements, abridged, with annotations and new material), Knopf, New York, 1963.

McDavid, Raven I. Jr.: "The Speech of New York: The Historical Background," Paper presented at the Annual Conference of the National Council of Teachers of English, New York City, 1977.

McKerrow, Ronald B.: "Typographic Debut," in *Books and Printing*, Paul A. Bennett (Ed.), World Publishing Company, Cleveland, 1951, pp. 78–82.

Mencken, H.L.: *The American Language*, Knopf, New York, 1919, Fourth revision, 1936, *Supplement One*, 1945; *Supplement Two*, 1948.

Messerli, Jonathan: *Horace Mann*, Knopf, New York, 1972.

Miller, George A.: "The Psycholinguists," *Encounter*, Vol. 23, July 1964, pp. 29–37.

Miller, Helen Hill: *The Realms of Arthur*, Scribner, New York, 1969.

Minkoff, H.: "Graphemics and Diachrony: Some Evidence from Hebrew Cursive," *Afroasiatic Linguistics*, Vol. 1, Issue 7, March 1975.

Minnich, Harvey C.: *William Holmes McGuffey and His Readers*, American Book, New York, 1936.

Monaghan, E. Jennifer: "Noah Webster's Speller," unpublished doctoral dissertation, Yeshiva University, New York, 1980.

Moore, Samuel: *Historical Outlines of English Sounds and Inflections*, revised by Albert H. Marckwardt, George Wahr, Ann Arbor, MI, 1951.

Moorhouse, Alfred C.: *The Triumph of the Alphabet*, Henry Schuman, New York, 1953.

Morgan, John S.: *Noah Webster*, Mason/Charter, New York, 1975.

Morris, John: *The Age of Arthur*, Scribner, New York, 1973.

Morrison, Coleman and Mary C. Austin: *The Torch Lighters Revisited*, International Reading Association, Newark, DE, 1977.

Mossé, Fernand: *A Handbook of Middle English*, Johns Hopkins University Press, Baltimore, 1968.

Mulcaster, Richard: *The First Part of the Elementarie...*, Thomas Vautroullier, London, 1582. Reproduced by Scolar Press, Menston, England, 1970.

Murray, James H. et al. (Eds.): *Oxford English Dictionary*, 13 vols., and *Supplement*, Oxford, 1933. (Originally published in 1884–1928 as *A New English Dictionary on Historical Principles*.)

Murray, K.M. Elisabeth: *Caught in the Web of Words*, Yale University Press, New Haven, 1977.

Noyes, Gertrude E.: "The First English Dictionary, Cawdrey's Table Alphabeticall," *Modern Language Notes*, Vol. 58, December 1943, pp. 600–605.

Ogg, Oscar: *The 26 Letters*, Crowell, New York, 1971.

Ong, Walter J.: "Backgrounds of Elizabethan Punctuation," *Publications of the Modern Language Association (PMLA)*, 1944, pp. 349–360.

Painter, George D.: *William Caxton*, Putnam, New York, 1976.

The Peabody REBUS Reading Program, American Guidance Service, Circle Pines, MN, 1969.

Pedersen, Holger: *Linguistic Science in the Nineteenth Century*, John Webster Spargo (Trans.), Harvard University Press, Cambridge, 1931. Reprinted as paperback MB40, *The Discovery of Language*, Indiana University Press, Bloomington, 1959.

Peters, Robert A.: *A Linguistic History of English*, Houghton-Mifflin, Boston, 1968.

Pike, Kenneth L.: *Phonetics*, University of Michigan Press, Ann Arbor, 1943.

Pike, Kenneth L.: *Phonemics*, University of Michigan Press, Ann Arbor, 1947.

Pitman, Sir James and John St. John: *Alphabets and Reading*, Pitman, New York, 1969.

Pomerance, Leon: "Phaistos Disc—An Interpretation in Astronomical Symbols." Lecture delivered at the Explorers Club, New York City, February 9, 1976.

Popp, Helen: "Current Practices in the Teaching of Beginning Reading," in *Toward a Literate Society: The Report of the Committee on Reading of the National Academy of Education*, John B. Carroll and Jeanne S. Chall (Eds.), McGraw-Hill, New York, 1975, pp. 101–146.

Potter, Simeon: *Modern Linguistics*, Andre Deutsch, London, 1957.

Putnam, George Haven: *Books and Their Makers During the Middle Ages*, 2 vols., Putnam, New York, 1896.

Pyles, Thomas: *Words and Ways of American English*, Random House, New York, 1952.

Pyles, Thomas: *The Origins and Development of the English Language*, Harcourt Brace Jovanovich, New York, 1971.

Quirk, Randolph and C.L. Wrenn: *An Old English Grammar*, Holt, Rinehart and Winston, New York, 1957.

Ramson, W.S.: *Australian English*, Australian National University Press, Canberra, 1966.

Ranow, George: "Simplified Spelling in Government Publications," *American Speech*, Vol. 29, February 1954, pp. 36–41.

Ravitch, Diane: *The Great School Wars*, Basic Books, New York, 1974.

Rayner, R.M.: *England in Early and Medieval Times*, Longmans, Green, New York, 1931.

Read, Allen Walker: "British Recognition of American Speech in the Eighteenth Century," *Dialect Notes*, Vol. 6, Pt. 6, 1933.

Read, Allen Walker: "The Spelling Bee: A Linguistic Institution of the American Folk," *Publications of the Modern Language Association* (*PMLA*), Vol. 56, No. 2, June 1941, pp. 492–512.

Reber, Arthur S. and Don L. Scarborough (Eds.): *Toward a Psychology of Reading*, Erlbaum, Hillsdale, NJ, 1977.

Robertson, Stuart: *The Development of Modern English*, revised by Frederic G. Cassidy, Prentice-Hall, Englewood Cliffs, NJ, 1954.

Robinson, H. Alan (Ed.): *Reading and Writing Instruction in the United States: Historical Trends*, ERIC Clearing House on Reading and Communication Skills, National Institute of Education and the International Reading Association, Newark, DE, 1977.

Rollins, Richard M.: *The Long Journey of Noah Webster*, University of Pennsylvania Press, Philadelphia, 1980.

Ross, Alan O.: *Psychological Aspects of Learning Disabilities & Reading Disorders*, McGraw-Hill, New York, 1976.

Rozin, Paul and Linda R. Gleitman, "The Structure and Acquisition of Reading II: The Reading Process and the Acquisition of the Alphabetic Principle," in *Toward a Psychology of Reading*, Arthur S. Reber and Don L. Scarborough (Eds.), Erlbaum, Hillsdale, NJ, 1977, pp. 54–141.

Sakamoto, Takahiko and Kiyoshi Makita: "Japan," in *Comparative Reading*, John Downing (Ed.), Macmillan, New York, 1973, pp. 440–465.

Sapir, Edward: *Language: An Introduction to the Study of Speech*, Harcourt, Brace, New York, 1921.

Saporta, Sol (Ed.): *Psycholinguistics*, Holt, Rinehart and Winston, New York, 1961.

Scargill, M.H.: *Modern Canadian English Usage*, McClelland and Stewart, Toronto, 1974.

Schlauch, Margaret: *The Gift of Language*, Dover, New York, 1955. (Former edition published as *The Gift of Tongues*, Viking, New York, 1942.)

Scott, Foresman and Company: *Scott, Foresman Reading Systems*, Scott, Foresman and Company, Glenview, IL, 1971.

Scragg, D.G.: *A History of English Spelling*, Manchester University Press. Published in the U.S.A. by Harper & Row, Barnes and Noble Import Division, New York, 1974.

Setton, Kenneth M.: "900 Years Ago: The Norman Conquest," *National Geographic Magazine*, Vol. 130, No. 2, August 1966, pp. 206–251.

Shaw, George Bernard: *Androcles and the Lion*, The Shaw Alphabet Edition, Penguin Books, Harmondsworth, 1962.

Sheldon, Esther K.: "Pronouncing Systems in Eighteenth-Century Dictionaries," *Language*, January-March 1946, pp. 27–41.

Sheldon, Esther K.: "Walker's Influence on the Pronunciation of English," *Publications of the Modern Language Association* (*PMLA*), March 1947, pp. 130–146.

Sledd, James H.: "Bi-Dialecticism: The Linguistics of White Supremacy," *English Journal*, Vol. 58, No. 9, December 1969, pp. 1307–1315, 1329.

Sledd, James H. and Gwin J. Kolb: *Dr. Johnson's Dictionary*, University of Chicago Press, 1955.

Sledd, James H. and Wilma R. Ebbitt (Eds.): *Dictionaries and* That *Dictionary*, Scott, Foresman and Company, Glenview, IL, 1962.

Smalley, William A.: *Manual of Articulatory Phonetics*, Practical Anthropology, Tarrytown, NY, 1963.

Smith, E. Brooks, Kenneth S. Goodman, and Robert Meredith: *Language and Thinking in School*, Holt, Rinehart and Winston, New York, 1976.

Smith, Frank: *Understanding Reading*, Holt, Rinehart and Winston, New York, 1971.

Smith, Frank (Ed.): *Psycholinguistics and Reading*, Holt, Rinehart and Winston, New York, 1973.

Smith, Frank (with Kenneth S. Goodman): "On the Psycholinguistic Method of Teaching Reading," in *Psycholinguistics and Reading*, Frank Smith (Ed.), Holt, Rinehart and Winston, New York, 1973.

Smith, Frank: *Reading Without Nonsense*, Teachers College Press, New York, 1979. (First published as *Reading*, Cambridge University Press, Cambridge, England, 1978.)

Smith, Nila Banton: "What Have We Accomplished in Reading? ... A Review of the Past Fifty Years," *Elementary English*, No. 38, 1961, pp. 141–150.

Smith, Nila Banton: *American Reading Instruction*, International Reading Association, Newark, DE, 1965.

Southgate, Vera (Ed.): *Literacy at All Levels*, Ward Locke, London, 1972.

Spinka, Matthew: *John Amos Comenius; That Incomparable Moravian*, University of Chicago Press, 1943.

Starnes, DeWitt T. and Gertrude E. Noyes: *The English Dictionary from Cawdrey to Johnson 1604–1755*, University of North Carolina Press, Chapel Hill, 1946.

Stenton, Sir Frank (Ed.): *The Bayeux Tapestry: A Comprehensive Survey*, Phaidon, New York, 1957.

Stenton, Sir Frank (Ed.): *Anglo-Saxon England*, Oxford University Press, London, 1971.

Stetson, R.H.: *Motor Phonetics, a Study of Speech Movements in Action*, North-Holland, Amsterdam, 1951.

Stevick, Robert D.: *English and Its History*, Allyn & Bacon, Boston, 1968.

Sturtevant, E.H.: *Linguistic Change*, University of Chicago Press, 1917.

Taylor, Insup: *Introduction to Psycholinguistics*, Holt, Rinehart and Winston, New York, 1976.

Thieme, Paul: "The Indo-European Language," *Scientific American*, October 1958, pp. 63–74.

Thomas, Isaiah: *The History of Printing in America*, 1st edition, 1810, 2nd edition, 1874. Edition of 1970, Marcus A. McCorison (Ed.), Crown, New York.

Thompson, Tommy: *How to Render Roman Letter Forms*, American Studio Books, New York, 1946.

Tiffany, William R. and James Carrell: *Phonetics: Theory and Application*, McGraw-Hill, New York, 1977.

Trevelyan, G.M.: *History of England*, Longmans, Green and Co., New York, 1945.

Trnka, Bohumil: *A Phonological Analysis of Present-Day Standard English*, University of Alabama Press, University, AL, 1966.

Tuer, Andrew W.: *History of the Hornbook*, Leadenhall Press, London, 1897, reissued by Benjamin Blom, Bronx, NY, 1968.

Vachek, Josef: "Review of the Structure of English Orthography by Richard L. Venezky," *Language*, Vol. 47, No. 1, 1971, pp. 212–216.

Vachek, Josef: *Written Language*, Mouton, The Hague, 1973.

Vallins, G.H.: *Spelling*, Revised by D.G. Scragg, Andre Deutsch, London, 1965.

Venezky, Richard L.: "A Study of English Spelling-to-Sound Correspondences on Historical Principles," unpublished doctoral dissertation, Stanford University, 1965.

Venezky, Richard L.: "English Orthography: Its Graphical Structure and Its Relation to Sound," *Reading Research Quarterly*, Spring 1967, pp. 75–105.

Venezky, Richard L.: *The Structure of English Orthography*, Mouton, The Hague, 1970.

Venezky, Richard L.: "The Curious Role of Letter Names in Reading Instruction," *Visible Language*, Vol. 9, No. 1, Winter 1975, pp. 7–23.

Venezky, Richard L.: *The Role of Orthographic Regularity in Word Recognition*, Working Paper No. 181, Wisconsin Research and Development Center for Cognitive Learning, November 1976.

Von Maltitz, Frances Willard: *Living and Learning in Two Languages*, McGraw-Hill, New York, 1975.

Warburton, Francis W. and Vera Southgate: *i.t.a.: An Independent Evaluation*, Murray and Chambers, London, 1969.

Warfel, Harry R.: *Noah Webster, Schoolmaster to America*, Macmillan, New York, 1936.

Warfel, Harry R. (Ed.): *Letters of Noah Webster*, Library Publishers, New York, 1953.

Webster, Noah: Letter to Thomas Dawes (Postscript), *Monthly Anthology and Boston Review*, Vol. 7, p. 208ff. Reprinted in *The Beginnings of American English*, M.M. Mathews (Ed.), University of Chicago Press, 1931.

Webster, Noah: *Noah Webster's American Spelling Book* (1831 edition), with an Introductory Essay by Henry Steele Commager. Classics in Education No. 17, Teachers College Press, New York, 1962.

Webster's Third New International Dictionary of the English Language, G. & C. Merriam, Springfield, MA, 1961.

Weekley, Ernest: "On Dictionaries," *The Atlantic Monthly*, June 1924. Reprinted in *Dictionaries and That Dictionary*, James H. Sledd and Wilma P. Ebbitt (Eds.), Scott, Foresman and Company, Glenview, IL, 1962, pp. 9–21.

Westcott, Roger W.: "Protolinguistics: The Study of Protolanguages as an Aid to Glossogonic Research," in *Origins and Evolution of Language and Speech*, Annals of the New York Academy of Sciences, Stevan R. Hamad, Horst D. Steklis, and Jane Alexander (Eds.), Vol. 280, 1976, pp. 104–116.

Whittaker, Kenneth: *Dictionaries*, Clive Bingley, London, 1966.

Wijk, Axel: *Regularized English; an Investigation into the English Spelling Reform Problem with a New Detailed Plan for a Possible Solution*, Stockholm Studies in English, Vol. 7, Almqvist and Wiksell, Stockholm, 1959.

Wrenn, C.L.: *The English Language*, Methuen, London, 1952.

Zachrisson, R.E.: "Four Hundred Years of English Spelling Reform," *Studia Neophilologica*, Vol. 4, Nos. 1–2, 1931, pp. 1–69.

Zachrisson, R.E.: *Anglic, an International Language*, Almqvist and Wiksell, Stockholm, 1932.

Appendix

OLD ENGLISH CONSONANTS

SPELLING   PRONUNCIATION

b   As in Modern English.

c^1 As *c* in *cat* except in these instances:

           1. Pronounced as the *c* in *cello* before front vowels *e* and *i*. (Old English *cild* was respelled as Modern English *child*.)

           2. In two different clusters:

              a. *sc*, pronounced "sh"

              b. *cg*, pronounced "dzh" and used instead of a double *g*. (Later, it evolved into *dg* or *dge*.)

d   As in Modern English.

f   As in Modern English except between voiced sounds, when it was pronounced "v." (*Wolf–wolverine* and *loaf–loaves* are Modern English examples that have been respelled with the borrowed symbol *v*.)

g^2 *In initial position:*[3]

           1. As *g* in *good*

---

[1]The three variant pronunciations of *c* developed from the allophones of the original Proto-Germanic phoneme /k/. In Old English, first the "ch" pronunciation developed into a separate phoneme, and then from it the "sh" pronunciation developed as yet another phoneme, occurring after the "s" pronunciation and eventually absorbing it—as the *sc* spelling cluster reveals. All three pronunciations retained the *c* spelling in Old English.

[2]The Old English form of *g* (corresponding to Old Latin as well as to Modern English *g*) was ȝ, adopted from a form used by Irish scribes. It lasted through most of the Middle English period as well, in a slightly modified form. It may have acquired the name *yogh* (rhyming with Scottish *loch*) from its shape: a sideways ŋ, or *yoke*, or, according to Scragg, may have been a word coined from the letters that replaced it: the *y* in initial position and the *gh* after a vowel. (Scragg, 1974, p. 22, n. 4.)

[3]There is some divergence of opinion on the pronunciation of Old English *g* in initial position. Moore (1951, pp. 20 and 74) ascribes the velar fricative pronunciation in *all* initial positions rather than only before *e* and *i/y*. Most other authors, however, ascribe the *g* as in *good* pronunciation before back vowels *a*, *o*, and *u* (Quirk and Wrenn, 1957, p. 16, for example).

a. before consonants
b. before the back vowels *a*, *o*, and *u*
c. before other vowels in words derived from words in which the vowel was *a*, *o*, or *u*. (For example, *geese* is derived from *goose* by umlaut so that the *g* in *geese* has kept the hard sound of *g* even though it is now followed by *e* and should ostensibly be soft.)
2. As *y* in *yes* before *e* or *i*.[4] (Old English *gear* became Modern English *year*.)

In medial or final position:
1. As a voiced velar fricative[5] somewhat like Modern Greek *gamma*, except:
   a. As *y* in *yes* when preceded by or between the front vowel æ, *e*, or *i*. (For example, *mægden–maiden* or *hunig–honey*.)
   b. As in Modern English *finger* when preceded by *n*.

h   *In initial position:*
As in Modern English. (There were also several initial clusters with *h*: *hl-*, *hn-*, *hr-*, and *hw-*, all voiceless, so that the *hw* was like Modern English *wh* and the *hl* was like the Welsh pronunciation of *ll*.)

In medial or final position:
Here, *h* represented either one of two harsh voiceless palatal[6] or velar fricatives, somewhat resembling the pronunciation of Modern Spanish *j* and Modern German *ch*, neither of which is found in Modern English.

j   Did not exist as a separate character in Old English. See pp. 39–40 for discussion of the development of *j*.

k   As in Modern English. Rarely found in Old English writings, but its use in Latin was known in Old English times.

l   The exact pronunciation is in question. It may have had more than one variation of Modern English *l*.

m   As in Modern English.

n   As in Modern English, except before medial or final *g*, when it was pronounced as in Modern English *finger*.

p   As in Modern English.

q   Seldom found in Old English. It had been used in Latin to precede *v* when the "kw" pronunciation was required. The *q* appeared occasionally in some early writings and in the Rushworth gospels, according to Venezky,[7] but *c* was generally used in its place during Old English times.

---

[4]Modern English words with the hard *g* pronunciation before *e* or *i* (other than those noted under 1c), are generally borrowed from the Scandinavian—e.g., *get* and *gill*.

[5]Velar speech sounds are those produced with the tongue touching or raised to the soft palate or velum. The *g* in *good* is a velar stop. A velar fricative is produced when some air is released as the tongue is raised to the velum.

[6]Palatal speech sounds are those formed when the tongue is raised to the hard palate. Modern English does not have any true palatal sounds, although the "h" in Modern English *huge* is close to it. Also "sh" represents an alveolar-palatal sound—a bit far forward for a true palatal sound, but it can be used as an indication of how a palatal is formed.

[7]Venezky, 1965, p. 110. Also, see p. 38 n. 12 for background on the development of the *q*.

r	Some divergence of opinion on this sound, as on the *l*. It was probably more consonantal than Modern English *r*, having either a velar (as in Modern German) or a trilled (as in Modern Spanish) pronunciation—or more than one pronunciation.
s	As in Modern English, except between voiced sounds, when it was pronounced "z," as in *leosan–to lose*.[8]
t	As in Modern English.
v	A difficult character to pin down. Modern English "v" pronunciation did not exist as a separate phoneme in spoken Old English, although there was an allophone of the Old English phoneme /f/ with that pronunciation found between voiced sounds (as in *heofene–heaven*). Occasionally, in written language, borrowed Latin words are found with the character *v*, written as *u*, although they may well have been pronounced as "f." The Irish, who were influential in all scholarly matters during this period, are known to have pronounced the letter *v/u* in Latin as "f," and the British may well have adopted the "f" pronunciation also.[9]
w	As in Modern English. It was written as a ligatured double *u* (*uu*) until the eighth century, when it was replaced by the Ρ (*wynn*) until the *uu* character, brought back to England by the Normans in the eleventh century, took over its functions by the thirteenth century.
x	As in Modern English, in medial or final positions.
y	Only used as a vowel and written in place of *i* or *ie* in final positions. (See p. 83 above on the list of Old English vowels.)
z	The Modern English phoneme /z/ was not a separate phoneme in Old English but was an allophone of the Old English phoneme /s/, occurring between two voiced sounds and written with an *s* (e.g., as above under *s*: *leosan–to lose*). In those rare instances—usually loan words—when the letter *z* did occur, it seems to have represented the "ts" and "dz" pronunciations.

The Eth and the Thorn

In addition to the alphabet characters just listed, two other characters used interchangeably in Old English are no longer in use today. These were the eth (or *crossed d*), written *đ* and the thorn, written *þ*. Each was used to represent either voiced "th" as in *there* or voiceless "th" as in *thick*. The voiceless pronunciation was used between vowels in spoken Old English. Venezky[10] describes the development of these

---

[8]The difference between the sound of *s* in *lose* and *loose* is accounted for by their different origins. *Lose* comes from the Old English word *leosan* and *loose* comes from the Old Norse word *lauss*. In both cases, the original pronunciation of the letter *s* has been retained.

[9]Pyles, 1971, pp. 125–126. In Classical Latin, however, the *v* was pronounced "w." It only acquired the "v" pronunciation in Late Latin, so we continue to be uncertain on this point. (See p. 40 above for background on the early *v*.)

[10]Venezky, 1965, pp. 120–122 and p. 140, n. 35. See also Quirk and Wrenn, 1957, pp. 7–9.

two characters in fair detail, also noting that there is a good deal of disagreement about the early usage of the various characters to represent the "th" pronunciations. He states that the characters *th* and *d* were used in the earliest writings, mostly with *th* in initial or final position and *d* in medial position. Both were allophones of the same phoneme. Then, in the seventh century, the *đ* was created or, perhaps, borrowed from Norse, to replace the written character *d*. By that time, the spoken "d" pronunciation had evolved as a separate phoneme and the written character *d* was needed to represent it. Thus, for a time, the written characters *th* and *đ* were both used to represent the same "th" pronunciations.

In the ninth century, however, the thorn *þ* was borrowed from runic writing, in which it represented the "th" pronunciations. It soon replaced the *th* and existed side by side with the *đ* for several centuries. In early Middle English times, the *þ* replaced the *đ* also and became the sole character for the "th" pronunciation until, in the fifteenth century, the *th* reappeared and replaced the *þ*. From that time on, the *th* has been the only written form of the "th" pronunciation.

In all this time, there was no written difference between the voiced and unvoiced pronunciations of "th." Each of the various characters was used to represent either pronunciation, just as the *th* digraph does today.

MIDDLE ENGLISH CONSONANTS

SPELLING	PRONUNCIATION
b	1. As in Old and Modern English.
	2. The *b* pronunciation in the final sequence *-mb* was lost (as in cli*mb*).
c	1. Pronounced "k" except for the front vowels *e* and *i/y*. Before *e* and *i/y*, the Old English pronunciation "ch" as in *child* gave way to French "s" pronunciation, first in borrowed words (*citee–city, cesser–to cease*) and then in English words as well. (Old English *sinder* became *cinder.*) The letter *k*—scarcely used in English before that time—was then adopted for the "k" sound before *e* and *i/y* (Old English *cetel–kettle*).
	2. After a fashion used by French scribes, the letter *h* was placed after *c* to form the digraph *ch*, as in *child*. (This *c* spelling was dropped in unstressed final syllables, probably because the sound was lost in pronunciation. Thus, the suffix *-lic* became *li/ly* as in *heofonlic–heavenly.*)
	3. The clusters *sc* (pronounced "sh") and *cg* (pronounced "dzh") were changed in spelling to *sh* and *dg*.
d	As in Old and Modern English.
f	As in Old and Modern English except that in southern dialects *initial f* was voiced and pronounced as "v." The Modern English word *vixen* (from *fyxe*) is one of the vestiges of this pronunciation.

g^{11}

In initial position:

1. As in Old and Modern English before consonants and before the back vowels *a*, *o*, and *u* as well as in words derived from words with those vowels (e.g., *geese* from *goose*).
2. Before front vowels *e* and *i/y* the *g* was pronounced in one of two ways:
    a. With native English words, the Old English *y* as in *yes* pronunciation, which had been written with the *g* (or *yogh*), until the middle of the thirteenth century, began to be written with the letter *y* (e.g., *giet–yet* and *geolu–yellow*).
    b. With borrowed French words, a new sound was introduced: "g" as in *gem*. This pronunciation was used not only in initial positions with such borrowed words but also in other positions as well before *e* and *i/y* (e.g., Old French *geant–*Modern English *giant*, and Old French *changier–*Modern English *to change*).[12] No native English word had or has since had the "g" as in *gem* pronunciation in initial position—it occurs only in loan words from French or other foreign languages.[13] In medial position, however, English with "g" as in *gem* pronunciation, was still used (altered in spelling to *dg*), as in *hedge* (Old English *hege*—also written in Old English as *hecg*, *hegg*, among other forms).

In medial or final positions:

1. The voiceless velar fricative pronunciation (see p. 220) became "w" after the consonants *l* and *r* as well as after back vowels (e.g., *halgian–hallow*, *borgian–borrow*, and *lagu–law*).
2. After the front vowels *æ*, *e*, and *i/y*, this pronunciation of the *g* became "i" or "y," forming a new diphthong (e.g., *mægden–maiden* and *hunig–honey*).

h

1. As in Old and Modern English in initial and medial positions.
2. The voiceless palatal and velar fricative sounds of the Old English letter *h* in medial and final positions became vowels and combined with preceding vowels to form diphthongs. The resulting pronunciation in any given word depended upon whether the letter *h* occurred after a front or a back vowel as well as whether it acquired the vowel pronunciation before or after the Great Vowel Shift (when long vowel sounds were raised). Post-Shift *h*-derived vowels retained their first vowel pronunciation, while pre-Shift *h*-derived vowels were raised to new pronunciations by the Shift.

---

[11]The written French form of the *g*, which is our present form, was imported after the Norman Conquest and slowly replaced the Old Irish 3 (see p. 219 n. 2).

[12]In Old French, this *g* was also pronounced as in *gem*. In France, however, the sound evolved into the Modern French pronunciation as in *rouge*, while the older pronunciation had been preserved in English.

[13]That accounts for the hard "g" sound before *e* and *i* in initial position in such words as *get* and *give*, which were in the language before the Norman Conquest.

Also, the change to a vowel did not occur until early Modern English times in words with final *t*, such as *night* and *thought*.

A complication in tracing the development of the Old English voiceless palatal and velar "h" fricatives is the fact that both these sounds were undifferentiatedly represented in many Middle English writings by the combination *gh*. Moreover, not only was *gh* used to represent these old voiceless "h" sounds, but it was also used in many Middle English words to stand for the *voiced* velar fricative pronunciation of the Old English *yogh* or *g*. As a result, the endings of Modern English words such as *sigh, enough, weigh, though,* and *laugh* refer to a variety of etymological histories and the *gh* in any given word can stand for any one of the three extinct palatal and velar fricatives that had been represented in Old English by *g* and *h*.

3. The *h* was silent in some French loan words (e.g., *hour, honest*). In such words, the *h* had been neither pronounced nor written in French until French scribal reformers of the thirteenth century restored the letter in writing so that the spelling would conform to earlier Latin derivations. When the *h* was restored in the French language, it was also restored in the words borrowed into English by the bilingual scribes of the time. In some cases, the *h* was eventually pronounced again (e.g., *hymn*). In other cases, because of the confused spelling of the time, words that never had an *h* were given one, and some of these *h*'s later acquired sounding as well (e.g., Modern English *hermit* and *hostage*).[14]

4. The *h* was dropped in Old English initial combinations like *hl-, hn-,* and *hr-*. Under Norman influence, *hw-* was modified to *wh-* in spelling as early as the thirteenth century. Its "hw" pronunciation became simple "w" except in the northern dialects. In Modern English, too, the simple "w" pronunciation is used, except in northern England, Scotland, Ireland, and in those parts of the United States influenced by northern British and Irish immigrants.[15]

j   As in Old English, *j* did not exist as a separate letter but was still considered a slight written variation of the letter *i*. See pp. 39–40 above for discussion of the development of the *j*.

k   As in Old and Modern English, but after being used only rarely in Old English, Middle English *k* was often used to replace *c* before *e*

---

[14]Venezky, 1965, pp. 96–97. Such sounding of a word according to an analogous written pattern rather than to its standard spoken form is called a *spelling pronunciation* and, as in this instance, has quite often superseded the standard spoken form. Examples of current spelling pronunciations (that may or may not become standard) are: pronouncing the *t* in *often* or pronouncing the word *a* with a *long a* rather than with the schwa in unstressed positions as in *a long time ago*.

[15]Venezky notes that although most Modern English words with *wh-* refer back to the Old English *hw-* spelling, there are exceptions whose origins are obscure. Among these are *wherry, whim, whimsey, whinny,* and *whip* (1965, pp. 127–128).

and *i/y* when the "k" pronunciation was needed. Thus, *cene* became *keen* and *cypera* became *kipper.* Also, the Old English cluster *cn-* became *kn-*, as in *cnocian–knock.*

l	As in Old and Modern English.
m	As in Old and Modern English.
n	As in Old and Modern English, except that *ng* was not a separate phoneme as it often is today, but an allophone of *n* before *g* or *k.* Also, final *n* very often dropped off in final unstressed syllables.
p	As in Old and Modern English.
q	Introduced by French scribes and used with *u* to replace Old English *cw-* as well as in French loan words (as Old English *cwen–queen*, Old French *queste–quest*).[16] Consistently pronounced as "k."
r	As in Modern English, although it was more consonantal, perhaps slightly trilled.
s	As in Old and Modern English. (Aside from certain exceptions such as *sure*, in Modern English.)[17]
t	As in Old and Modern English.
v	Became a separate phoneme as a result of numerous, newly acquired French and Latin words. (Also, initial *f* was pronounced as "v" in Southern dialects. See above, p. 222, under *f*.)

w[18]

1. As in Old and Modern English in initial and some medial positions.
2. As part of a diphthong (*aw, ew, ow*) used alternately with the letter *u* in these cases to differentiate the *u* from the *v* before another vowel. Also, *w* replaced *u* in final position in these diphthongs.
3. In words where the *w* followed a consonant (generally *n, s,* or *t*) and preceded a back vowel, its pronunciation was often lost (e.g., Modern English *not* was changed from Old English *ne wot,* while Modern English *answer, sword,* and *two* are examples in which the "w" pronunciation was lost but the spelling remained.)
4. There were three clusters with *w* in initial position: *wh-, wl-,* and *wr-.* Of the three, only the *w* of *wl-* was dropped. The other two clusters continued on into Modern English times. (The *wh-* was newly formed during Middle English times from *hw-.* See *h* above, pp. 223–224.)

x	As in Old and Modern English.
y	

1. The *y* acquired its current consonantal pronunciation (as in *yes*) during this period from several sources:
    a. From French borrowings, in which it had the soft "g" sound (as in *gem*) just as the letter *i* did. (See p. 223 above.)

---

[16]See p. 38 n. 12 above for further information on the development of *q.*
[17]Moore, 1951, p. 139.
[18]The Old English Þ (*wynn*) was replaced by the *w* character in the thirteenth century. (See p. 221 above for further information.)

b. In initial position, the Old English *g* (or *yogh*) became *y* during late Middle English times. (Old English *gear* became *year.*)

2. The written form of the letter *y* resembled the form of the Old English *thorn* (*þ*) (pronounced "th"). During the Middle English period, after the *þ* had gone out of use, the *y* was substituted for it in certain written abbreviations, although the "th" pronunciation was retained. The word *yᵉ* was really *the*, and the word *yᵗ* was really *that*. (For this reason, in appellations like "Ye Olde Curiosity Shoppe" the first word should be pronounced as Modern English "the.")

z   The *z* symbol came to represent a separate phoneme and was used with much greater frequency in Middle English than it had been in Old English because it appeared in French loan words. In addition, in late Middle English times, the *z* symbol was substituted for *s* in a number of native English words where the *s* had been voiced (e.g., *amasian–to amaze*).

MODERN ENGLISH SPEECH SOUNDS

The nonspecialist may be confused by the different written phonemic and phonetic representations of Modern English speech sounds that appear in the literature. While there is agreement on many forms, there are enough disagreements for Gleason to state that even among those writings "that purport to describe English phonology on a scientific basis, there are considerable and often perplexing differences. It seems almost as though no two authors can agree, and that few even approach agreement."[19]

In the main, such authors fall into two categories: those deriving from the phonemic systems of descriptive linguistics and those deriving from the International Phonetic Alphabet (IPA). In the tables of Modern English consonants and vowels that follow, forms from both kinds of systems are listed. Where more than one IPA form is given, they represent allophonic variations that are not significant for understanding English but have implications for the phonetician.

For the phonemic forms, the sources were mainly Gleason's *An Introduction to Descriptive Linguistics* (1961) and Bolinger's *Aspects of Language* (1975). For the phonetic forms, the prime sources were Gray and Wise's *The Bases of Speech* (1959) and Borden and Harris's *Speech Science Primer* (1980). These sources reflect the mainstreams of opinion and the forms they give appear in many writings.

---

[19]Gleason, 1961, p. 312. See Chapter 19 of his book for a discussion and comparison of the various phonemic and phonetic notations used by different authors.

Modern English Vowels

Monophthongs

SOUND IN A WORD	MODERN ENGLISH PHONEMIC TRANSCRIPTION	IPA PHONEMIC TRANSCRIPTION
bat	/æ/	æ
bet	/e/	ɛ
bit	/i/	I
bock	/a/	ɑ, a, ɒ
but	/ə/	ɜ, ə, ʌ
beer	/ɨ/	ɨ
bought	/ɔ/	ɔ
bold	/o/	o
book	/u/	ʊ

Diphthongs[20]

SOUND IN A WORD	MODERN ENGLISH PHONEMIC TRANSCRIPTION	IPA PHONEMIC TRANSCRIPTION
bate	/ey/	e, eI
beet	/iy/	i
bite	/ay/	aI
boat	/ow/	oʊ
boot	/uw/	u
beaut	/yu/	ju
bout	/aw/	aʊ
adroit	/ɔy/	ɔI

[20]There is divergence of opinion on the designation of Modern English diphthongs. Generally speaking, the vowels of bate, beet, and boot are considered diphthongs by descriptive linguists and monophthongs by phoneticians.

Modern English Consonants

SOUND IN A WORD	MODERN ENGLISH PHONEMIC TRANSCRIPTION	IPA PHONEMIC TRANSCRIPTION
*b*at, mo*b*	/b/	b
*d*ot, re*d*	/d/	d
*f*it, ree*f*	/f/	f
*g*ap, le*g*	/g/	g
*h*at	/h/	h
*k*it, *c*at, lu*ck*	/k/	k
*l*et, fa*ll*, nob*l*e	/l/	l, ɫ, ḷ
*m*at, he*m*	/m/	m
*n*et, pi*n*	/n/	n
*p*at, mo*p*	/p/	p
*r*at, pu*rr*	/r/	r
*s*at, ye*s*	/s/	s
*t*ot, pu*t*	/t/	t
*v*at, lo*v*e	/v/	v
*w*et, *wh*ich[21]	/w/, /hw/	w, ʍ
*y*et	/y/	y
*z*ed, qui*z*	/z/	z
*th*in, nor*th*	/θ/	θ
*th*at, brea*th*e	/đ/	đ
*sh*ot, ru*sh*	/š/	ʃ
*g*enre, bei*g*e	/ž/	ʒ
*ch*at, ri*ch*	/č/	ʧ
*j*et, ca*g*e	/ǰ/	ʤ
—si*ng*[22]	/ŋ/	ŋ

---

[21]In some dialects, *wh* as in *which* is pronounced "hw." The question of whether *wh* is a consonant cluster or a separate phoneme has merited considerable discussion.

[22]In English, the ŋ does not appear in initial position. Some linguists consider it to be an allophone of /n/ rather than a separate phoneme. (Bolinger, 1975, pp. 81–82).

Index

Page numbers followed by *n* indicate footnotes; those followed by *t* indicate tables.